THERAPY FOR COUPLES

A Clinician's Guide for Effective Treatment

****

BILLIE S. ABLES

in collaboration with

Jeffrey M. Brandsma

THERAPY FOR COUPLES

Jossey-Bass Publishers
San Francisco • Washington • London • 1978

THERAPY FOR COUPLES
A Clinician's Guide for Effective Treatment
by Billie S. Ables in collaboration with Jeffrey M. Brandsma

Library of Congress Catalogue Card Number LC 76-50698

International Standard Book Number ISBN 0-87589-312-0

Manufactured in the United States of America

JACKET DESIGN BY WILLI BAUM

FIRST EDITION
First printing: April 1977
Second printing: February 1978

Code 7710

✹✹✹✹✹✹✹✹✹✹✹✹✹✹✹✹✹✹✹✹✹✹✹✹✹✹✹✹

The Jossey-Bass
Social and Behavioral Science Series

Preface

After a number of years of slow growth, family therapy has rapidly emerged on the psychotherapeutic scene as an extremely important treatment approach that is based firmly in theory, accepted, and widespread in use. The work and contributions of a number of prominent family therapists who have become leaders in the field are well-known. By contrast, couple therapy, a stepsister to family therapy, has remained a poor relation. Lacking leadership and shadowed by family therapy, it partakes of family-therapy knowledge but has developed less clearly as a discipline in its own right. With the increasing divorce rate and the vast changes in mores eroding the traditional family structure, the need for new modes of help for spouses under marital stress is now clear. Individuals attempting to assist couples are becoming more aware of the difficulty and limitations of coping with marital disharmony with the more traditional individual-treatment approach. With this growing recognition, the need emerges for the systematic development of a couple-treatment approach distinct from individual therapy in its methodology and theoretical basis.

This book is directed toward creating such an approach. Drawing from clinical experience and years of teaching and supervising

mental health professionals working with married couples, we hope
to develop in this book a way to work with couples whose discomfort
lies primarily with their interaction. Our hope is that much of what
has been learned and practiced can be communicated to others who
wish to help couples in a structured and useful form.

We have chosen to focus on the work of the therapist rather
than on the kinds of individuals or marriages with which the therapist works. Within this context, the book brings together theory and
practice as they relate to the therapeutic goals. Theory is employed
as a means of understanding and appraising individual dynamics
shown in present and interactional behaviors. These dynamics not
only pose certain problems for the marriage but also relate to advantages for or limitations to a couples' approach; an understanding of
such dynamics guides therapeutic interventions and aids the therapist in adopting realistic goals. The emphasis of the book, however,
is not theoretical but practical. The book is designed to bring the
reader into the therapy session to see how the therapist works—why
a given way of working is chosen and what its relevance is for the
couple at the moment. Although the orientation presented for
understanding behavior is a psychodynamic one, the reader who
does not subscribe to our theory may apply his own to the raw data
and interventions of the treatment sessions. Thus the book can be
of benefit to clinicians with various training and theoretical back-
grounds who choose to work with couples.

Since marital or couple therapy as currently conceived is not
a unitary phenomenon and many approaches are used, we would
like to describe our vantage point. The approach reported herein is
usually conjoint (with variations as necessary or indicated), consisting of both members of a dyad with the therapist(s) and using a
variety of conceptions and techniques that can only be termed
eclectic. The issue of using a cotherapist is left open; there are
advantages and disadvantages, but our interventions can be made
by one individual or by cotherapists.

Consistent with our heavy emphasis on therapeutic interventions, numerous verbatim excerpts from actual therapy hours are
included. In the few instances when sessions were not taped, material was dictated immediately after the sessions. In some cases,
excerpts have been chosen from tapes of beginning therapists to
show the errors or difficulties posed by less successful interventions.

To highlight the tenets of the text as they relate to the specific problems at hand, comments are interspersed within the dialogue, which has been edited for relevancy and brevity. Details of content have been altered only for purposes of confidentiality; otherwise, examples are faithfully reproduced. Throughout the book, the terms psychotherapy and treatment are used interchangeably.

Writing this book has been labor, but not without rewards—for example, those of friendship and of sharing our views and insights about life and marriage. We believe that a careful reading of the book will be of value for the novice and the more experienced clinician. We offer this effort in hopes of a growing understanding of people systems and psychotherapy in general; we trust it will fill an important niche and enable others to better aid spouses in distress.

The authors wish to acknowledge the faithful and steadfast assistance of Wendy Van Meter and Donna Wilkie, who typed the manuscript. Appreciation is also extended to Alan Church, who carefully read the manuscript and offered many valuable suggestions. Various mental health workers who attended seminars on couple treatment with one of the authors over the years contributed to the formulation of many of the ideas in this book with their interest and provocative questions. The authors are particularly indebted to those therapists who graciously allowed the inclusion of their taped sessions in the book. The greatest debt of all is owed to the many couples who, together with the authors, embarked on a journey to explore new ways of living that would increase their mutual well-being and satisfaction. Their willingness to allow use of verbatim tapes made this book possible.

Lexington, Kentucky   Billie S. Ables
February 1977   Jeffrey M. Brandsma

Contents

Preface   ix

The Authors   xv

1. Marriage and Marital Dysfunction   1
   The Nature of Marriage, 2 • Theoretical Stance and Overview, 7

2. Assessment and Its Implications   16

3. Early Phases of Couple Therapy   33
   Varying Vantage Points of Spouses, 33 • Telephone Calls, 36 • Beginning Sessions: The Importance of Structuring, 37 • Issues of Control and Misconceptions, 57 • Tribulations of Early Therapy, 59 • Therapeutic Alliance, 66 • Face Saving, 69

4. Helping Couples Negotiate: Obstacles and Interventions   72
   Assuming Personal Responsibility, 75 • Role of Blame and How To Deal With It, 90 • Anger and the Tug-of-War, 100 • Compliance and Deadlocks, 112 • Resistance to Change, 114 • The Heavyweight versus the Lightweight, 118 • Separating Issues, 121 • When the Cognitive Negotiating Approach Fails, 121 • Sample Session, 125

5. Facilitating Couple Communication:
    Problems and Methods   136
    *Talking and Learning to Listen, 136 • Stating Needs and
    Expectations, 146 • Expression of Feelings, 152 • Priorities
    in Feeling Issues, 155 • Ongoing Communication of Dissatis-
    factions, 156 • Positive Strokes, 160 • Avoidance of
    Abstractions, 167 • Avoidance of "Why" Questions, 173 •
    Red Flags, 174 • Mind Reading and Vengeance, 175 •
    Modeling, 178 • Nonverbal Communication, 179 • Working
    in the Here-and-Now, 179*

6. Reeducation: Altering Attitudes,
    Perceptions, and Misconceptions   190
    *"The Real Problem," 190 • Interaction of Individual with
    Marital Problems, 192 • Separating Feelings and Intentions
    from Behavior and Outcomes, 204 • Expectations from
    Marriage, 208 • Extramarital Affairs and Vendettas, 225
    • Threats, Control, and Tolerance Limits, 231 • Limits of
    Power in Marriage, 234 • Reframing into a Positive
    Context, 236*

7. Continuing Therapy and Termination   240

8. Specific Problems in Therapy   299
    *Married versus Unmarried Couples, 299 • Living Arrange-
    ments—Together or Separate? 300 • Children from Previous
    Marriages, 301 • The Mate Who Refuses to Attend, 302 •
    Divorce as Blackmail, 303 • Advice about Divorce, 304 •
    Individual Therapy and Secrets, 307 • Spouses Who Have
    Previously Been Patients, 310 • Monologues, 313 • Sexual
    Problems, 313*

9. Therapy with a Divorced Couple   325

10. Couple Therapy: A Summary   339

    Appendix: Personal Data Form   353

    Index   359

The Authors

Billie S. Ables is an associate professor of psychiatry at the University of Kentucky Medical School in the Child Division of the Department of Psychiatry. She is a member of the American Psychological Association and the Academy of Psychologists in Marital and Family Therapy, a diplomate in clinical psychology, and she has a joint appointment to the Department of Psychology, University of Kentucky.

Ables received her Ph.D. in psychology from Purdue University in 1954 and was a postdoctoral fellow at the Menninger Foundation in 1956. She taught at Washburn University, Topeka, Kansas, for three years and was affiliated with the Family Service and Guidance Center for four years before coming to Kentucky. She has spent the past twelve years at the University of Kentucky Medical Center, where she is director of the Clinical Psychology Internship Training Program. In addition to therapeutic work with couples, families, and individuals, she spends a major part of her time teaching and supervising psychiatric residents, child-psychiatry fellows, psychology interns, and social-work students. She is married and resides with her husband and two children in Lexington, Kentucky.

Jeffrey M. Brandsma is an associate professor of psychiatry and psychology of the University of Kentucky Medical School. He is a member of the American Psychological Association (Divisions of Clinical Psychology and Psychotherapy) and the Society for Psychotherapy Research. He coauthored with Frank Farrelly the book *Provocative Therapy* (1974) and is presently writing *The Outpatient Treatment of Alcoholism: An Empirical Study.*

Brandsma received his Ph.D. in psychology from Pennsylvania State University in 1971. After a clinical internship at Mendota State Hospital, Madison, Wisconsin, he accepted a position at the University of Kentucky Medical College, where he became an associate director of the Psychiatry Outpatient Clinic in 1972. He has done research and writing in the area of multiple personality, rational therapy, and the treatment of alcoholism. In 1972 he and his co-authors received the Roy M. Dorcas award from the Society for Clinical and Experimental Hypnosis for "the best clinical paper on hypnosis in the past year." Brandsma and his wife Anne, a registered nurse, live in Lexington, Kentucky, with their three young children.

To Our Families
Past and Present

✳✳✳✳✳✳✳✳✳✳✳✳✳✳✳✳✳✳✳✳✳✳✳✳✳✳✳✳✳✳✳✳✳✳✳✳

THERAPY FOR COUPLES

A Clinician's Guide
for Effective Treatment

1

Marriage and Marital Dysfunction

Marriage is a complex relationship that can be viewed from many perspectives—sociological, biological, cultural, anthropological, religious, legal, and, of course, psychological. Obviously, the legal document of the marriage is the clearest empirical referent of marriage, but just as obviously, the relationship that this document is grounded on is more complex and meaningful than a simple legal license indicates. Because many authors more expert than ourselves have commented on marriage from these perspectives,[1] we will not reit-

[1]*See* W. J. Lederer and D. D. Jackson (*The Mirages of Marriage,* New York: Norton, 1968); N. W. Ackerman (*The Psychodynamics of Family Life,* New York: Basic Books, 1958); T. Lidz (*The Family and Human Adaptation,* New York: International Universities Press, 1963); I. Boszormenyi-Nagy ("A Theory of Relationships: Experience and Transaction," In I. Boszormenyi-Nagy and T. L. Framo (Eds.), *Intensive Family Therapy: Theoretical and Practical Aspects,* New York: Harper & Row, 1965); B. L. Greene (*The Psychotherapies of Marital Disharmony,* New York: Free Press, 1965); and V. W. Eisenstein (*Neurotic Interaction in Marriage,* New York: Basic Books, 1965).

erate their insights. We hope to make our contribution largely from a psychological perspective that is tempered by the intimate experience of doing couple treatment. We have tried to account for those variables that seemed most crucial for making the relationship work for the individuals involved.

The Nature of Marriage

The following is a brief discussion of our assumptions regarding marriage or intense dyadic relationships, and why with time marriage so often is disillusioning. Marriage is a relationship that proceeds from a romantic, intensive, infatuation stage to a problem-solving, extensive relationship. One might characterize the early stage of being in love as one in which reality recedes and fantasy dominates. Although the element of conscious choice is important, strong unconscious needs are also at work in determining attraction. The individual projects his or her own needs and symbolic perceptions onto the loved one in such a way that this person becomes overidealized far beyond whatever reality qualities are possessed. In addition, marital choices are usually made under the sway of strong sexual strivings. It is no wonder that the contrast between the early state and the later state of marriage, after reality looms more significantly, produces major problems.

Let us look at what happens. In the "in-love" or honeymoon stage, the lover lives only for giving to the chosen one. The paradox is that the partner demands little but gets everything, since the other partner is at the same vantage point, that is, giving all and asking nothing but to bestow one's love on the partner—a position that nevertheless garners unheard-of treasures of love for the self. Under the sway of intense feelings and distorted perceptions, each responds optimally to the other's needs and, because of this, does not have to work to gratify his or her own needs. However, with time, this divine state of madness changes. As reality becomes preeminent with the exigencies of closer living, the symbolic holds less sway. When there were fewer demands by the extensive complexities of living, attention could be focused almost exclusively on each other; such romantic issues as "when can we be together again," the exquisite pain of separation, and the elation of reunion are replaced with mundane problems like changing diapers and balancing the checkbook.

A strange paradox now unfolds. Spouses or lovers who were originally sufficient unto each other are no longer so. In addition, they begin to be perceived in terms of their own reality characteristics rather than in terms of their mate's needs. Most importantly, as the demands of living intrude, each begins to give less and to focus more on self-needs. However, because life is now more complex, with more external responsibilities required of each partner, each expects more of the mate. The dependency fostered by living together increases both expectations and frictions. It is this coinciding of giving less and expecting more that seems to be at the heart of the inevitable conflict of needs.

To make matters worse, each wants one's own needs to be met first before one meets the other's. It is no wonder that so many marriages strain under these pressures. Conflict-management skills become increasingly important. To be able to balance one's own needs along with all that is required of one, to remain attuned to another's needs, to be able to give when one feels more like getting, to be able to protect one's own interest, all these require a certain level of maturity, that is, a resolution of the various developmental tasks along the road to adulthood that may not have been completed. Thus, many individuals who enter marriage are often looking for a way to resolve unmet needs and are handicapped in their capacity to give. The normal stresses of a changing relationship affect these people more intensely.

A quel point les besoins sont-ils névrotiques?

One other fact should be mentioned because of its frequent occurrence. The very characteristics that are the most appealing initially and that pull the couple together inevitably become sources of major irritation later. On superficial glance this seems puzzling, but a closer look reveals why this is so. For example, the gay, dashing, adventurous, risk-taking male may captivate the more demure, conservative, somewhat inhibited female. These qualities in the male may offer the female a vicarious route of satisfaction and a fulfillment of unexpressed desires. However, once they are married, fun, pranks, adventures, and dangerous pursuits may now irk and disgust the female, because they interfere with the predictable, conservative style of life that she feels is necessary for comfort and security. With the exigencies of marriage (such as aging, addition of children, increase in responsibilities, and changing needs), perceptions of and values attached to behaviors also change—much to the difficulty of the couple, who now suddenly conclude that they are horribly mismatched.

The following comments from couple treatment illustrate both the increased expectations after marriage and how the initially appealing qualities later became problems. In the first example, the wife had been complaining that she had not had as much closeness with her husband as she wanted and felt largely excluded from his life.

T: "I was wondering when you married your husband, what were some of the things that were most appealing to you?"

W: "That he was an independent person."

T: "Then what?"

W: "That he was an independent person and that he was loving. That was really the big thing."

H: "How did I share my love then when I'm not sharing my love now? What things didn't I give?"

W: "Well, probably, I think you did the same things. I just think that maybe I expect more now. Maybe it's just that being married to you, being in the same house with you all the time, or not all the time, but rather than having a date with you or something, you know, being with you there, I just feel like I really want to be closer to you, and so I think you probably do the same things, you know, but. . . ."

The preceding illustrates well the increase in expectations with marriage.

H: "You just expect me to do a lot more?"

W: "Well that really sounds horrible when you say that I expect you to do a lot more. It's just that I feel I want to be closer all the time. If not, I want you to do things more and feel differently and act differently, do things more. It's just that, I don't know, maybe I just want a closer bond with you . . ."

T: "This is backing up a little bit. The reason I asked the question of what appealed to you most was because I was curious as to what you would say, and the first thing you mentioned was 'independent' and that is one of the reasons you married him, because he is very different from you. You are much more emotional and your feelings show quickly, whereas he has things much more under control and is more on top of it, and I think that gave you some feeling of strength, and that was much more appealing, and it is appealing. However, now you're saying that's the very thing that makes you feel shut out, because he is not sharing all his private thoughts and feelings."

The therapist's comment illustrates how an initially attracting characteristic becomes a problem for the couple.

H: "Well, when we got married, I thought that she was . . . well, you know, it's kind of funny because when we got married, I liked her because she was kind of dependent."

T: "Well, that's what I thought. You see I wanted you to say that to her. Because the very thing that you have been bemoaning now is the thing that was most appealing at first."

One of the husband's major complaints now is that his wife is too dependent, requires too much of him, and makes him feel guilty for not giving more. Again note how the very qualities that first drew the people together later caused problems.

This phenomenon is shown by another couple whose major complaint is that they can no longer talk to each other. The following comment by the wife is most revealing:

W: "Well, Tom and I first got started very largely because of long conversations about everything and anything in his apartment over drinks and snacks, and I must say he found me or professed to find me literally spellbinding. Either I've lost my touch or he's changed his mind or something."

With sufficient growth and maturity, individuals may change so that irritating characteristics are better modulated and do not clash so strongly with the mate's. When this does not occur, major marital problems arise. The husband gives the following sad and bitter commentary on the course of events that have led from two people who were thoroughly intrigued with each other to two who can no longer talk together.

H: "One thing that happened was she wasn't at home—another thing that happened was that when she came home she would be reading when I'd try to talk to her. [To wife] You'd find something to do elsewhere. You sometimes were tired—or whatever reasons, you were exhausted and would have to go to bed. . . . [Readdressing therapist] That's not much chance for communication—Zelda and her reading and not me. She was exhausted from sex . . . from having . . . from her guilt feelings. She'd come home and be exhausted. She'd either have to go to bed or get away from me—one or the other. She invited people in just to have something else going on—she had her reading and people of no consequence to her and even less to me."

Realistically, people get married for social, economic, complementary, sexual, romantic, or other reasons; idealistically, they take a risk, not often consciously considered, that they will grow and change in similar directions throughout the life cycle. The probability is great that two people may not fit well with time. As one wife put it, "I'm not the same person I was, and I don't feel the same. Maybe you can't change. I don't know that, but I have changed enough that I think for us to be happy together that either I am going to have to reverse fields or you're going to have to make some fairly important changes."

Another aspect to the disillusionment in marriage is the fact that characteristics that maintain their value in the eyes of the spouse often occur in clusters with other, less desirable characteristics. For example, a husband who admires and enjoys his wife's charm and vivacity may become thoroughly disgusted when she continually entices other men. In other words attractiveness, a positive attribute, may be highly correlated with seductiveness, a more negative one. Thus spouses buy package/deals in marriage, not all of whose contents are equally desirable. The reality that no one person can have all the ideal attributes to satisfy another may grate increasingly with time and eventually become a major disruption of harmony.

Theoretical Stance and Overview

Marital treatment, like all psychotherapy, is still very much an art form. Nevertheless, it can be subjected to scientific inquiry, and efforts have begun in this direction.[2] Tentative research data suggest the efficacy of marital therapy within a dyadic context and with a relatively modest investment of professional time. With this kind of research support and with our own convictions arising from clinical experience, we have little doubt about the use of conjoint couple therapy as an important treatment modality. It is with this bias that we have proceeded to formulate a couple-therapy treatment approach.

It is a difficult task to conceptualize the essence of one's therapeutic orientation, especially if it does not adhere closely to a specific theoretical model and is not allied with a known school of therapy. A first step in resolving this dilemma is to proclaim one's eclecticism, which hopefully will at least point out the broadness of one's approach and acknowledge the fact that it has crystallized

[2]*See* A.S. Gurman and D.P. Kniskern. "Research on Marital and Family Therapy: Progress, Perspective, and Prospect." In S.L. Garfield and A.E. Bergin (Eds.), *Handbook of Psychotherapy and Behavior Change: An Empirical Analysis.* (2nd ed.) New York: Wiley, in press.

under the influence of varying theoretical persuasions, different individuals, and the winnowing of experience. Although technical eclecticism seems to be currently in vogue,[3] many rightly frown at theoretical eclecticism because it can cloud communication, inhibit intellectual growth, and be used defensively to rationalize anything. We hope that we are not considered to be that kind of eclectic, and so we will state our biases, assumptions, and principles within the context of our experience in doing therapy. First, however, we must acknowledge our intellectual debt to William Lederer and Don Jackson, Virginia Satir, Rubin Blanck and Gertrude Blanck, George Bach, and various gestalt proponents.[4] These have all had their impact upon us.

Our couple-therapy approach is essentially an ego-psychological, problem-solving approach that relies heavily on a cognitive orientation. Its underpinnings are drawn from psychoanalytic developmental psychology. More conventional therapeutic techniques that are used, such as confrontation, clarification, interpretation, reeducation, encouragement, and support, are directed toward the ego, that is, the cognitive and rational parts of the individual that will be able to join in a therapeutic alliance to work toward mutual goals.

Some might detect an inherent contradiction in this viewpoint, that is, if the therapists work at a cognitive level, they may overlook the operative unconscious attitudes as they conceptualize a couple's behavior and shape interventions. We admit the possibility of contradiction but see no necessary incompatibility in working with both levels where necessary. For example, therapists may become aware of unconscious problems and thus modify their largely cognitive intervention to take these into account. Similarly, therapists can shift the focus between the interactional and the intrapsychic as

---

[3]P. M. Friedman. "Personalistic Family and Marital Therapy." In A. Lazarus (Ed.), *Clinical Behavior Therapy*. New York: Brunner/Mazel, 1972.

[4]W. J. Lederer and D. D. Jackson (*The Mirages of Marriage,* New York: Norton, 1968); V. Satir (*Conjoint Family Therapy,* Palo Alto, Calif.: Science and Behavior Books, 1964); R. Blanck and G. Blanck (*Marriage and Personal Development,* New York: Columbia University Press, 1968); G. Bach and P. Wyden (*The Intimate Enemy: How to Fight Fair in Love and Marriage,* New York: Morrow, 1969); and E. Polster and M. Polster (*Gestalt Therapy Integrated: Contours of Theory and Practice,* New York: Brunner/Mazel, 1973).

the problems dictate. Our position is to use knowledge of unconscious processes where necessary as counterpoint to the main symphony of therapy.

In addition, we rely heavily on present transactions to guide us in our therapeutic interventions. Our theoretical orientation allows us to make inferences about the kinds of etiological factors that have shaped present behaviors, and with this frame of reference we are further guided in adapting appropriate therapeutic interventions. However, our primary emphasis is always on how the assumed failures of past developmental conflicts are reflected in the present and how we can best deal with these.

In less abstract terms, we as therapists proceed cognitively to the extent that a couple will allow, that is, we utilize a problem-solving approach dealing with issues in terms of helping the couple to communicate and to be aware of the other's feelings, thoughts, wants, and needs. How far one can proceed is largely determined by the health of the couple. Psychological health in a marital couple means such things as their adaptive strength and flexibility in dealing with problems, their capacity for separateness yet mutuality, the strength of their individual identities, and their capacity for recognizing and responding to the needs of each other. The more these factors are present, the more efficacious is the cognitive approach. Indeed, the cognitive approach is particularly suited for resolving temporary crises in otherwise well-functioning marriages. In these cases, the problems presented can be negotiated and solved without attending to and altering more basic conflicts.

There is a certain paradoxical element to these statements, for the more the individuals have achieved these adaptive characteristics, then the less likely it is that they will need to seek help. Of course, individuals do vary, some being better equipped in certain areas than others. In those areas where a spouse is most vulnerable, unresolved issues are likely to be brought into play in times of stress. Shifting problems are posed externally as one progresses through the different stages of life, and these tap into varying unresolved problems. These stages are likely to be encountered even by generally well-functioning individuals.[5] The interplay of such

---

[5]G. Sheehy. *Passages: Predictable Crises of Adult Life.* New York: Dutton, 1976.

external problems with internal problems within the context of marriage may produce a crisis that needs attention.

At the other extreme, in the case of a spouse or a couple with few individual assets and strengths and pathological behavior that has remained fixated along the developmental path toward maturity, some of the techniques to be discussed may not be workable. At such times it is incumbent upon the therapist to be aware of the limitations of any cognitive, problem-solving approach and of the necessity for modifications and additional techniques in working with spouses. At this extreme of couple pathology, the cognitive, problem-solving approach may have little chance of effecting the changes necessary for such ingrained pathology. We will illustrate in later material how modified goals and techniques are employed and how at times the couple's best interest can be served by encouraging individual therapy for one of the spouses.

We by no means see marital therapy as the solution to all problems in a marriage. Indeed, with some couples it may be completely inappropriate. The nature of the individual pathology may be such that it requires forms of treatment that cannot be accomplished well in a couple context. The next chapter will expound more fully on this point. However, although marital therapy may not always be best suited for working with individual pathology, it does offer opportunities for individuals to learn more about themselves within the marital framework and in this sense become more knowledgeable about their individual problems.

The reader may wonder why we frequently refer to the need for individual therapy in a book on marital therapy. The question might be asked, "Why marital therapy at all?" Our answer is that marital therapy is of undisputed value because some marital problems can only be worked on with both spouses present and because some work on individual problems can also be done in a marital context. If attention to the points of conflict in a couple's interaction can alleviate some stress, then marital therapy is warranted.

Individuals without undue pathology can be helped in a fairly efficient way by focusing on the points at which their individual needs clash. Even where the convergence of individual pathologies produce pronounced marital problems and the resolution of the

[handwritten margin note:] excellente occasion pour une thérapie Relationnelle — dont certains points sont applicables, par le client, à toute relation humaine c.f. communication, conflits

individual problems by an individual approach might be considered optimal, often the time, effort, and financial drain may not be within the couple's capabilities. In addition, many individuals with grave pathology come for marital therapy with their spouses but refuse individual help. There is less stigma, less identification as a patient, and less implication of "being crazy" if a couple wish to work on marital problems together with a therapist. This is probably because most people in our society can acknowledge marital problems more readily than personal problems.

Marital therapy also has the advantage that a spouse is seldom able to remain silent and uninvolved. The presence of the mate serves as a catalyst for working on problems. Even if one spouse prefers avoidance and denial mechanisms, it is unlikely that the mate will behave similarly, and the less willing spouse is often forced to confront the dissatisfactions of the mate and to deal with these in some way. Indeed, this is one of the main therapeutic leverages the therapist has.

In cases of severe pathology, one is well advised to begin with the marital focus, especially if this is the couple's choice. One would then hope to pave the way for encouraging individual therapy or, better still, for the spouse to recognize its desirability and to seek it. Even where pathology is not grave and conflicts are more in the neurotic realm, we have had the frequent experience of spouses after or during couple therapy wishing to seek further individual treatment for themselves.

Thus, in our treatment of a couple, we move back and forth between staying in the here-and-now with conscious problem solving (giving this greater emphasis) and, when necessary, evolving different ways to further awareness. In essence, the individuals determine how we work (as in all therapy). The personality of each spouse and the spouses' relationship will influence the nature of the treatment. Thus, each case of treatment will be unique; nevertheless, we hope to elucidate in this book a set of effective, general principles or commonalities for all couples.

Chapter Two on assessment will illustrate the importance of a developmental approach based on psychoanalytic concepts in assessing spouses and guiding therapists in their therapeutic interventions. To the extent that one can be more knowledgeable about and better able to use such understandings, we believe that the therapeutic work will be enhanced. On the other hand, and especially when dealing with less maladjusted spouses, many of the therapeutic techniques that will be described can be used successfully by professionals who have not had psychodynamic training. A fuller understanding of the importance of how less than successful resolution of earlier developmental tasks are played out in present behaviors, with a full appreciation of the ingrained nature of such maladaptive behaviors, however, does help one appreciate more fully why certain reality-oriented, "obvious" solutions do not work; this awareness may lead to more effective interventions and realistic goals.

As a bridge between the more abstract notions presented above and the exposition of techniques that will follow, we shall briefly present an overview of the book, noting some of the crucial ingredients of our approach. Foremost, we try to address ourselves to the ego, recognizing the limitations of doing this and being aware that many unconscious attitudes and developmental flaws may be at work to defeat such efforts. We work to support initiative, responsibility, reality testing, curiosity, inquisitiveness, and the courage for spouses to disagree. We encourage spouses to work toward understanding their conflicts and exploring possible solutions. We stand by to aid and direct without taking over these tasks for them or attempting to assuage their anxiety too much or to gratify them unduly. We acknowledge to them the difficulty of the task they undertake and the discomfort that accompanies it.

With due recognition of personality deficits, we use several ego-building devices. For example, we work to sharpen the differences between the self and others, thus promoting autonomy and separateness between spouses. Also, we attempt to promote greater awareness of self by helping a given spouse to integrate cognitive capacities with the experiential level of feeling, thus strengthening the coping skills of the ego and paving the way for a better capacity for interpersonal relations. In addition, through support and emphasis on cognitive mastery (that is, interposing thought for action) efforts are made to increase the spouse's capacity for coping with anxiety and learning how to delay impulse gratification. Overall, we attempt to ally ourselves to whatever extent possible with the capacity of the person for further growth and development, with due respect for the regressive as well as progressive wishes and needs of each spouse.

The foregoing sums up the bias we bring to the office wherein we meet the couple. Within this frame of reference, much effort is directed toward working with communication, a readily available vehicle to utilize as we attempt to foster better handling of many kinds of problems. In other words, communication is seen as the means whereby the couple express their various discontents. It may also be used as a means of minimizing or eliminating some of these discontents. We suggest that communication be viewed as only one aspect of behavior and acknowledge the many variables that underlie its expression; then one is not likely to see couple therapy simplistically as "improving communications," although this is indeed an important part of the whole.

Focus is also directed toward the nature of the transactions and the couple's overt behavior in the hope that these will be changed. One way we do this is through helping couples to give up the typical viewpoint of "who's to blame" and to adapt a more useful negotiating style. Shifting from this blaming, argumentative style toward one of accommodation and compromise represents one of the major tasks for the spouses as they work toward mutual gratification. Therapeutic efforts toward providing a safe, nonjudgmental climate will be essential if spouses are to feel sufficiently comfortable to state their grievances and what they would like changed. To further these aims the therapist will need to promote hope and belief in the attainment of individual satisfaction through the recognition of differing needs of the spouses and the importance of attending to these. This concept of mutuality will have to be learned as respect for the self and the spouse, along with accepting responsibility for working constructively toward gratifying the needs of both.

The therapist will be working with communication (Chapter Five) to achieve such goals. Many steps can be defined along the way. For example, spouses will need to learn how to communicate their needs so that they will be heard and attended to. Typical problems in communication will be identified and discussed later.

Spouses will also need to become more fully aware of the ways they are presently using to work toward gratification that are counter-productive. As they become more aware of such behaviors, they can learn the extent to which such behaviors are more individually determined as well as how they interact with behaviors of the spouse to intensify friction. This promotes the individual's assuming responsibility for his or her own behavior and ultimately greater appreciation for the limits of the individual in effecting overall change.

In addition to communication, the therapist will want to promote reeducation of thinking processes (Chapter Six) by challenging either faulty hypotheses or what may be manifestations of childhood, omnipotent fantasies. Successful negotiation can only proceed as unrealistic misconceptions are corrected; that is, misconceptions about spouses, their roles, how they should behave, and what marriage should be like must be altered along realistic and functional lines. Many couples continue to seek and work toward fulfilling an image of marriage that is impossible to achieve; their efforts can only lead to frustration.

Along with direct attention to manifest thinking and communication, equal importance is given to internal expectations, beliefs, attitudes, and feelings, of which the spouses are usually less aware. In any interchange there are many levels of meaning conveyed beyond the verbal. Thus, while we may ostensibly be working on a surface level (that is, discussing ways to change external behaviors, communication, and thinking), much may transpire in the interchange that is not expressed in words. We are continuously recognizing the need to remove barriers that prevent us from dealing with the feeling component of the encounter both in terms of awareness and expression. To focus on the transactions exclusively would fail to attend to many more important aspects of the spouses, such as the subjective and emotional aspects of an encounter as well as the unconscious attitudes influencing these which may not be readily apparent. Latent meanings may be only tenuously connected to manifest cognitions.

Thus, there are many levels that may be focused on—overt, transactional, cognitive, subjective, perceptual, and affective—all essentially figural or unconscious. Focus will vary as we tread our way through this complex web toward effecting changes that will improve the relationship. Efforts are directed toward whatever levels are more accessible for change, while recognizing that changing behavior at one level may influence behavior at another—but not necessarily. For example, one often notices how spouses will make certain efforts to change external behaviors, but negative feelings persist. There is no simple or predictable path to success.

In short, we work for the couple in whatever way they are ready to work and thus can use our help. This may change as we proceed together. We may give up on methods that become futile and shift toward different methods that appear to offer more opportunity for success. In addition to the marriage, we may shift our focus between the individuals at times, coming back to the marital focus as soon as the couple see how their individual problems coalesce to make trouble. A successful therapy has to fit the individuals, and the mechanical use of the principles herein or elsewhere is doomed to failure.

Successful therapeutic work requires knowing the spouses, what the particular conflicts of each individual are, as well as how the individual characteristics converge to produce the specific marital problems. The frictional interface that has brought the couple for help and on which they initially focus may be only one indication of a more extensive pathology. At such times proper assessment is crucial for establishing both appropriate goals and some efficient methods. This will be discussed in the following chapter. In succeeding chapters the more general overview presented above concerning negotiation, communication, and reeducation as key concepts in therapeutic work will be detailed with emphasis on the obstacles and problems encountered by the therapist and how these may be dealt with.

2

Assessment and Its Implications

Despite working in a medical setting for most of our professional lives, we have not seen the need to evaluate a couple prior to treatment. Operationally defined, evaluation is the administration of a mental status exam and the securing of a selective history so as to assign a psychiatric diagnosis. In some settings, this would also include a psychosexual history, dynamic formulations, and a characterological and symptomatic picture of each spouse. Except for knowing that an individual is psychotic, we have not found previously assigned diagnostic labels helpful. People diagnosed as psychotic are usually not able to work in the fashion we propose. Overall, our position is that assessment evolves from the process of therapy, the experience of which we put into a framework of developmental understanding of the individuals. Conversely, evaluation apart from treatment is not helpful or useful, and often proves detrimental.

The usual procedures for diagnosis present problems that

are best avoided. They require, if not actually seeing the individuals separately, at least focusing on them separately. This approach impedes focus on the marital transactions. Among other things, the emphasis on fact-finding contributes to expectations that the therapist's understanding will eventually dictate solutions that can be related to the couple. This is antithetical to our usual way of working and to our firm beliefs of how help should be rendered.

For these reasons, we focus on what is going on between the couple as we begin the first session and encourage them to begin talking and negotiating with each other. To direct the interchange away from this in order to secure information would at least be awkward. As treatment proceeds, the gestalt of the couple and the necessary information for treatment usually emerge. Where some piece of information would foster a better understanding of a given interchange or lead to a more sophisticated intervention, the therapist may briefly ask for it. However, it is best to make clear by the manner of inquiry that this is a parenthetical interchange not meant to interfere with the flow of the ongoing discussion. Often, one of the spouses senses when some information would make their discussion more understandable and supplies it spontaneously.

To emphasize again, it seems least useful to use a medical model, wherein after sufficient detective work, the illness is diagnosed and prescribed for. We view marital problems as psychological in nature, having transactional and individual determinants. Usually the individuals are worked with as spouses, not patients. If psychological problems are extreme, we may think of an individual as a patient, but this does not imply illness in any physical sense.

One obvious implication of this approach is that treatment is begun without our being aware of some information; yet we have not found this to be a handicap. For example, after treating one couple for several months, it emerged that the husband had previously been hospitalized briefly and had received electroshock therapy. His tendency toward depression had already been apparent and therefore taken into account. Not knowing this information neither helped nor hindered the work, nor did it affect what transpired thereafter.

Let us stress that we do have a diagnostic interest in the spouses, but our way of assessing is different from a medical model, and the information we find useful may differ from what is often considered important. What we often deem helpful at the outset of therapy is to have each spouse fill out a questionnaire separately before or after the first session; the form we use is shown in the Appendix. Data secured from this form include demographic characteristics, general information, and some history regarding childhood and family relationships. Each spouse may also be encouraged to write a brief synopsis of his or her life. Although the answers may provide useful information, they cannot all be taken at face value, since they may be misleading. Much that is conflictive and leads to distress may not be in conscious awareness; and individuals intent on being cooperative may not be able to reveal significant conflicts.

Because of this factor, an individual's description of major current problems may not be as revealing as inferences one may make from other reported information. For example, one would want to look for evidence of any early trauma in the first year of life, paying particular attention to feeding schedules and related problems, the consistency of available mothering, and any abrupt changes concerning the mother figure, including loss. Rapid changes and early losses, if persistent, would make the mastery of normal developmental tasks very difficult. In some cases, individuals may inadvertently reveal their own developmental flaws by their manner of attributing blame to their partners. A description of sexual problems may include information from which one can infer a persistence of immediate need-gratification, which would signify incomplete symbiotic resolution, for example, a spouse who demands immediate sexual gratification irrespective of the state, needs, and availability of the mate. The data form is a limited but occasionally useful adjunct to the main data on the ongoing diagnostic and therapeutic process.

 To reiterate, assessment is best when it evolves naturally from the process of therapy. Couple treatment begins with some working assumptions and methods; should they fail, diagnostic acumen and understanding are increased, leading to the modification of treatment procedures and strategies. However, what occurs in treatment must be put into some conceptual framework in order to make it understandable and useful. For this purpose we have found a developmental understanding of the individuals essential. The remainder of this chapter contains some generalizations on individuals and marriage in this framework. Although one may consider many of the methods and principles set forth by us as important and use them in working with couples without sharing our theoretical assumptions, we think that couple treatment can be greatly aided with knowledge of psychoanalytic developmental psychology. This enables the therapist to become more fully aware of the problems posed and why some methods have little chance of succeeding.

In order to put our experiences and methods in a meaningful framework and to explicate our basis for treatment further, we shall delineate what have become the most important concepts and theoretical understandings for us. Not only do they ground our methods, but they also relate to the use of various treatment procedures and the determination of appropriate goals for couples.

We view marriage as a continuation of the psychological development process that begins in infancy and proceeds through childhood and adolescence (see Erikson[1] for a discussion of the conflicts attendant throughout the life cycle). Although the adulthood stage evolves more slowly, the marriage phase, like each of the other stages, has its special characteristics and problems.[2] To understand problems apparent in an adult (especially an adult in a close relationship with a partner), it is helpful, as therapy proceeds, to become aware of the ways in which previous developmental tasks have been unresolved or only partially resolved and thus contribute to present disharmony.

Marriage entails many realistic burdens that are made heavier when spouses bring to it the frustrations and failures of the past. Often they hope to use their relationship to remedy or undo their previous unfortunate experiences. In this sense, marriage may serve as an attempt to solve early conflicts or as a defense against anxiety associated with problems rooted in earlier life (for example, the spouse who suppresses homosexual desires).

If the partners have sufficient adaptive ability and skills, much

[1]E. H. Erikson. "Identity and the Life Cycle." In G. S. Klein and others (Eds.), *Psychological Issues*, 1959, *1* (1). New York: International Universities Press, 1959.
[2]G. Sheehy. *Passages: Predictable Crises of Adult Life*. New York: Dutton, 1976.

may be accomplished as the therapeutic work addresses incompleted developmental tasks. Often, a spouse who has reached a greater level of psychological maturity or is not handicapped by the same problems as the partner can catalyze growth in the mate. If the capacity for surmounting difficulties is sufficient, the result is mutually rewarding. On the other hand, the frustrations that result from unrealistic desires and an inability to deal with disappointment whenever the mate fails to "make up for past disappointments" and "make it all better" can lead to excessive quarreling and deadlock any personal growth. Success with the approach described in this book, or with any approach, will be minimal when interactional problems are deeply rooted in severe developmental flaws in both spouses.

Blanck and Blanck[3] have singled out five major areas of personality growth potentially available for individuals within the context of marriage. Each of these areas provides opportunity to work through previous problems toward greater individual maturity and thus to enhance the couple's relationship. At the same time, incompleted developmental tasks may manifest themselves in these areas to the detriment of the marital relationship. These areas are: (1) the establishment of a sexual relationship, (2) the establishment of a new level of interpersonal (object) relationships, (3) completion of psychological separation from the parents, (4) increased opportunity for the exercise of autonomy, and (5) new opportunities for identification.

In assessing marital problems in terms of these five areas, the therapist will be aided by understanding three earlier developmental stages[4] that the individual must successfully negotiate to reach a level that allows mastery of current problems and the use of the opportunities offered by marriage.[5] In addition to discussing these early stages and some of the tasks required for subsequent development, the concepts of fixation, regression, anxiety, and defense are employed to evaluate the relative success in completing

[3]R. Blanck and G. Blanck. *Marriage and Personal Development.* New York: Columbia University Press, 1968.
[4]M.S. Mahler, F. Pine, and A. Bergman. *The Psychological Birth of the Human Infant.* New York: Basic Books, 1975.
[5]See Blanck and Blanck.

the developmental tasks of each stage and to guide the therapist in his or her work. Although the three stages are presented as discrete entities, they actually represent a continuum with one stage blending into the next. In the discussion that follows, we will describe these stages and then give some examples of marital problems that can result from their incomplete resolution. Some additional comments will be made relative to therapeutic approaches, although this emphasis on intervention will not be the major thrust of this chapter.

Briefly stated, the infant progresses through three predictable early stages: the autistic, symbiotic, and separation-individuation stages. If biological maturation and mothering are adequate, the infant moves from primary narcissism through need-gratification to "object constancy."[6] In the autistic first stage, which occurs in the first few weeks of life, it is assumed that there is no perceptual differentiation of the mother from the self and that sensory awareness is primarily focused inward on the bodily states of pleasure or tension. The initial ministrations by the mother are not distinguished by the infant from his own tension-reduction efforts, such as, coughing, vomiting, eliminating, defecating, and sneezing. The mother-infant dyad functions as a psychological unity, sleep predominates over waking, and simple tension reduction is primary. Physiological functions predominate over psychological ones.

Successful development in the symbiotic second stage, which begins in the second month, depends upon a predictable balancing of frustration-gratification; optimally, frustration stays within manageable limits for the infant and gratification is preeminent. Out of this context, and with the occurrence of memory traces of the good and bad qualities of experiences, the infant develops a dim awareness of a self and of something outside the self. Initially, this something (the mother) is experienced as part of the self (a dual unity). From the point of view of the infant's cognitive-affective life, primitive mental images are assumed to be of "oneness," of fusion with mother. Since the child's needs are primary, this outside person is experienced as existing solely for the purpose of im-

---

[6]S. Hartman. "The Mutual Influences in the Development of the Ego and Id." *Psychoanalytic Study of the Child.* Vol. 7. New York: International Universities Press, 1952.

mediate gratification. Thus, during this second phase, in which differentiation of the self from the mother begins, need-gratification remains primary.

It is primarily in the symbiotic stage that the foundation for an individual's ability to trust others is laid down. This requires a mother who is sufficiently attuned and responsive to the signals sent out by the infant, to be able to administer appropriately. As a result of reliable gratification, rudimentary memories and images of the "good" mother are formed, which form the foundation for basic trust. The attachment figure is thus conceived as being trustworthy and ready to help. It is this confident expectation that ultimately underlies emotional valuing of others, object constancy, and social interaction.

Progression to the third stage, separation-individuation, which extends into the third year of life, depends also on the nature of the mother-child relation. If a sufficient closeness has evolved, a gradual process takes place whereby the infant-toddler disengages from the mother and establishes individuality and autonomous functioning. This does not refer to a physical separation but to a psychological separation, so that the toddler can experience a sense of separateness from the mother and, through this, from the world at large. The development of the perceptual apparatus and the increase in wakefulness prepare the way for active scanning of the environment. The infant's previous manner of responding to the mother by molding to her body is replaced by new behaviors of manual, tactile, and visual exploration of the mother's face and body. This facilitates a successful differentiation of self-perceptions, particularly of body boundaries, from perceptions of the mother as well as an eventual discrimination of the mother from others. With the continued process of differentiating inner stimuli from outer and of self from others, an internal representation of the mother occurs (that is, making part of oneself that which is external). In a broader sense, a working model is built up in the individual consisting of stable perceptions, beliefs, attitudes, and expectations with regard to relationships, the world, and the self as an agent in it. This internalized model becomes the guide to the world in general.

Thus, by this gradual internalization process, the normal three-year-old achieves a state of emotional object constancy, that

Sécurité acquise

is, the child can sustain an inner image of a positively valued mother. This inner image supplies comfort to the child and offers continuity in the relationship without the physical presence of the significant figure, thus promoting independence. For this to occur, the child must have had good experiences of gratification and tension reduction in the symbiotic phase that will facilitate trust and confidence as well as sufficient cognitive development for symbolic representation via memory and fantasy to occur. With this accomplishment, temporary separations can be lengthened and better tolerated, paving the way for autonomous functioning; the mother then acquires value as a person independent of the state of need.

With the successful psychological separation of the self from the mother and the consolidation of individuality, the individual ultimately proceeds to develop mature interpersonal relations. This necessitates not only the capacity to value others independently of services rendered, but also the ability to suspend individual needs at times in favor of another's—true mutuality. This stage has important implications for the development of willfulness, free choice, and cooperation, which will be weakened if basic trust has not been established.

Successful negotiation of the separation-individuation phase is a gradual process of the infant absenting himself or herself from the mother so that anxiety can be tolerated and eventual separation may take place (concomitant with the internal representation of the mother in her absence). As the toddler moves back and forth between the mother and the world, the emotional attunement and availability of mother, who must encourage separation but also emotionally "refuel" the toddler when needed, is crucial. Individuals who have never achieved a sense of constancy (internal representation of the mother) sufficient to feel secure when the mother is no longer physically present may be plagued in later years by anxiety and terror when disruptions occur in meaningful relationships.

There are many other developmental tasks to be accomplished beyond separation and differentiation—for example, internalization of parental rules and standards (superego development), development of social skills, and reaffirmation and maintenance of identity during adolescence. The degree of success in accomplishing these developmental tasks will have major implications for the problems posed in marriage and the potential for resolution and

further growth. For our purposes here, we will give greater emphasis to problems originating in the second and third stages, since
such problems, if fairly fixed, deeply affect couple-therapy treatment. Individuals with problems rooted in the first stage would in
all likelihood have such serious problems that they could not maintain an extensive dyadic relationship and consequently would not
be candidates for couple therapy.

A significant portion of marital problems are rooted in the
failure to resolve early symbiotic ties and the subsequent failure to
complete successfully the separation-individuation stage. For some
individuals, such problems may occur primarily in times of stress;
for others, failure at these stages has more profound consequences.
For example, failure in gender identity, which may provide the
basis for homosexuality, often results from an unsuccessful resolution of symbiotic wishes; the self and the mother are experienced
as the same and gender distinction is not made. Milder problems,
such as a constant need for reassurance through frequent contacts
with the spouse (reminiscent of the "refueling" of the toddler) may
result from an incomplete resolution of symbiotic ties, which disrupts subsequent successful differentiation. The spouse who experiences all requests of the mate as infringements on his or her autonomy could have had difficulty in the late separation-individuation
phase, because of a mother who discouraged efforts toward independent functioning. An individual whose mother discouraged
and disapproved of disengagement because she perceived it as
rejection may have difficulty in asserting his or her own individuality
in marriage, fearing that separateness would bring loss of love.
In this case, the individual may believe that love and approval can
only be achieved by denying self-needs and subjugating the self to
others.

The symbiotic desire for fusion, when intense, will result in
more marked marital problems. The spouse who has not achieved
a sufficient degree of separateness and identity will have great difficulty in a close dyadic relationship. This may be manifest in a
number of ways. One is an abnormal need for closeness with the
partner and a total inability to tolerate the partner's absence. A common problem is the wife of the graduate student who feels left out
and jealous when her husband's time and energy are invested in
work outside the home. Another case is the married adult who can-

not separate from the mother and who uses the mother to fulfill the spouse or parental duties. A further example is the spouse who experiences the successes or failures of the partner as a direct reflection of personal glory or disgrace, or expects exclusive attention from the mate. She will often press for greater participation in her spouse's work, social life, and activities.

In all these examples, the lack of psychological separateness and the desire to maintain a feeling of oneness underlie the behavior. At the pathological extreme are those individuals, commonly referred to as borderline personalities, who have grave difficulties in their dyadic relationships and who often suffer from acute separation anxiety. Although such behavior may appear selfish, the therapist will need to keep in mind the anxiety aroused in the absence of the symbiotic partner and, characteristically, the degree to which it is overwhelming and less subject to defensive alleviation. Many patients remain fixed in symbiotic union, fearing that separation will destroy both the self and the other. The therapist will find that these severe problems will not be readily resolved in couple treatment.

In some ways, men are more likely to use marriage to fulfill symbiotic wishes, since women characteristically play the mothering role and may attract the mate by offering nurturance. The very structure of marriage, in which the wife's role is cast as the caretaker of the home and family, reinforces the symbiotic pull. However, once married, the husband will face frustrations when symbiotic needs cannot be totally met. Even the best wife cannot exist solely to serve her husband's needs. The appearance of children usually compounds the problem, since the wife, as a mother, must now turn her attention to the infant, leaving the husband feeling even more left out and ungratified.

The unconscious wish for symbiotic fusion and the failure to establish individual autonomy are unlikely to diminish in response to a cognitive treatment approach, whereby the therapist stresses the importance of each individual's need for separateness. However, through such an approach, one provides support for both spouses by protecting autonomy. Through this help, the spouse, overly encumbered with symbiotic wishes, may become more aware of them. Awareness may also be increased by encouraging spouses to understand the initial choice of the mate and the needs that underlie overt, clinging behavior. Even if greater awareness cannot be achieved, the therapist can clarify the untenableness of certain assumptions within the current relationship and encourage verbal communication to foster better understanding and to help meet realistic expectations. The more that a spouse's behavior is governed by conscious, rational motives, the more the therapist can help. By supporting individual rights, the therapist can promote a better understanding of the nature of the anxiety for both spouses. What may be viewed as an irrational and selfish approach by one's spouse may be viewed differently if the behavior is better understood, for example, if the partner realizes that the spouse's behavior represents a primitive fear of abandonment and that the spouse feels that, if left alone, he or she would literally no longer exist.

Marital difficulties also arise out of the opposite problem— fear of the desire for symbiotic union; often strenuous defenses are erected to guard against the gratification of this desire, lest identity be obscured. To preserve the self-image of autonomy and separateness, the longed-for state is often defended against by substitution of its opposite. Thus, we see the cold spouse who is overly independent and maintains great distance from the mate. For example, one spouse (who was also seen individually) who became aware of his intense need for distance had progressed to the point of allowing some preliminary sexual play as a form of closeness. However, he did not want his wife to acknowledge this change on his part, so great was his fear of commitment and union. This intense need for distance is difficult to treat in couple therapy. A small goal that may be obtained is to help the spouse who seeks greater closeness to appreciate the defensive nature of the mate's behavior and to realize that it does not indicate a lack of caring; this may prevent the spouse from becoming discouraged and withdrawing the closeness previously offered. Adjusting closeness to fit with the level of tolerance is necessary but hazardous. In some cases, however, a spouse capable of greater closeness may terminate the marriage out of frustration.

An assessment of the level of development in mature interpersonal relations that each individual has reached is often difficult. Although couples will readily declare their love for one another, it is crucial to determine whether each partner's love consists of some wish to give, or if the partner seeks mainly to be given to. Marriage can be used to be taken care of and to be supported rather than to share with both giving and taking. Many individuals who have never received sufficient love remain fixated in a passive-receptive position, seeking those who will support and take care of them. They are unable to provide any mutuality and are unlikely to be able to gratify their partner sexually or in other ways. Even in less extreme cases, the therapist will need to be aware that the very closeness of marriage involves constant stimulation of symbiotic wishes. Since resolution of these wishes is never complete, regression under stress is likely. For example, at times of great fatigue or sickness, the wish for a symbiotic fusion with the mother is prominent; at such times, we all feel childlike and tend to seek the reassurance and protection of a more powerful and nurturing individual.

The maintenance of separateness while still being attuned to the other's needs and the ability to retain one's own identity within a context of closeness and mutuality are the foundation for any successful union. The couple are continuously faced with the task of maintaining "optimal distance"[7] in their daily give-and-take, sexual relations, and parenting. Furthermore, the nature of marriage fosters an interdependence, yet this very dependence may serve as a threat to autonomy. Thus, in marriage, couples must constantly deal with the varying aspects of coming together and being apart, which involve their identity, autonomy, interdependence, separation, and mutuality. The interplay of these variables can be seen in the sexual act. Coming together sexually may provide immense gratification for some individuals, but for those who have not successfully separated from the mother and have not solidified an autonomy and identity, this very union may provoke harsh anxieties of being consumed or of merging.

Since fluctuations in functioning are common, it is useful to assess not only the kinds of developmental deficits that are reflected in present behavior, but also how firmly entrenched these problems are. Do the maladaptive behaviors represent only temporary regression in the context of generally more adequate functioning? Under the various pressures of life, spouses may occasionally manifest behaviors that are characteristic of earlier stages of development. For example, in times of stress, a partner may go to bed and

[7]M. Bouvet. "Technical Variations and the Concept of Distance." International Journal of Psycho-Analysis, 1958, *39*, 211–221.

insist on being pampered even with minimal physical discomfort; at other times, however, this same spouse may show a high level of coping with work and other activities. Therapeutic goals can be ambitious in this case and optimism greater. The therapist would want to reinforce the individual's positive achievements wherever possible as well as to help the individual to find ways to employ regressive behaviors that would be tolerable to the partner. Helping individuals to understand regressive needs and to accept them in a way that does not seriously impair either partner will relieve guilt and foster a closer relationship.

Entrenched patterns of behavior that cause stress for the individual and the mate will provide useful diagnostic and prognostic information. The therapist will want to note how rigidly a spouse maintains a pattern of behavior that excludes the mate's needs. The therapist may gain an even broader perspective of the fixity of specific maladaptive behaviors by noting the functioning in areas besides marriage, as in work or with friends. If such data are not indicated on the data sheet or do not emerge spontaneously in the interchange, the therapist may make pointed inquiries.

Further assistance in determining the fixity of pathological behavior will be provided by noting the spouse's capacity to develop a therapeutic alliance, to hear therapeutic interventions, and to use interventions to show some modification of behavior in the session. In one case, the wife failed to alter her behavior in response to almost any intervention offered in the opening session. Since she was determined to deliver a long diatribe blaming her husband for all their problems, there were many therapeutic efforts to redirect her—all to no avail. The wife did not get what she wanted (the therapist's compliance with her wish to force her husband to change), and it was easy to predict that the chance of any successful work was slim, despite the therapist's efforts to hear her frustration and to intervene and encourage a different way of responding. In this case, the wife's minimal frustration tolerance interfered with the development of trust in the therapeutic relationship; we could infer a substrata of tremendous frustration in achieving need-gratification and a built-in expectancy of disappointment with its consequent rage. Thus, by carefully noting a spouse's responses to therapeutic interventions and to the mate's behavior, one can learn a great deal about the fixity of pathological problems and the capacity for change and for working relationships. The data base of diagnosis is essentially the experience in therapy, which will provide valuable cues for intervention and guide the ongoing process of therapy.

Once the nature and fixity of unresolved problems are understood, the therapist is in a good position to determine how to proceed. Significant fixation, particularly with developmental problems relating to the second and third stages, limits the use of couple treatment. The therapist may choose to focus on helping the partner who has more adaptive capacity. If both partners exhibit significant developmental deficits, which are reflected in the marital clash, the therapist may wish to work toward furthering understanding of the problems of each individual. Although this may not eliminate their individual problems, it may encourage the exploration of ways to deal with them as they affect the spouses that will lessen the stress for both. In other words, although the therapist recognizes the urgency of the unconscious fears or wishes, he or she can still support problem-solving attempts to the extent of the couple's capability. If this is not promising, the therapist can steer the individual with the more fixed problem toward individual treatment.

The therapist may need to focus on an individual with severe developmental problems and prepare him or her for individual treatment by developing the individual's trust, helping the individual to abandon excessive projection (blaming), and encouraging greater frustration tolerance and delay of gratification. Although success may be limited, the couple format offers some opportunities for such work. For example, attention to interactional patterns in times of stress and emphasis on discussion versus action, as when spouses resort to physical attack, will increase the capacity to deal with anxiety and to refrain from impulsive expression. Helping the individual with *greater* delay capacity to understand, control, and disengage can reinforce the efforts made by the individual with *less* capacity. Nevertheless, individuals diagnosed as borderline personalities are ill-equipped to develop the therapeutic relationship necessary for success within the couple format. For these individuals, the therapist should terminate couple treatment and encourage the spouse to obtain individual treatment.

Other useful diagnostic information is obtained by noting

the extent of anxiety and the nature of the defenses, that is, the characteristic ways of dealing with anxiety. Regression has already been noted. Other kinds of defenses may be conspicuous. For example, a spouse may consistently refuse to acknowledge blatant reality problems with the partner and thus not be amenable to problem-solving through negotiation. It is difficult to invest energy in the latter process when all energy is invested in denying or ignoring what is unpleasant and might engender anxiety. Such a strong denial, one of the most primitive defenses, would imply severe obstacles to be surmounted in therapy.

Particularly common in marriage is the use of displacement and projection as defenses. Some spouses have difficulty in experiencing anxiety as emanating from within and tend to perceive its sources as externally derived. When anxiety is extreme, the mate will often serve as a ready displacement object and will become the object of blame. In some cases, spouses will attribute to their mates their own bad feelings that cannot be owned, or the opposite may occur; the mate is perceived as faultless and the self becomes the reservoir of the bad feelings. Whatever the manifestation, couple treatment lends itself readily to projection and displacement. With sufficient support, these defenses will hopefully be relinquished. When they are not, diagnostic and prognostic cues will indicate early developmental problems that are relatively pathologically ingrained. Again, whatever the defenses typically used, it will be important to assess how rigidly they are employed.

In addition, the therapist will want to note whether the defensive system can be mobilized in dealing with anxiety and how successfully the defenses maintain equilibrium. A stable defensive system may be employed that will permit alleviation of anxiety associated with primitive wishes by substituting acceptable behaviors, such as orderliness and cleanliness in reaction to wishes to mess. Where such behaviors are not carried out to extreme, they may be very functional. If, however, a stable defensive pattern is not available, an individual will be more vulnerable to anxiety and its debilitating effects, which can be overwhelming in extreme cases. If anxiety is intense, the spouse will need supportive measures, and confrontations that would add to the anxiety will have to be postponed. Thus, the therapist will want to pay special attention to the spouse's capacity to withstand anxiety and carefully guard against using confrontations too frequently or too soon. This will be especially difficult in a couple context, since the mate will inevitably be confronting the spouse with behaviors deemed undesirable. The therapist must also avoid experiences that would arouse so much anxiety in a spouse as to promote disintegration. When an individual lacks internal regulating mechanisms for dealing with anxiety, the therapist must be even more alert to the role he or she plays in influencing anxiety in therapy, with the ultimate goal of helping the spouse to learn how to cope with anxiety better.

A spouse's ability to tolerate anxiety greatly limits the procedures to be utilized in couple therapy. Since couples frequently vary in this ability, it is important not only to elicit possible solutions to problems from the spouses (as opposed to giving solutions didactically), but also to assess the tolerability of a solution for each spouse. What may appear to be a perfectly obvious, appropriate solution may prove to be extremely anxiety-producing for one spouse and thus totally unacceptable. Gauging the comfort of each spouse as work progresses is mandatory for effective help.

The above discussion has included some of the developmental problems that might be encountered in couple therapy. In the following chapters we will highlight behaviors that suggest developmental failures and unconscious determinants that contribute to problems and how they affect the therapeutic work. Clearly, being aware of problems emanating from developmental arrests or incomplete resolution of developmental tasks will immeasurably contribute toward understanding a couple's problems and aid in adapting to them therapeutically. It will be of particular value to the therapist to be able to recognize present behaviors that are rooted in unconscious assumptions, wishes, and fears that will not yield to rational persuasion or "reasonable" solutions.

The previous discussion belies the complexity of the subject matter, but hopefully exposure to a way of thinking that may not be characteristic of all individuals doing couple work will promote further study and understanding of a theoretical framework that can be helpful. We have emphasized problems arising in the earliest developmental stages because of their crucial role in determining an individual's capacity to form relationships with others. The relative success in identity formation in the separation-individuation stage has a special implication for marriage. Since identity is not clearly established, it must be worked out and reaffirmed in the close relationship with the spouse. Further, even in normal development, resolution of symbiosis and separation-individuation is never complete in any absolute sense. Varying aspects of earlier problems will emerge to shape present behaviors and must be attended to and understood even if not pathologically entrenched. Because identity is never completely established, even the relatively "normal" individual in the early years of marriage will be engaged in further work in establishing the self as uniquely different from the spouse and others. The closeness of marriage with its pull toward merging and union will prove hazardous as the spouse attempts to tread his or her way separately but also with "togetherness." Thus earlier developmental problems always cast some shadow, however pale, on further adaptation.

In summary, it is important to diagnose what problems have impeded development, how intractible they are, and how they contribute to marital disharmony. There must be some capacity for separateness between the spouses and some capacity for mutuality for the therapist to help the couple learn negotiating skills as well as to establish a therapeutic alliance. This means that, for both spouses, basic trust will have been established and development will have successfully proceeded beyond the level of immediate need-gratification. The capacity to perceive one's partner as being independent from the self and having separate needs is necessary for our cognitively oriented couple therapy. Without this capacity, the individual may need major preparatory work to correct the developmental flaws. The reader will note that we say *some* capacity for separateness and mutuality. This is by way of pointing out that the establishment of trust, object constancy, and mutuality occur in relative degrees, as does resolution of the other normative developmental tasks. The therapist thus should expect some ramifications of early developmental snags to be present in therapeutic work; this does not necessarily forecast a poor outcome. When problems are mild, one can expect the spouses to respond well to a primarily cognitive-oriented therapy.

3

Early Phases
of Couple Therapy

Varying Vantage Points of Spouses

Couples come to a therapist for various reasons. How they come is a major factor to be considered when one begins therapy. Often they have been sent because someone (a mental health professional, minister, or friend) has told them that they should seek professional help. Even though they may recognize their distressed marital relationship, being sent by someone else is vastly different from the couple taking the initiative themselves.

For example, patients hospitalized for psychiatric reasons usually evidence strain in their marriage. Frequently individuals working with such patients will identify "marital troubles" and refer the patient and spouse for help. The couple often arrive with only a vague idea of why they were sent, even though an explanation may have been given. As a result, they do not have the set or motivation to involve themselves in a therapeutic process as described in this book. This is not to say that they cannot be helped; but it is essential when beginning treatment to determine what the couple's understanding is of why they have come and what will ensue, because this will determine how the therapist should set the early structure of the therapy.

Sometimes one or both of the spouses come because "it's the thing to do." They may be sophisticated enough to know that "marital counselors" exist and feel obligated to make use of their services, not so much out of any conviction or belief in possible help, but to conform to middle-class values. Again, although this does not preclude help, recognition of this alerts the therapist to specific problems likely to be encountered early in therapy. These often involve a spouse's readiness to appeal to a higher authority to settle disputes, and the proneness to fall into the common trap of assuming that if somehow the therapist can be convinced of how bad the spouse is, then he or she will reform this spouse and reduce marital stress. Much more will be said about this later.

A variation of this attitude is when one spouse has decided to dissolve the marriage but "saves face" by seeking therapy. This alleviates any personal guilt one may have for not trying and prevents the other spouse from saying, "You haven't really given it a fair chance." Helping a couple early in therapy to clarify their positions, what they want to work toward, and what their attitudes are toward these goals brings individual preferences and differences into focus more clearly.

Often a spouse has been forced to come by the partner and is unwilling to participate, typically feeling exposed and defensive in response to accusations of the mate. The therapist will need to be particularly sensitive to this feeling of vulnerability and make extra efforts to minimize it.

Occasionally a spouse comes out of desperation, fearful of losing the mate. In this case neither spouse really comes voluntarily; the frightened spouse feels pressured to come lest the marriage crumble, while the other spouse may accompany the mate out of obligation. One should specifically note which spouse is less enthusiastic, since this may provide helpful information. For example, the husband complying with his wife may feel his masculinity is compromised and be ready to defend himself rigidly against anticipated threats. Here the therapist must work toward minimizing the husband's defensiveness.

Two related variables seem important in determining the attitudes of the spouses regarding treatment: the extent to which they feel helpless to improve their marital situation, and their degree of enthusiasm or pessimism that help can be achieved through a third person. For example, even though expressed with many doubts, a spouse who says "*I* want to save our marriage and will do whatever it takes," is quite different from a spouse who says "I don't think there's anything that can be done." Notice that in the latter case help is viewed as beyond the self, while the former assumes personal responsibility. A statement of experienced helplessness does not necessarily foretell doom. However, it does alert the therapist to the feelings and expectations of that spouse. It may reflect the characteristic stance of an individual who feels a victim of circumstances beyond his or her control. In such cases, it will be one of the therapist's major tasks to help the spouse *experience* that he or she does help determine what happens in the marriage.

Equal enthusiasm is hardly to be expected nor is it necessary, although it is delightful when it occurs. No overt recognition of the varying degrees of enthusiasm need be made. However, recognition of such aids in the assessment and therapeutic tasks. Statements often suggest early developmental problems that have prevented optimistic anticipations toward dyadic relationships. Individuals with such expectations will be more difficult to help than those who assume a positive attitude with magical expectations of the omnipotent parent-therapist, although these people present a problem that also must be dealt with.

These vantage points unfold as the therapist begins to work with the couple. Identifying different vantage points of spouses for the potential therapist is by way of stressing the importance of being aware of the different attitudes and feelings with which the couple arrive: compliance, defiance, desperateness, ambivalence, fright, anger, or dependence. The therapist is then better prepared for the various problems that will ensue. This is not to suggest that the spouses should be confronted with their viewpoints; this may make matters worse, particularly where there are sharp differences in their positions. It is enough that both spouses be present and that the therapist be aware of their respective stances.

We must add that although any of the negative feelings mentioned above may be present, there can still be some concern for the partner and for the marriage, even though for reasons of self-interest. If one can discern such concern, it is most helpful to focus on its positive aspects. Occasionally, what may appear to be resistance to help (for example, an oppositional or negativistic attitude) may in fact be a positive struggle of that spouse to establish and maintain identity, in itself a worthy goal.

We might mention here one prevalent vantage point that will be discussed in detail later. Many individuals arrive with magical, unrealistic expectations of the therapist, who is viewed as possessing varying degrees of omniscience and omnipotence. The therapist may be imbued with powers and strength beyond any capacities he or she could possibly have. Varying therapeutic moves will be necessary to dissipate such perceptions.

Telephone Calls

Therapy often starts when a spouse calls the therapist to make an appointment. At this time, the therapist should do the following: make known the therapist's availability, determine if the spouse has discussed the proposed meeting with the mate (if not, suggest that this be done first, with a subsequent call to the therapist by either partner), set up a working time that all three agree upon, and minimize the discussion of problems. Usually only the last presents any problem. Spouses frequently need to unburden and thus try to discuss their dissatisfaction and unhappiness over the telephone. The therapist can supportively acknowledge these feelings but should state that since the distress concerns the spouse, it would be better to wait until all three can meet together. It is preferable not to relate extensively at this time to an individual spouse because of the therapist being perceived as more allied with one spouse than the other. Most spouses will accept this and limit the call to the particulars necessary for setting up the meeting. When the spouse continues to vent complaints, comments should be limited to acknowledging that the need for help and the urgency of his or her feelings are the reasons for the spouse's difficulty in waiting for an arranged session. However, one can reiterate that waiting for the actual session would be most helpful.

A problem often arises when a spouse calls but has not yet talked with the partner about engaging in therapy and feels unable to do so. One should encourage the spouse to talk to the partner; if the spouse is unwilling to do this, the therapist may (although not enthusiastically) agree to call the partner. If this is done, it is important to avoid any blame when mentioning that the spouse has called; rather, stress the relationship problem. The therapist should explain that he or she is calling only to see if the partner and the spouse will meet with the therapist to explore whether the three might wish to work together. If the partner refuses, no further effort should be made except to convey this to the original spouse and, if desired, to offer services for individual help.

Beginning Sessions: The Importance of Structuring

The first sessions are extremely important and demanding. Because there has been little or no previous contact, the problems that the triadic relationship poses will stand out. At this point, the therapist has the opportunity to lay down the ground rules of how the couple and therapist will proceed and to assess how well this structure is received. By their responses, the therapist will learn much about each spouse's willingness and capacity to work in this mutual way and can begin to assess strengths and liabilities, with the diagnostic understanding growing out of the therapeutic tasks. As one attempts to elicit interest and participation in the mutual work to be done, one begins to foster a therapeutic alliance with each spouse. This provides additional information for assessing possibilities for help.

The first order of business after initial introductions is to inform both spouses of what one knows about them and how this is known. Usually the therapist opens with a comment like, "As you know, your wife called me about the two of you coming in, and essentially what I learned was that things haven't been going well between you." One may add more detail if this has been relayed. The following example from an actual first therapeutic session illustrates this point. In this case, because of working in the same setting, the husband had stopped by the therapist's office to discuss the possibility of help.

> T: Your husband came in a few weeks back. That was my first contact with him. My memory of what he said to me at that time was that you had some problems and that you were thinking of coming for help. And then he came in today. . . . Your husband spent just a little time telling me about the marriage. I don't know very much about it other than it's not going too well and he's upset, and would like some things better. . . . He talked a little about you, and I think it's fair to your wife for me to be able to tell her, if that's O.K. with you, what you said about her, [to wife] because then you'll know where I'm starting at. He told me you had had a job, but now that you weren't working, you were at home, and you have some concern about doing something worthwhile or not doing something worthwhile . . . maybe some concern about your status with respect to the people you associate with. . . . So that's kind of mostly what I know. I'm telling you so you'll know what has transpired between us.

Another example is that of a patient who had been hospitalized: "Dr. George, your doctor on the ward, suggested that since you two have been having some difficulties that it might be helpful to talk to someone about them." One may want to add parenthetically to the hospitalized spouse, "I know from your doctor that you have been in the hospital for the past few weeks feeling depressed."

The following is an opening comment from a first session where, in addition to relating what she knows of the relationship and how the knowledge was gained, the therapist begins to structure how the couple are to work.

> T: Now all I know about you is that your wife called, and the only thing she said to me was that you were having trouble

with your marriage. I did talk with Dr. X [referral source]; he did not tell me anything other than that you were having trouble with your marriage. So that's all I know about you. I just want you to know where I am. Maybe you could start talking together about what you think the trouble is.

Although this instruction is fairly simple, contrast it with a comment such as, "Why don't you two talk together?" This comment does not sufficiently structure what the couple should talk about and could be easily misunderstood. Since the therapist who made the above comment had already heard some initial complaints, a more focused comment might have been, "Maybe it would be helpful if you two could begin to talk now about the problem of who does the checks, and perhaps work toward some solution of this; perhaps it would be helpful to let each other know how you feel and what you would like." As the discussion begins, the therapist may need to give additional structure from time to time.

An example of another undesirable early structuring question is, "What's the main thing you see that has fouled up your marriage?" Although focusing on the interaction, it implies there is a primary problem that the couple must discover before they can achieve help. The spouses may not know how to approach such a formidable task. Furthermore, the comment tends to begin therapy with a negative focus, suggesting blame and points away from the spouses' responsibility for their problems.

Opening comments should emphasize two things: The problem to be focused on is what is happening between the spouses, and the therapist has no alliance with either spouse and is available to both. This cannot be overstressed, since maneuvering for alliance with the therapist is one of the earliest and most persistent problems in couple therapy (see the section on blame in Chapter Four).

After the opening comment about what one knows, one usually attempts to direct the beginning of the session by suggesting to the couple how they may start. Without a structure, one spouse will inevitably begin to criticize the mate, who in turn seeks to redress with a subsequent argument. Even with the initial structuring toward talking together, the couple often start to talk to the therapist, voicing their complaints and criticisms.

T: The way I would like for you to start is for you two to be-
    gin talking together about what you're concerned about
    in your marriage—what kind of problems you're having.

W: Well, I think we ought to tell *you* why we're here and let
    you ask us things from there.

Notice the wife's need to direct the flow of communication to
the therapist so that the therapist can then find out more about the
couple. The wife proceeded to relate that her husband had been
talking of wanting a divorce for a long time and that she decided
they needed help; this immediately elicited a complaint from the
husband about the wife.

Talking only to the therapist should be avoided for it is rarely
productive and often destructive. Very early one should set the
structure for problem-solving rather than talking about each other.
In talking about each other, the couple avoid any real confrontation. Spouses will frequently comment, "That's all we've done is go
over and over this, time and again, and it doesn't help"; or "We've
talked till we are blue in the face and it always ends the same—in an
argument"; or "That's the trouble, we can't talk together." A usual
therapeutic answer is to agree with the spouses that they probably
have talked at length, but that now it will be different because the
therapist will be with them as they talk and will help them learn
more about the nature of their difficulties and help them learn
how to talk together so that they can better deal with some of their
unresolved problems.

This is illustrated below. After the therapist's opening comments and structuring, the spouses begin to talk to the therapist.
The therapist points out that the spouses are not talking to each
other.

T: I was hoping . . . you two could talk together about what
    you see that is going on between you.

W: We've done an awful lot of talking between the two of
    us, so. . . .

T: Right, I'm sure you have. The different thing you will be
    doing now is with a third person here and there may be

> some things going on that I can help you with as you talk
> together and try to understand better, to do something
> about this trouble.

It is important to acknowledge whatever feelings spouses are
expressing in their opening comments, be they discouragement,
helplessness, or whatever. Although one can recognize that the
spouses have lost faith in their own abilities to solve their problems,
one can also point out that since they have chosen to come, it is to
their advantage to use the time to see how they can work together
with the therapist to better their relationship.

The therapist should not promise to take over but should convey the willingness to use therapeutic skills to help the couple, stressing that all three will be working together. The stage is being set for
the spouses to assume more responsibility in the therapy. The therapist is also trying to convey that help lies in the mutual work, not
with the therapist. One should be careful to avoid making promises
which may feed into omnipotent wishes. The therapist attempts to
foster hope and provide encouragement, but the promise is not help
per se, but help to aid the spouses to learn how to deal more effectively with their problems.

In a case where the couple say that they cannot talk to each
other, one might respond that this probably means that they cannot
agree when they do talk together and perhaps have given up trying.
At any rate, the therapist should encourage them to begin talking
together now.

The next common stage is that the couple will appear confused and say, "But we don't know where to start; there is so much."
The therapist can agree that there must be much going on between
them that cannot be quickly conveyed, and then suggest that they
decide on something that is uppermost in their minds at the moment
that is particularly troublesome in their relationship and that they
can begin to talk about together. The therapist may add that in time
it will be possible to talk more about the many things that are contributing to their dissatisfaction, but that it is necessary to start somewhere. Sorting out which are the more important issues to work on
is part of the therapeutic task. The therapist hopes to give a couple
the feeling that although it may all seem complicated and hopeless,

"We will take our time and do what is necessary to see if we can get things going better."

It is preferable to let the couple decide what to begin talking about; a specific topic is rarely suggested. It makes little difference what material the couple choose to begin with; what is important is that they accept the responsibility for beginning and are free to begin with whatever problem they wish to focus on, however they may see it. If need be, it might be added, "You both have told me that things are not going well—maybe you can begin by each of you telling the other how you see the things that are going badly."

A common problem is the couple who have no trouble beginning but cannot be channeled in a way that would be helpful. Often when they begin it is like opening a dam, and remarks explode forth without focusing on an issue. The therapist must modulate this process by commenting on it and then helping the couple to pick one issue to begin working on; otherwise, the session will begin to sound like a free-for-all and may well become one. The therapist should quickly intervene with a comment like the following:

> T: You know one of the problems we're having is that we can't [don't] stay on one issue and try to work for resolution, and what you're doing is moving from one thing to another. You don't get a chance to find out what you can do when you have a point of difference.

Occasionally, rather than beginning to talk to the spouse, the mate begins to talk about personal problems not related to the mate. For example, one wife began to talk of some of the ways she felt different from her husband and their friends; she felt out of place, as if she should be doing or being something different than she was. Her comments were addressed to the therapist. The therapist might deal with this in several ways. In one instance, the therapist said:

> T: I have the feeling you are talking to me. What I want you to do is [talk with your husband about what you see as points of difficulty between the two of you,] because that's the kind of thing we can work on here. Now the things you started talking about are maybe things of your own,

concerns which maybe you could work with individually
with someone—if they bother you sufficiently—but you
see your husband can't do anything about the fact that
you are of a different race, or have less education.

If these factors grated on the husband, they would be quite pertinent; but this did not appear to be the case, and the therapist chose
to redirect the therapy to an interchange between the couple about
their dissatisfactions with each other. The actual reality of the wife's
race and education did not appear significant for the interactional
problems other than indirectly as they contributed to the wife's low
self-esteem.

When the therapy is initiated by one spouse, the partner often
assumes that the spouse has already given biasing information to
the therapist. The assumption may be revealed in the initial comments: "Well, I suppose she told you what a bastard I am." The
importance of this statement is not the assumption about the spouse,
but the assumption that the therapist would believe the spouse and
that the partner is already in a disadvantaged position. It is essential
for the therapist to respond in a way that does not indicate prejudice
and that recognizes that there are differences between the couple
that are causing problems. At this point, it is often helpful to rephrase what the wife or husband originally said in terms of his or
her own needs or hurts and to focus on the assumed mutuality of
the problems: "Yes, I understand from your comments that your
spouse is unhappy, and I am sure that there are things you *both* are
unhappy about with each other—that's what we want to try to
understand better, to see what the two of you can do about the
situation." Here, one sets the stage for each spouse seeing the therapist as someone who can appreciate both persons without taking
sides or blaming. Most importantly, it must be established that the
work will not consist of each partner compiling a long list of complaints about the other; instead, they will look at what is happening between them. By better understanding this, the spouses can
then explore what they may and are willing to do to change the
relationship.

The following is an excerpt from a first session. Note the difficulty the couple have with using therapeutic suggestions and in

talking together, and the persistent need of the husband to justify himself. Note also the therapist's opening remark, which seeks to establish neutrality and the therapist's previous knowledge of the couple; also, note the focus of successive interventions. The emphasis is on the couple talking together and beginning to express what they see as problems, and on countering any unrealistic expectations that they might have.

T: I don't know anything about either of you. You probably know your husband called me. So all I know . . . [to husband] I just want to tell your wife so she knows where we stand, you and I . . . the only thing I know is that you were having some marital problems and that someone had suggested that you call here, so that's where I am. So maybe we could start by you two trying to talk together about what you see is going on between you that's making things not work out for you.

W: Well, I suggest . . .

H: [Interrupting] I think my wife thinks that there isn't really much problem. Or if she thinks there is a problem, it's concentrated on our sexual problem. This is not really true.

Note that the husband is talking for his wife. Eventually the therapist will have to encourage each to speak for himself or herself.

T: O.K., maybe then you two could start by talking together about what you think . . . whether you think there is a problem, or some problems or not. I'm hearing there's not a seeing eye to eye on this, and maybe you could start about that."

H: Well, you want me to talk?

T: Now I want you two to talk together . . . about your differences—about whether or not you have a problem or maybe about what it is, if I'm reading you right, what some reasons are.

> H: Well, I don't hardly know where to start. I would rather just state my case.

This is a common response. Many spouses would rather "state my case" than talk to each other. This way of trying to present evidence for an ultimate judgment alerts the therapist to the spouses' expectations about how help will come.

> T: Well, if we're going to work together, it's going to be important to have you start talking together. Because that's where the help is going to come. It's not going to come by each of you stating your case to me. So what I want you to start doing is talk about what you've already introduced to start with, as a difference in the way of seeing something—that is, whether or not you have a problem or what the problem might be. And I'd like for you to start talking together about that.
>
> H: Well, I just don't know hardly where to start.
>
> W: Well, it seems that all of our problems that we've ever had have been about sex; he seems to put so much emphasis on sex.

The wife begins to talk but addresses herself to the therapist and talks about rather than to her husband.

> T: Since your husband is here maybe you can talk directly to him, rather than referring to him . . . because when you refer to him, you're talking to me, and I'm trying to get you to talk directly to him—in other words, your feelings about this business about whether you have a problem or not over sex. Am I coming through clear?
>
> W: Well, we've discussed this and . . . so many times, you know. It just seems so futile to go over it all again.

This is a very typical response and reflects the discouragement that often accompanies it.

> T: All right, I understand that. . . .

The therapist was interrupted by the husband. The reply should have acknowledged the discouragement shown in the wife's comment and should have helped the wife feel that the therapist would be an ally and lend strength to help the couple.

H: I believe it's almost going to be necessary for us first to talk to you, and then maybe we . . .

T: I thoroughly understand that. You're saying we've discussed this so many times, but what you haven't done though, is discuss it together in the presence of a third person who can then help you learn how to talk about it together so you can work on your problems. I'm here and I'm listening.

[Several minutes of dialogue intervenes, in which the husband begins to state that the problem resides with the wife. The therapist intervenes several times to help the husband stop blaming the wife and state his feelings, frustrations, and needs more; he was not successful. The next two remarks are quoted to illustrate the husband's persistent need to maintain control and his difficulty using therapeutic interventions.]

H: I still feel like it might be better if I was to lay all my cards out on the table to both my wife and you, and then you would . . .

T: Well, then you would expect me to do something I probably would not be able to do for you, and I don't want to mislead you that I have some magical solutions.

difficulté de H.
à parler pour
lui-même - renvoie
Responsi. Au T.
Résiste à se Rapprocher
de w. pour résoudre
problèmes

The following excerpt is given to contrast with the previous example and to illustrate errors in beginning sessions. In both examples, progress is difficult, but it is more the result of the therapist in the second case, as opposed to the severity of the problem in the first.

T: [To husband] Your wife called me up the other day and asked me to make an appointment for marital counseling for the two of you to come in today. How do you feel about coming?

The therapist appropriately begins by informing the couple of his knowledge about them and how it was gained. His final question, however, evokes defensiveness in the husband.

H: Well, I don't really know very much at all. It's her idea. She's got the problems. I don't know why I was called in here. And I'm willing to come along if it will be helpful for her.

In his defensiveness, the husband does what spouses often do— identify the problem as the mate's.

T: You are willing to come into couple therapy?

H: Well, I want to; I'm willing to do that. If that's what is indicated—you feel and they feel that that's what we ought to do—I'll do it.

The husband exhibits conformity rather than assuming any responsibility. The therapist misses an opportunity to deal with this issue by turning to the wife:

Importance pour le T. de miser sur le Here and Now

T: How does it feel to you?

The wife now begins to defend herself.

W: Well, I feel really good about coming. But he says it's my problem and I just don't buy that. It's just as much his problem as it is. . . . I mean I think it's more his fault than it is my fault. I feel really good that we decided to come.

T: I was wondering if there were any particular expectations involved in what can happen here?

The therapist does not deal with the spouses blaming each other and changes the subject.

H: Well, I figured that we'll tell you what's going on and
     you'll explain to us why we're not getting along as well as
     we could, and after a few sessions, you know, we'll under-
     stand what the problem is, and everything will be all
     right

The husband clearly reveals his infantile wishes for an omnipotent
parent who will straighten things out by telling them what to do.

T: You think it will take a few sessions though?

H: I figure . . . you know.

T: [To wife] Is that pretty much what you. . . .

W: Yeah, I think that we could get some suggestions on how
     we could get along better.

T: I think it would probably be a good idea to tell you how I
     do want to approach things before we do get into things.
     Really, the way I see my role is more of a conductor than
     anything else. In other words, helping you to arrive at
     whatever kind of solution to whatever problems you feel
     you have and as particularly as possible. I don't see my
     role as trying to impose anything on you—you know,
     tell you how to solve your problems—but to help you
     communicate with one another as effectively as possible
     so that you can solve your problems the way you want to
     solve them. Do you understand what I mean? Because I
     am an outsider, it's a little easier for me to see the prob-
     lems and how the two of you are communicating with
     each other. I think that's the way in which I can be valu-
     able to you. So if there's really no particular feelings that
     you have that you feel like you need to talk about now,
     maybe one of you can give me an idea of what you think
     the problem is.

The therapist begins to structure therapy but is somewhat general.
Then he asks what the problem is, promoting the erroneous idea
that there is one big problem to be found, and encourages lines of
communication from the therapist to the patient and back.

W: O.K., we'll start. I think Jim [the husband] thinks I'm
really weird because I like to . . . I really get into things
and I enjoy things, and when I get excited about something, I like to share it, and he won't share anything with
me. He just stares off and kind of looks at me like I'm
crazy, and then that starts me thinking, "Well, maybe I
am a little weird," and I get depressed, and it's a cycle
that keeps going on.

The wife assumes feelings about the husband, and the therapist fails
to begin the process of encouraging separateness and each spouse
speaking for himself or herself. Although the husband does correct
her perceptions, the therapist has failed to help her learn the process
of checking out assumptions, many of which may be wrong:

T: [To husband] Do you see things the way she sees them?

The therapist focuses too much on whether there is a problem. This
reinforces the husband's defensiveness, and he again disclaims personal responsibility:

H: I see it as a problem, but I see it more as her problem.
And I'm naturally concerned that she gets upset, and I'd
rather she didn't, but I don't see what I do. I don't know
what there is I can do to make things different
T: Who could tell you?

Although a simple question, it is somewhat challenging, and the husband again defers to the therapist's authority:

H: Well, I don't know, maybe you can—you're the expert.
T: So you think I can tell you what to do?

The therapist is not stating his position and is not making his role
clear to the spouses. The husband gets more defensive:

H: Not now, but maybe when you get to know us . . . maybe

you can. I don't see what I can do to change; I don't see
it at this point. I don't see how she can get so upset.

T: If you know what to do, would you want to do it?

The therapist becomes more provoking, insinuating that the husband does not want to do anything. At this point the therapist and
the husband are mildly sparring.

H: Well, I . . .

T: Would you be interested in giving it a try?

The therapist attempts to elicit cooperation.

H: It would make things better, yeah, as long as I don't have
     to change myself too much. I'm pretty happy with myself,
     I mean, I don't get as happy as Jane [the wife] does but,
     you know, I don't get as depressed.

The husband states his position clearly—to conform as long as there
are no demands. Up to this point, the therapist has failed to structure the session so that the spouses learn that the therapist cannot
help them by himself or herself:

T: So you see it as a problem. You're not sure whose fault
     it is or who has to change. You really don't know what
     to do.

The therapist keeps discussing the notion of who is at fault rather
than restructuring in terms of the failure in mutual gratification.

H: I don't know what to do. I see it as more Jane's problem.

T: Do you understand what he's saying?

W: He's saying that he doesn't . . . he's willing to go about it,
     but he doesn't want to change anything that he does. I
     mean all I want him to do is show a little feeling once in a
     while, and I don't see that now, [to husband] and I don't
     see you willing to do that.

T: Is she right in what she says? I mean, is that what you were saying?

The therapist misses an opportunity here to help the wife with her request for affection. He could have redirected her comment to the husband for a response. Instead he continues to discuss the issue of blame.

H: Well, I guess it is, but I don't think of it that way. I wouldn't put it that way.

T: [To husband] You know how she said it in the beginning? You remember what she said?

W: Yeah, that's what I said. I don't think you make an effort, because you said you were happy in the way you are, and you don't want to change.

T: That's the message you meant to say?

H: Yeah, that's right.

T: Then you were a little bit confused about something else as the problem?

This is an unproductive remark likely to be heard as critical.

H: I was confused?

T: Well, you went on to talk about feelings, and I think you were trying to say something else about that before.

H: Well, I guess I don't like to think that I'm unwilling to give an inch. I guess that's why I said it, I guess. That's what I mean—I don't really see why I should. I mean as far as I can see, I'm O.K.; I behave O.K. We don't happen to fit together sometimes, [To wife] but you're the one that gets upset, not me. I don't see that I do anything to upset you. I'm just being me. And if I don't happen to respond to your feelings or something, then I don't know what I can do to change. You have to accept the fact that I'm just that way.

Because the structure so far is on blame and who must change, therapy is likely to be stymied. Finally the husband, in desperation, pulls out the final stopper: "You'll just have to accept me the way I am." The therapist has not picked up on the husband's frequent comment about not knowing what to do, which could have been done earlier, when the wife was expressing her wish for more affection.

> T: [To wife] How big a problem is that for you?

It would have been more appropriate here to request that the wife tell her husband how important the issues are to her. The wife needs to communicate the importance of her feelings and her wish to have her husband hear her pleas and respond to them.

> W: Well, I think right now it's a pretty big problem, because I get very depressed when I can't share my feelings with somebody who won't show some feelings anyway, and when I don't have someone to share those feelings with, I get very depressed—so it's a big problem.
>
> T: Would you say it's the most important problem you have as a couple now?

The therapist continues his therapist-to-spouse approach, failing to encourage interchange.

> W: Yeah.
> T: Did you know she felt that strongly?
> H: No.
> W: Well, you knew I was getting depressed.
> H: Yeah, but you're kind of always been depressed. Sometimes you're depressed; sometimes you're happy. I just wasn't aware that it was such a big problem. I didn't know it had to do with me, or with us.
> T: How do you think you're coming across to your wife right now? How do you think she's characterizing you?

It is hard to discern the therapist's purpose for this question; it seems unrelated to the previous interchange.

H: How would she . . .

T: How would she describe the way you've been acting?

H: Well, she'd probably think that I'm here . . . I was kind of forced to come . . . but that I'm here and trying to be understanding . . . making an effort. And I'm willing to be open-minded about the whole thing. She probably feels that.

T: [To wife] How would you describe him?

There is an invitation to criticize here; perhaps by encouraging differing views the therapist hopes to correct perceptions, but he only seems to be furthering the rift.

W: [To husband] Just the opposite of what you said. I think that you're being your typical, unemotional self and being cold. You're not showing at all that you're willing to change or do anything. I don't think anything that you said was true.

The therapist misses an opportunity to help the wife learn that her needs will be heard better if she stops criticizing her husband. She needs to learn to talk about her needs (defined behaviorally) rather than to blame her husband. Her comments will only strengthen her husband's defensiveness; it is obvious that he already does not welcome the demands for change. The therapist has not helped the couple so far; the issue before them remains who has the personality flaws, or who has the problem. Therapy has started badly.

H: [To wife] You have a tendency to exaggerate.

T: I'm wondering if I can interrupt here for a minute. You know, I think that it would help if you would say all that again but talk in terms of how you see him, not just what he actually is.

The therapist attempts a valid therapeutic technique of having the spouses tell how they feel or think rather than what the other spouse is.

W: O.K., I see you as . . .

T: Instead of saying he's cold or . . .

W: I see you as uninvolved and unemotional, and I see you as not willing to or not appearing to try very hard to change anything. Is that true?

H: Uh, that's pretty good.

The husband seems to be demoralized at this point.

The above interchange consumed approximately a third of a beginning session. Thus far, the therapist has not been very successful in helping a couple new to therapy to learn its procedures.

Certain aspects of beginning the first session pertain to later sessions. One usually waits for the couple to begin. Couples who have worked long enough so that the therapeutic alliance is solidified usually begin to discuss what they wish with no waiting. Others who are still new to therapy or resistive to assuming responsibility may turn to the therapist for guidance. An appropriate comment to them is, "What do you want to work on today?" Often this helps them to focus on an issue that they wish to pursue.

The opening of a session is extremely important because it sets the stage for how the time will be spent and where the focus will be. It also determines who will assume responsibility for what follows. In listening to tapes of different therapists, we have noted widely varying ways in which therapists begin their sessions. We will comment on the following three examples: "We were talking last time about some of your work problems; how are things going on that?"; "What have you two talked about since our last meeting?"; and "What would you like to work on today?"

Although one might feel that the first comment would get the session started, we see it as the least productive. What actually transpired after this comment, in fact, was a long, detailed account of previous problems at work. This kind of question produces much verbalization but minimal therapeutic interchange; we consider this opening as filler material.

The second comment is an improvement in that it focuses on the interaction between the couple, but it is still quite vague and does not direct the couple toward an important interchange. In the actual session, the couple replied that they had not talked much, and the momentum died. Since the therapist had assumed the initial responsibility for directing, he now had to come up with a new comment. Our preference is for the third comment if silence has been unproductive. It focuses on the interaction; it implies that the couple have come to work on problems; it places the responsibility with them on how they will proceed; and it allows them to focus on what is most important for them as a dyad.

A frequent opening question asked by many therapists is: "How have things been going?" Although this question may be useful, it can have three undesirable effects: It may elicit from spouses an effort to please the therapist (it may suggest that the therapist is looking for evidence that the therapy has been useful and that things are going better); it may invite a glossing over of the problem (frequently, responses are often vague, such as, "Oh, O.K., I guess"); and it may encourage summarizing progress when this may not be appropriate, especially early in therapy.

In one case, although the couple presented the usual problems in beginning the session (their third), the therapist kept the focus on the couple interaction, leaving the responsibility for work with the couple. At the start, the wife commented that she did not know where to begin and looked at her husband and then back to the therapist for help. The therapist replied that since they knew best what was uppermost in their minds that was troubling them, they might begin there. The wife began to expound on some of her problems at work, but this topic went nowhere. The therapist clarified, "When I said what was uppermost in your minds, I meant in terms of what was going on between you that is troublesome that you might want to work on." The wife then began to talk about her feelings of anger and frustration after the last session, when she had expressed a need for her husband to seek her out more, and he had not done so. This then led to a fruitful discussion.

The following example of opening comments from a session after therapy had been underway for some time illustrates less successful therapeutic structuring. Note the therapist's way of beginning the session, the early comments, and what happens.

T: Well, I see you're both here, so tell me what's been happening.

W: Progress report. [laughs]

T: Well, I guess so, yes.

H: Well, not a lot, just plugging along. We've got a lot of irons in the fire—business to transact. It's been a relatively uneventful week, [to wife] wouldn't you say?

W: Yes, I guess so.

T: When you left, there was a sort of an unresolved question hanging in the air that was . . . I think you were working on the idea of making some decision about . . . if your house, or option, or something of that sort . . .

[The husband and wife proceeded to talk of business. The therapist asked more questions and talked of the agent who helped them with the deal.]

T: Well, the problem is not between the two of you but between you and somebody else.

W: No . . . as long as we have somebody else to fight with we don't fight with each other.

H: A common adversary unites us. [laughs]

T: Well, maybe a new technique here . . .

H: It's well-known in diplomatic circles.

W: [To therapist] Sometime I feel we lead you into a bad condition. Do we undo you ever?

T: Well, I know I've been through an hour.

W: That's what I thought.

[Much chitchat follows.]

T: Well, you say things have been sort of rocking along, I take it, no major problems . . .

Notice that the therapist's initial remark is very unstructured and does not assist the couple to begin working in the session. Consequently, their responses are general. The therapist's third remark is more structured but does not help the couple focus on meaningful dyadic problems. On the contrary, it leads them into a discussion of business issues, which the therapist unfortunately supports by asking questions related to the topic. Because of the lack of direction, approximately the first quarter of the session is wasted.

Occasionally, the therapist may want to ask a pointed question relative to the previous session, for example, "How did the things you worked on last week pan out at home?" This may be important for assessing whether the couple are working outside and how successful they are; if they are not successful, it allows exploration of what obstructed their efforts. A possible problem is that this question may detour the spouses from something that is much more important to them at the moment.

A good example of the therapist beginning the session with a structural comment was a suggestion that the couple pause and try to recall ways in which each had been trying to please the other to make things go better since the last meeting four weeks earlier. This was done at a time when the couple seemed discouraged and was intended to be supportive, so that they could gain sufficient strength to renew their work efforts.

Issues of Control and Misconceptions

Some couples refuse to talk to each other no matter how hard the therapist may encourage them. They want to talk to the therapist and only to the therapist, because they want to tell the "judge" what is wrong in the marriage, why it is wrong, what the spouse is doing to make it so, and what this spouse needs to do to remedy it. Often there is a desperation that forces them to tell how it is. They seem to think that if only the therapist could understand, then he or she would be able to correct it at once. This kind of communication can also be viewed as an effort to control the exchange and to manipulate the therapist into assuming responsibility for solutions. A problem for the therapist is that any blunt interpretation or confrontation may alienate the spouse in the beginning session before there has been time to cement the therapeutic triad.

Problems can also arise when the therapist immediately takes control and directs the spouses. Some may complain that the therapist does not know them yet and therefore cannot know what to do. Although agreeing he or she doesn't know them well, the therapist can communicate that his or her way of getting to know them is different from what they might have expected. Regardless of whether this is acceptable to them, they may insist on telling the therapist about their spouse. The therapist must weigh the problem of resentment and possible early alienation against the problem of allowing the spouses to control the interchange in an unhelpful way.

With more experience, particularly when a spouse is desperate, the therapist can permit (by this is meant not interrupting or unnecessarily redirecting too hastily) some of the complaining to continue. However, responses should be restricted to recognizing the hurt rather than accepting the perceptions of the other spouse. Hopefully, one can provide some support through such patience and understanding, and then try to redirect the work toward the spouse interchange as soon as possible.

Even when couples have learned the protocol for talking with each other, they frequently forget. The therapist needs to interrupt them and to remind them whenever it seems crucial to the interchange. When a remark is addressed to the therapist that is not talking about the spouse, one should listen and reply appropriately. Talking to the therapist should be discouraged primarily when it is used to avoid talking with the partner. If a spouse needs to tell the therapist of some pain or hurt, this is appropriate and deserves attention; usually, one can then redirect the comment to the spouse by saying, "Were you aware that your mate felt so badly about that?"

A frequent misunderstanding underlying the need to control the interchange through blaming is the belief that the therapist will serve as a judge. (Eric Berne has called this the "courtroom" game.) Spouses tell the therapist their side of the story (and if they are magnanimous have their mate do likewise), expecting that the therapist will then see the glaring errors of the partner. We cannot overstress how often this occurs, whether to a small or, as in many cases, an extreme degree. One of the continuous tasks of the therapist is to confront the spouses with expectancies they might have that conflict with the therapist's conception of the therapeutic relationship. In essence the therapist says to the spouses, "I won't be a judge nor serve as a jury. I don't want to hear evidence in order to weigh it with respect to who is the guilty culprit. This is not the way that I can be helpful to you. I understand the need each of you has to have someone hear your side in what appears to be a formidable battle between you, but I want to be in a position to help you both be able to get more of what you are seeking, and if it is a better marriage that you both want, then I will be working on the side of the marriage."

How this is communicated will depend on how the couple portray their position, what ploys they use, what their willingness to hear and understand is, and what their ability is to change their course of action. But it is imperative that the therapist encourage the couple not to work from a context of blame but to focus on what is happening, how it can be understood, and what can be done.

Tribulations of Early Therapy

If the therapist and couple have worked through the issues described above, one can tell the spouses at the end of the first session how the work will proceed. Continued clarification will, of course, be necessary in subsequent sessions. We do not require any contract other than the couple's willingness to return. If they have doubts, one can suggest that they try a session or two to see how it goes and then decide whether to continue.

The following is the therapist's concluding remark in a first session:

T: We only have five minutes left. We've had a hard struggle here trying to begin work, and it's always hard—and you've had some kind of feeling about what it would be like, you know, if you continue to come. So I guess I need from you some kind of feedback about how you feel about this kind of process for helping you and what you want to do. It probably is somewhat different from what you anticipated. Most people when they come feel like they can state their cases; each one is going to present their side, and they kind of expect that a third person will tell them something that will resolve it, but it's not really that way that help comes. The only way it's going to come is by my trying to help you learn how to work on your differences, and it is hard work, and it can help.

W: How often do we meet?

T: Usually once a week and sometimes I have you listen to tapes in between.

H: I think it's excellent because Margie is much better with you because she's able to verbalize the way she feels much better than I can, but I think it's helped—it would help.

The following remarks conclude a session of a couple who are much more anxious about the prospects of therapy and reveal their fears and anticipations:

T: We don't have too much time left. I would like for you both to focus on whether you'd like to continue or not. This is kind of the issue we started on—your apprehension and dread about coming and concern about maybe it would make things worse. That was my interpretation of what you said; it would stir up things and make you come to grips more with some of the pains and dissatisfactions, and maybe some lack of sureness about whether you want to go on. I think I picked that up from both of you. I think we ought to spend the last part of the time trying to at least focus on this and see where you are.

W: O.K.

[A long pause follows.]

H: [To wife] Do you have any feelings about it?

W: I'm not sure. When I came in here I was very apprehensive; in the past I've felt very defensive.
[The wife goes on to say she had anticipated a program to change her and if that were the case, she would not want to continue.]

T: You thought it was more one-sided—more directed at you and . . .

W: Yes, I even stated that and if it was going to be that way I frankly cannot handle it. If my husband said either do this or we'll divorce, I'll handle it because I have such great needs for my husband, but . . .
[The wife goes on to talk of the difficulty she would have if efforts were made to change her.]

W: I'm willing to continue.

[The husband voices his fear that his wife may not be able to handle it.]

T: You're afraid something bad will happen?

H: Yeah, I'm afraid she'll just get up and say screw it and walk out.

T: Yeah, she might really just cut you loose and say to hell with it—no more. So you're really afraid you'll lose her— it might break up the marriage?

H: [To wife] 'Cause when you say you can't handle it, I believe you and I hear what you're saying that you can't . . . right now I know that you can't. I think maybe if we set some goals for the session so you'd know you wouldn't be the target, maybe that might be helpful.

W: I don't have any idea, I'll leave it up to you. I don't know.

H: Is that even possible? Could we set the goal of not changing your behavior? But frequently that becomes the issue.

[The therapist points out problems with the wife's anxiety over feeling pressured to change.]

T: [To wife] I don't feel any intention personally to modify you at all; I'm trying to help you both express your needs and see wherein you two can move to help each other satisfy them. It may be only this far or that far; that's for you to work on, to decide—not for me. I don't feel any pressure to modify you in any direction. You can stay right where you are if the relation can sustain it and you both can live with it; that's O.K.—so I can agree with that fine 'cause I don't even conceive of that as what I'm trying to do anyway. I see the problem as one of when [to husband] you state your needs, [to wife] hearing them and attending to them, implies maybe some change. I think that's where the trouble comes in.

H: I don't see counseling as possible without behavior changes on both parts, whether they're asked for or not.

T: You may be asking for them; it's implicit when you say these are the things you want.

H: O.K., so for us to say we're not going to ask any behavior

W: changes of each other, that we're going to come back here
      every week—what for?

W: I didn't say it that way. Now, I said behavior changes of
      me alone.

T: I heard that.

W: I said of me alone.

H: And I said if both of us . . .

W: And if I'm clear it's coming in one direction, I'll say let's
      wait. I'm not going to sit here and listen to a one-sided
      record.

H: O.K.

T: Of course, that seems very appropriate to me. I think
      anybody would feel resentful if they thought you're the
      one that has to do all the changes and everything over
      here is just fine.

Occasionally, after a beginning session, one of the spouses
may refuse to return. Although one may proceed with individual
therapy, when the marital problems remain the focus, there are
some inherent dangers in working with a spouse alone. What we
have seen happen is that the therapist helps the spouse to respect
his or her own needs, learning to become more independent, and to
get some desires met. When the spouse tries to do this at home, the
partner blows up. The spouse may return to therapy but is likely
to be intimidated, more discouraged, and less willing to work. When
the therapist is trying to help a spouse to be assertive toward effecting a change in the partner, this is best done when both are present,
because the therapist will need to help the partner appreciate how
this will also best serve him or her in the long run. If burdened by
fewer resentments, a spouse may evidence fewer annoying or objectionable behaviors; thus the partner stands to gain as well. Without this, the partner is unlikely to tolerate the new behavior of the
spouse resulting from individual therapy.

If a couple returns, there will frequently be some improvement
after the first few sessions of therapy. Often after the first or second
session, couples say that things are better. Apparently, these spouses

were able to alter some behaviors to the benefit of the relationship. However, as therapy continues, these changes prove superficial, and the couple become aware of the difficulty in effecting significant change and of the amount of work necessary. The initial spurt of optimism is often followed by a halt in progress and by discouragement. At this point, the therapist should discuss with the couple their feelings about what has happened and provide support and encouragement: "This kind of bogging down after initial gains is frequent but often temporary. Things can get better with further work."

As therapy continues, couples commonly become anxious; by focusing on their disagreements, more dissatisfactions emerge. Spouses will often mention their mounting anxiety as they leave home for the therapy session. With the intensification of anxiety, there is often a need to avoid discussion of disagreements and working on issues as they arise. The comments below were made at the end of an arduous early session, in which the wife had great difficulty voicing her feelings. One can see her ambivalence and anxiety about continuing.

> W: I feel like we still haven't hit the basic difficulty, like we're just shoving things out of the way.
>
> T: Would you like to get down more to your real feelings?
>
> W: Yes and no. I'm frightened about it.
>
> T: See, I think we started on that briefly today, and it's a difficult kind of thing to do. It may require saying to each other things that are really scary and experiencing things in yourself that shake you up quite a bit.

In some cases spouses express their wish to discontinue therapy. They fear that unearthing all the problems will shatter the marriage beyond repair. As one wife commented in an early session, "I have the feeling we're going to get a divorce, and all we're doing is delaying it. And all this digging is going to lead us into it."

It is important to indicate to the spouses when one becomes aware of such fears. One should encourage spouses to explore the anxiety and to understand it as much as possible. This ability, of course, varies with different spouses. For example, one spouse was plagued with anxiety about being put on the spot and of having to defend herself. Encouraging the spouse to express this feeling gives the therapist further cues on how to proceed. In this case, an effort was made to help the spouses explore what kinds of interchanges were contributing to this spouse's feelings. The spouse was then asked to suggest how the triad might minimize the anxiety.

It is desirable to tell spouses that some anxiety is inevitable as they begin to work seriously and to look more closely at the tensions and disagreements between them:

> T: There is one thing that does happen—and I understand the feelings people have—it does bring out into the open problems that lots of people don't like to focus on because they *are* problems, and it makes you aware of the pain, and unless you can get past that stage to work things out better, all you're stuck with is the pain. Treatment does stimulate a lot of feelings, a lot of discomfort at times.

Understandably, spouses will wish to avoid experiencing unpleasant feelings. One can acknowledge their fear of exposing problems, but also point out that addressing the problems is necessary if the spouses are to achieve the help they came for. To ease the anxiety and fear that are aroused, the therapist should stress the benefits of solving the problems as opposed to avoiding or denying them. By seeing how they can actively determine how things go for them, the spouses can feel more optimistic.

> T: What it requires is caring enough to make the effort. . . . First knowing what it is you need to do—which is part of what we're trying to do—and then caring enough to make the effort. What it means is trying to think about somebody's needs as well as your own.

In the following illustration, the couple, who have had only a few therapy sessions, are well into the hour and have begun to wrestle with a disconcerting issue. The therapist is trying to assist them in working on the problem of how their communication breaks down. The husband has expressed his perception that his wife doesn't "hear" him; the therapist is trying to help them identify what gets in the way of this. The wife, encouraged to analyze her interchange with the husband, begins to cry and comments that she is "tied up in knots."

T: [To wife] Like you said in the beginning, one of the things that does happen here in contrast to being outside where you can put things aside and not resolve them and sometimes act as if they don't exist, is that the nature of what we're doing is to take a look at them. And it's inevitable that it's going to make you uncomfortable; it's going to make most people uncomfortable. They'd just as soon not look at it. I can understand how you'd rather keep it pushed under the rug and not deal with it.

W: But we've been dealing with it for twenty years.

T: You haven't dealt with it in a session like this in which you've both decided you both really want to work and have resolved to make an effort. It *is* work looking at things like this, at what you're doing as you interact, and it is difficult, and it is painful.

The therapist supports the wife through this temporary breakdown by recognizing the difficulty and pain.

Should therapy prove too disruptive, which happens occasionally, the therapist should go along with the couple in the direction they choose. If the pain and fear seem too great, the couple may choose to terminate therapy; it may be that at some future time they will be able to resume. Should the therapist be overzealous in encouraging them to continue, their fears will inevitably interfere with the process of focusing on conflicts during therapy, and no work is likely to be accomplished. Even worse, they may quit shortly thereafter, feeling worse about their marriage and its prospects.

The following remarks sum up the precarious situation of one couple and indicate the therapist's acceptance of their way of dealing with their stress (a decision not to work for change) as a solution they feel comfortable with at the moment, lest they press for changes and break up the marriage.

T: [To husband] And that's where you're stuck 'cause you
feel if you press, your wife will blow up and leave you,
and that's where you're caught. You feel like the relation
is so precarious now and it may be. [To wife] You literally
can't take any kind of pressures from expectancies. [To
husband] You may be reading it quite correctly; I know
you're scared of that possibility. I can sense it when you
retreat very fast. You give up your needs in a hurry and
that may be the only solution at the moment for the total
situation you're both in, the solution in the sense of keeping the marriage together.

It seemed better to terminate couple treatment, once the precarious-
ness of the situation had been brought into focus and the spouses
were aware of and hesitant to encounter the hazards of further therapy. Terminating at such a point with mutual agreement leaves the
door open for help at a later time.

Therapeutic Alliance

We cannot overstress the importance of establishing a working
alliance with both spouses if treatment is to proceed successfully.
Most important, the therapist must be viewed as a nonjudgmental
person. The therapeutic climate must be benign but not overly
gratifying, and the reliability of the therapist unquestionable. A
reluctance to discuss certain problems or feelings should be accepted and respected; forcing compliance will not foster growth.
The therapist also should operate from the premise that each spouse
is entitled to his or her feelings—these are not and cannot be wrong.
Prohibitions and moralistic directions will infantalize the spouses
and offend their adult status. In the interest of respecting autonomy
and the spouses' capacity for change, the therapist would best avoid
these. In addition, from some framework of understanding which
one can make known to both spouses, a given spouse's feelings make
sense. The therapist must not challenge feelings; rather, they are
important data to be given attention. Nor can they be readily legis-
lated. Respecting this principle is important for both spouses, who
hope to change not just behaviors but also feelings. Behaviors are
easier to change than feelings. This does not preclude acknowledg-

ing that given behaviors may in fact stem from certain feelings and often do cause difficulties with the spouse. Once the importance of respect for each spouse's feelings has been emphasized, there is a greater chance for the triad to focus on troublesome behaviors without the judgmental implications that cause difficulty. Spouses will then be less defensive and be able to address behaviors that they feel they can and should change.

It is extremely important that any therapeutic suggestions be responded to freely by the spouses and voluntarily rather than from a need to conform to authority. Unless the therapist can foster this kind of mutual participation, little of value is likely to be accomplished. The goal is to promote a feeling of sharing the workload. The success of the therapeutic alliance can often be gauged by the frequency with which the therapist and spouses can simultaneously laugh at and share the humor of a situation.

Even with the best of efforts and intentions of the therapist, misunderstandings often arise and disrupt the therapeutic alliance. An example of this was when a therapist, who was trying to encourage a spouse, remarked, "You have to be willing to try," referring to trying to use the help and guidance provided in the session. However, this was not made clear and the spouse felt criticized, misunderstood, and resentful. The spouse responded, "You just don't know how hard I've tried," and went on to defend himself by emphasizing the extent of his efforts. This problem occurs often and is a potential pitfall for the therapist if it is not dealt with appropriately. It is extremely important that the therapist acknowledge the awareness of a spouse's sincere interest and degree of emotion and energy invested in wrestling with the problems of the marriage, lest the spouse feel misjudged. What the therapist must communicate is that there may be some new ways of dealing with problems that the spouse may have been unaware of and that the triad should try to identify what the spouses have been doing that has not worked. This will enable all to become more creative in problem-solving. In short, to avoid resentment and undermining the alliance, the therapist must be sensitive to the spouses' tendencies to feel criticized or chastised.

Because of the necessity to shift the focus between the spouses, there are more fluctuations in the therapeutic alliance in couple therapy than in individual therapy. Even at the best the therapeutic alliance is not always reciprocal. It is not uncommon for spouses to hasten to the defense of each other if they perceive that the other is under attack. The therapist who hopes to remain an ally must regularly work against efforts to dislodge him or her from a neutral position. If the therapist does avoid taking sides or prevent confrontations beyond the tolerance level of an individual, the working relationship will be fractured and the work disrupted.

At times, the therapist may take a position that is more agreeable to one spouse. The purpose behind the position must be made clear lest it be interpreted as taking sides. For example, to promote separateness, the therapist may stress respect for each spouse's needs to keep some time for the self at a time when one spouse is complaining about the unavailability of the other. It is imperative that the comment be understood as in the best interest of *both* spouses. Unless the therapist is perceived as an ally by both, therapeutic progress will be damaged.

The problem of taking sides is always a danger to establishing a therapeutic alliance. This may be amplified by natural occurrences in therapy. Sometimes, for example, one of the spouses will arrive before the other. We prefer to wait until both arrive before beginning. With one spouse alone, the therapist is faced with the dilemma of engaging in chitchat or of beginning therapy without the second spouse. If one begins, the problem of how the other spouse may feel because he or she misses what transpires must be considered. Feelings of exclusion, jealousy, resentment, or suspicion may be aroused, which will interfere, at least temporarily, with the therapeutic alliance. If the couple are also seen individually, this will not likely present a problem.

Inevitably, with some couples, the therapist will be perceived in alliance with one spouse. If the therapist is aware of this, the offended spouse can be encouraged to detail *how* the therapist behaves and what comments lead the spouse to this conclusion. The spouse can be invited to call attention to any behavior that indicates the therapist is taking the side of the partner so that the triad can consider the accusation and its validity. If the therapist feels that the accusation is unwarranted, he or she should help the spouse understand how this may have occurred. One should acknowledge the perception as a problem and invite suggestions how it can be dealt with better. Needless to say, if the spouse is in a struggle with the therapist, he will not be able to focus on his individual or marital problems very long.

Although rare, for one spouse the feeling of being jointly opposed by the partner and therapist was strong enough to disrupt therapy. Although this problem may have been compounded by the fact that the therapist was a man and the spouse was a woman, the therapist felt that couple therapy was not the most appropriate format for treatment. Couple therapy had proceeded on a trial basis with grave reservations by the wife in the beginning and, as a result, by the therapist as well. Even with strenuous efforts and forewarnings of the spouse's vulnerable position, it was impossible to offset her attitude sufficiently to proceed with therapy. After a few sessions, it was mutually agreed upon that the wife would resume individual therapy and that couple treatment would be terminated.

Face Saving

In establishing and furthering the therapeutic alliance, it is important to help the spouses "save face." A problem particular to couple therapy is that a spouse often feels exposed and condemned as embarrassing aspects of his or her behavior are brought into focus. The therapist must be especially careful when this occurs that the knowledge of a spouse's problems is not used as ammunition by the partner to attack the spouse.

For example, in a fight in which a spouse is trying to get the partner to be aware of some behavior allegedly committed, if one chooses to focus momentarily on the partner's difficulty in acknowledging wrongdoing, the spouse may see this as a triumph. ("I knew you were lying—you never will admit you've made a mistake.") If, however, the therapist can talk from a hypothetical viewpoint ("Suppose you really knew you had done so and so, what would you anticipate if you acknowledged it?"), then it might be possible to promote a fruitful discussion of both the individual problem and the transactional one, hopefully with the spouse recognizing his or her own part in the partner's unwillingness to acknowledge the "faulty" behavior. By not actually saying that the partner is guilty, he or she is spared from being caught by the spouse and saves face; the possibility for continued communication on the problem is strengthened.

Similarly, exposing through confrontation feelings that you suspect a spouse is experiencing that he or she is not ready to admit may place the spouse at a disadvantage. It is preferable to avoid confrontation as a way of facilitating expression until the spouses feel that there is little to fear and are thus ready to admit their thoughts and feelings.

The above is tantamount to saying that a one-to-one focus is useful in therapy within the couple context, as long as certain considerations are kept in mind. The foremost of these is that one must be sure that the couple are sufficiently dislodged from a blaming orientation to be ready to listen from a more sympathetic perspective. At that point the work focused on individual problems has the possibility for aiding both spouses; for example, the fellow spouse may come to feel less responsible for a given bit of overdetermined behavior, view it as more independent of the self, feel less guilty and more empathic, thus rendering this spouse in an unhooked position where it is possible to be perhaps more helpful—at least supportive and sympathetic.

Sometimes when couples argue, the therapist will want to help one spouse save face by supporting his or her good qualities, so that overall communication does not break down. An example of this was a couple where the wife was trying to explain to her husband some of her thoughts and feelings. The husband, who took pride in his ability to think rationally and logically, made what under other circumstances would have been intelligent, considered remarks, but they were not in tune with what his wife was saying. Exasperated, the wife launched into a number of critical remarks about his inability to carry on a conversation, stressing that he was not listening to her and not really communicating with her. The husband was baffled and hurt, since he had been listening and responding as best he could. It would have been helpful for the therapist first to have commented on the husband's capacity for logic and worthwhile opinions and then to point out that his remarks were misfiring and that this was a shame after all his effort. Then the therapist should have helped the husband to understand *why* he was not making meaningful contact with his wife. In other words, support of his good qualities may have helped him to learn what he had done that hindered communication. (In this case, the husband's comments were too intellectualized, impersonal, and did not take into account his wife's feelings.)

Granting the resistance spouses have acknowledging blame and accepting responsibility for change, it is interesting to observe how couples on return visits frequently report improvement without acknowledging any personal responsibility for this. A spouse will often say that it happened because the partner behaved in a different, more desirable fashion and not because of any difference in his or her own responses; any personal changes were seen merely in response to the partner. Just as often, the partner will take the reverse position. It is as if to acknowledge change is to admit guilt. One can minimize this by saying, "Apparently you both were able to do things differently that made things better for you; it is important for us to explore what these things were so that you can go on doing them." Then one can ask each spouse to relate how he or she experienced the mate as well as the self as being different. It is important for spouses to acknowledge any efforts made by their mate and to reward these whenever possible. (Refer to the section on positive "strokes" in Chapter Five for further illustration of these points.)

4

Helping Couples Negotiate: Obstacles and Interventions

In the following chapters, we will further describe the principles and methods we have found useful in working with couples. We have no definitive, set techniques; as Freud pointed out with regard to chess, the opening and end-game permit more exhaustive systematic presentation than the infinite variety of possible moves in between. So it is with couple therapy. We shall try to delineate what has emerged from our work, recognizing the need for continuous creative innovations by the therapist as he confronts each unique situation.

In the next three chapters, for purposes of convenience different points have been included under three main headings: (1) Negotiation; (2) Communication; and (3) Reeducation. This division is recognizably arbitrary and at times points discussed under one heading also have relevance for other headings. The same is true for examples, that is, they may exemplify other points than the key one being focused upon. Our purpose is to include what we feel are important principles. The order of presentation and at times the groupings are of secondary significance.

A major therapeutic task for the therapist is to help the couple shift from an argumentative style to a negotiating one. By negotiation, we mean that both sides are encouraged to voice their complaints and to constructively work for change in the status quo. In diplomatic terms, this is referred to as a quid pro quo; it means that I am willing to do something (that will make things better) if you will do something for me in return.

In the comments below the therapist begins the work of educating the spouses in the process of negotiating. The spouses have been talking about behaviors they find objectionable, and the therapist has been encouraging them to request changes.

> T: Well, the point I want to try to make is that you've got some requests for your husband and he has some for you. And if each of you can accept that you're more likely to get some of yours honored if you can honor some of the others, then you can at least start working on some of these little things, as we pick them up. Obviously, that's not all of what's going on but you have to start somewhere, and we're trying to just begin to identify some sore points and how you can move in to where you can work to change some of your behaviors to make things go better.

The couple must learn how and be willing to assert their own positions, their reasons, and the importance of their feelings and needs, and then to decide on compromise solutions that are reasonably satisfactory to both. The particular problem the couple may be focusing on at the moment is not as important as the fact that by focusing on any problem the therapist can help them learn how to negotiate with each other. How they resolve their differences is the crucial issue—not whether they completely resolve a specific problem.

It may be noted that this is a reality-oriented, problem-solving approach; however, its simplicity is deceptive. Helping couples learn to negotiate can be an arduous task that requires sustained therapeutic efforts. Often much of the major therapeutic work will have been accomplished before the couple can use this approach for resolving problems; in other words, in the process of working toward the use of the negotiating style, one brings into focus what gets in the way of negotiation, that is, resistance and the underlying conflicts behind the resistance. Herein lies much of the therapeutic work. More about this later.

In learning how to negotiate, it is useful for some couples to write down, either in the session or at home, some of the problems and solutions that they have reached. No matter how intense the involvement and how difficult the battle, agreements finally developed in the triadic sessions have a mysterious way of fading once the couple have left the therapist's office. Written commitments may avoid misunderstandings about what was previously agreed upon and allow review of what the spouses have been attempting should their efforts prove to be unsuccessful. This enables them, both at home and in the session, to reexamine the issues and to explore whether their solutions proved tenable or not. Misunderstandings about the meanings of agreements can thus be clarified, and hopefully whatever is blocking cooperation will be removed.

In addition to record keeping, it is often profitable to ask a couple how agreements made in previous sessions have been working. Do not be surprised if the couples report that they have not tried any of their proposed solutions. The therapist can then discuss with the couple what prevented their efforts. Often one finds that by doing nothing and by coming to therapy, the couple hoped some magic would be worked. The therapist then should reemphasize that change will come by virtue of their own efforts and that it may prove to be very hard work. If doing nothing resulted from feelings of helplessness, then one will need to cultivate hope, perhaps by reminding the couple of efforts they have already made that were successful.

The therapist will also find useful review of agreements, rehearsal, and verbal reinforcement of efforts in promoting new behaviors after the couple leave the office. For the hazy thinker with a poor memory, it may be helpful to encourage note-taking in the office to provide something concrete to focus on once the individual goes home. It is important to stress that a major part of the work will have to be done outside the therapist's office.

We often find the use of taped sessions valuable for many spouses; this permits an automatic review of what has transpired, providing that the spouses are willing to listen to their tapes. Listening can serve as a valuable reinforcement to the therapeutic work; in addition, the recording provides an objective monitor. Spouses often comment that they become more aware of certain aspects of their behavior through the tapes, and that they can better identify how feelings may have colored perceptions. Now let us look more carefully at some of the problems encountered as one begins the work of helping spouses learn to negotiate.

Assuming Personal Responsibility

If the negotiating style is to succeed, the spouses must be willing to assume or to learn to assume responsibility in the therapeutic work under the guidance of the therapist. As Kaiser has noted,[1] it is the therapist who must work toward inducing in the patient a sense of responsibility. It is the patient's responsibility to work, but it is the therapist's responsibility to teach him how—in other words, what responsibilities, or work is expected of him. These responsibilities are to be willing to voice one's complaints and needs, to use one's assertiveness and anger for the protection of self-interests, to be willing to listen to and to try to understand the spouse's position, needs, and feelings, as well as one's own, and, ultimately, to negotiate differences. One example of a facilitative comment by a wife trying to persuade her husband to assume more responsibility for affirming his needs is the following: "Say 'I

[1] L. Fierman (Ed.) *Effective Psychotherapy: The Contribution of Hellmuth Kaiser.* New York: Free Press, 1965.

want.' . . . Say, 'I want' for a change, not 'do you want?'." Here, the
wife tries to reinforce her husband's efforts to use his assertiveness
constructively to request what he needs and not to be attuned solely
to her needs.

The therapist's responsibility is to help each spouse take responsibility. This means helping both to become aware of their own
feelings and needs, and then communicating these to the partner.
In this manner, they will work toward a mutually satisfactory way
of gratifying these wants, with each standing ground without detriment to the partner. Spouses must learn that unless they respect
their own prerogatives and work toward having these honored, they
will be unable to gratify their partners. If the spouse has difficulty
in communicating his or her wants, the therapist must facilitate the
process. Without help, spouses often flounder, become discouraged, and give up.

The therapeutic process below illustrates the problems one
wife had in taking responsibility for communicating her needs to
her husband and the therapist's failure to help her. The therapist
had been trying to help the wife spell out to her husband what the
husband needed to do for her to feel better. The husband had said
that he did not know and was soliciting an answer. The wife usually
responded that she did not know, sounding helpless and defeated
as she spoke. The husband would then renew his demands, protesting that he had tried everything and that he did not know what she
wanted. Since the wife seemed able only to repeat herself about not
knowing, the husband was then in a position to feel exonerated, as
if he'd done his part and could not be held responsible for his wife's
dissatisfactions. Because of the impasse of this interchange and its
belabored nature leading to nothing productive, active intervention
on the part of the therapist was needed to facilitate matters. Several
things might have been done: suggest to the wife that perhaps it was
not because she did not know, but because she had become discouraged that she could not verbalize her wants, (2) try to help the husband assume some of the responsibility for getting his wife to open
up, or explore with the husband if there was something in the way
he responded when his wife made requests that contributed to her
reluctance to do so. Depending on the therapist's relationship with
the spouses, he or she might have made other interventions; obvi-

ously something needed to be done to improve their interchange.

As the session proceeded, it became clear that the wife did know what she wanted—she wanted more time together, specifically a vacation; but when she had approached her husband, he had thrown the vacation brochures in the wastebasket. What also became clear was that the husband felt shut out and needed more affection (also one of the wife's complaints); he referred to his wife as a "cold fish." As is often the case, each felt that they were reacting to the other's behavior.

It would have been helpful for the therapist to explain that both seemed to be hurting, both felt needy, and both wanted more from each other. They were reacting to each other in somewhat different ways, the wife giving up and feeling depressed and the husband becoming angry, but both were obviously discouraged about trying to do things for each other. The therapist might then have focused on the unsuccessful ways they had been trying to negotiate their desires and raised the question of what they might do differently. In the actual session, the therapist spent most of the time trying to get the wife to "speak up" and did not acknowledge the husband's frustration. The wife became increasingly frustrated and the husband, feeling attacked, defended himself. The session was deadlocked. The therapist failed to help the spouses learn how to assume responsibility for stating and hearing each other's needs.

Somewhat different is the spouse who feels already defeated and has given up hope after long years of frustration in failing to have needs met. The husband below is an example. He had literally given up hoping and talking about his wants, and in fact tried to deny having them. He would rather do without than to want and ask for something, only to be let down again.

H: I guess what I'm feeling is I don't really have any with her—expectancies.

T: You have a lot of needs, but I think you've given up. [The husband goes on to talk of the many times his wife has assured him she would do something but has let him down.]

T: That's the problem—she's saying she would like to do it

and intends to do it, but something comes up . . . and
you're saying I don't want to hope. I don't want to be let
down.

[The wife gives rational reasons why events occur such
that she fails to comply with her husband's requests.]

H: Yeah, I guess I'm just afraid to hope; she's [the therapist]
right, so therefore I won't ask you to . . . unless I really
don't care if you do it or not.

In this kind of situation the chances for any successful outcome are
slim unless the wife can provide her husband with hope to keep trying. The husband has given up any attempts at negotiation and is
attempting, with great pain, to live with a bad situation. The status
quo is completely unsatisfactory for both.

It is the therapist's responsibility to convey to the spouses that
what one does can influence the other and that we are not helpless
recipients of bad luck; that, to a large extent, we determine the
course of our lives by our behavior. Out of fear or helplessness,
spouses often expect that an unhappy course of events is inevitable.
Although their fears are logical in view of their present situation,
the conviction that the situation is unalterable is not necessarily
justified. The therapist will need to point out to both spouses their
single-minded pessimism and to support their strengths in order
to alter their behavior.

The following interchange occurred after the husband's statement that he felt that they were "marking time" and that divorce
was inevitable:

T: I would think it [divorce] would be a realistic fear that
both of you would have a hard time saying doesn't exist
now—it is there—you've both talked about it . . . but it
doesn't mean it's inevitable. From time to time when
things go bad, it's going to be a natural tendency to think
"It's no use, we're not going to make it anyway," but it
still is not inevitable. You still have some say in what happens to you; you have some power to change things . . .

and my intent is to help you try to make things go better.

[The therapist then responds to comments by the husband.]

T: I hear you saying, "I'm afraid to work, because I'm afraid it'll make the divorce more inevitable." . . . It might be pertinent if you [to wife] would respond to that, because that really is his fear.

[The wife acknowledges similar fears and then continues.]

W: If you could get some resolution to the differences or each of us learns to live with them more comfortably, then . . . we'd be more satisfied.

[The wife takes heart and refocuses on the work necessary.]

Because many people are convinced of the inevitability of certain life events, the therapist has to help the spouses see that regardless of the conditions that influence them, their behavior represents a choice they make in dealing with these conditions. For example, a husband may drink or gamble because his wife is having extramarital affairs, but this is a choice; he does not have to do either. Notwithstanding the power of unconscious forces, much can be done to educate people to see that they have choices and to help them experience themselves as active agents who can make their own decisions and who can work for change.[2] When one can help spouses to make their own choices and to learn how to regulate their own behavior, while taking into consideration both individual and other needs, then the therapist has gone a long way toward building and supporting healthy personality functions.

One of the complicating factors that contributes to a perceived lack of choice is that once initial choices have been made, other behaviors necessarily follow. Spouses often forget that they initially made a choice and experience the consequences as unrelated to their own efforts. It is helpful, where possible, to clarify this con-

---

[2]*See* H. Greenwald. "Direct Decision Therapy." *Voices,* Spring, 1971, 38–42.

fusion. For example, to a husband who was complaining about the lack of free time he had as a result of his job, it was pointed out that he had chosen this job, which was especially constricting in its demands; other ways of structuring his work were possible. In addition, his extra work (he always went to work on Saturdays) was experienced as a requirement, when in fact this was not so—again, the choice was there.

It is interesting that once one feels there are no choices, then one protests about external pressures that actually originated within and tries to meet the excessive demands. In such cases, a major therapeutic task will be to help the spouse to relax stringent self-expectations.

Related to this is the spouse who feels trapped in a marriage which he or she regrets and who thinks that no options are available to correct the original "mistake." For example, note the husband's conviction in the following comments:

H: I don't really think there is any choice now, you know, the choice should have been then. Now there is no choice.

T: I don't see what you mean by that, there is no choice. I think there are choices now.

H: Well, I feel like now is certainly not the appropriate time to say to Sandy "I want to pursue other relationships" or "I want to go back to school to do this or be trained to do that," because we have been married fourteen years, and we have three children, and life has gone in one direction for fourteen years, and it's just no time to change now. And it depresses me from time to time.

T: I am a little concerned about your statement that this is no time to change. I wonder how you got to that conclusion. I see that you are making efforts to change.

W: And to have a better relationship.

T: You are struggling to do something for yourself. You are making some waves and some efforts.

H: Well, I feel like the waves I am making are bad.

T: Bad from whose point of view?

H: Everybody's, I suppose, even partly my own.

T: You don't think you should make waves, is that what you are saying?

H: No, if it's going to hurt Sandy and the kids and my family.

T: But you think it would be better not to make waves and hurt yourself as an alternative?

H: I don't know.

T: Suppose you can find another way out of all that where you don't really have to hurt anybody, and you can find some things for yourself?

H: Yeah, except I have no idea what that is.

T: Okay, that's all right. All you have to have is the desire to do something about it and the willingness to explore, at least for starters. Now why don't you just talk to Sandy about this dilemma you feel yourself in, and see if she can help you.

Preferably, Sandy will not give her husband license to pursue romantic liaisons, but the therapist hopes that she will agree to help her husband explore options for meeting some of his needs, which he does not now see possible. The therapist does not know what solutions are available, but it is certain that some options are open for changing attitudes, feelings, and patterns of living if the couple are willing to take the necessary steps to find them.

It is also the responsibility of the therapist to help spouses appreciate more fully how they determine what happens to them. Only to the extent that they can understand this will they be in a position to change. Then they may or may not choose to repeat these patterns, depending upon the degree to which they are free from unconscious influences and are able to perceive possibilities and their consequences.

A brief excerpt from one therapy session illustrates other issues regarding personal responsibility. The husband has just remarked, "If I'm allowed to get away with anything, I will get away with it. . . . I will generally push a person as far as that person will be pushed." He has indicated that this was his wife's fault.

T: Can I clarify something, because it seems important to me. You put it in a sense of responsibility back over there—she's letting you get away with things. That's the way I heard it.

H: That's probably true.

T: I wanted to point out two things. One is that whatever you're doing, you're responsible for, and she can neither start nor stop you. Not really, I mean, if you want to do it, you will do it, and that's your responsibility. I want you to take responsibility for it. If you're pushing people and overriding them—you're doing it. It's you.

H: O.K.

T: [To wife] But I wanted you to take responsibility for an obligation to do something which is, if he's doing something which you think is bad for you, you should stand up and say something. . . . You could say "Look, you're pushing in this area and I don't like it. It doesn't make things right between us." And I think it's your responsibility to express loud and clear how you feel about the issue.

[The therapist goes on to say that the husband will then be in a position to know how she feels, and if he's trying to work on the marriage, he will take her feelings into consideration.]

A different problem is the spouse who assumes too much responsibility for the mate's frustrations and problems. Just as the therapist must work to encourage spouses to assume responsibility for themselves, he or she must also help them to avoid undertaking responsibility that only the other can appropriately bear. In the following, the husband has been focusing a great deal on his wife's problems.

T: Well, you see that's not helpful. It would be better if you would quit talking about problems and talk about specific behaviors and what you can do to work on these. [To wife] If there are problems about your feelings about yourself, that's probably not something you [to husband] can help her with directly, but you can help her by loving her, you can help her by supporting her, you can help her by asking her if there's anything you can do, you know, specifically.

Another example of undue responsibility, in this case through overidentification, is illustrated below. The husband had been complaining about the fact that his wife "throws temper tantrums" at home in response to various frustrations and demands, sometimes independent of the husband's behavior. The wife admitted that she had felt irritable and angry lately and pressured at work. The husband protested vehemently about his wife's behavior, stressing how often it occurred and his not wanting to hear it. In defense, the wife stated she did not fuss at her husband about things but fussed about things to her husband.

T: Could you accept her temper tantrums better if you didn't feel like you had to hear it all . . . if you felt free to leave the room?

H: I guess, I guess if she didn't kind of direct . . . she doesn't yell at me, but she yells about it at me, and like sometimes there's nothing I can do—it's just something that there's no way I can deal with it. It doesn't make me feel any better.

T: Can you hear why it's difficult for your husband to hear you at those times?

W: Sort of.

T: If you pull it all together, what would you hear?

W: I guess he's saying that he doesn't want to hear about it because he feels like it's something that he can't do anything about anyway—it's unpleasant to him.

T: Makes him feel helpless.

W: Right.

T: Most people don't like to feel helpless. See, the more of those things you direct at him, the more—if he assumes it's his responsibility, which is another issue . . .

[The wife interrupts and says that she does not ask for help.]

T: Well, see, you don't even have to say anything directly to him; apparently you [to husband] are assuming it's your responsibility to do something. Otherwise you wouldn't feel so helpless, and that's something you're going to have to struggle with, and that's not easy to change. But what I'm saying to your wife is if you [to wife] can see the end result of what that's doing to him, you give him more times of feeling helpless, and he's already told you he's weighted down with problems of not feeling important. I'm just trying to help you see one thing he is saying . . . are you willing to do anything about that?

W: Yes, the problem is that the times I get really mad, I'm not so rational so it's hard for me to commit myself about what I'm going to do to help our relationship. I think recognizing that it makes him feel helpless is a useful thing, and I think I can make an effort.

In this case, it seemed helpful to promote in the wife a better understanding of why her husband got so upset at her outbursts, since essentially they did no harm and were confined to the home. One might also want to help the husband accept his wife's right to be angry which often seemed legitimate. (This was done in the hour.) The husband's tendency to be overly responsible for his wife's frustrations was as much a problem as her outbursts. Since this seemed a more difficult task to accomplish at the moment, the therapist chose to assist the husband in telling his wife when he did not want to listen and in leaving the room if the situation were too upsetting. The therapist encouraged the spouses to distinguish between the husband's not telling the wife she should not get mad and his right to protect himself if he felt helpless. In support of the husband, the therapist also commented as follows:

T: That's a very common reaction, when somebody is continuously complaining about something that the other person has no power of doing anything about. It leaves you often with a helpless feeling . . . and it takes a great deal of work not to assume responsibility and still be able to hear it.

The following is a similar situation in which the individual hearing the complaints feels burdened and responsible for solving the plight of the spouse.

W: When you came home from work, I listened to you gripe.

H: But you finally said you didn't want to hear it anymore.

W: I just pointed out [that] I didn't want to hear it anymore. I just said if it's that bad, perhaps you should get a different job.

T: I think to the extent you hear the other person's bitching as something you feel required to do something about, it makes it difficult to hear. If you don't feel that you have to do anything, you can hear it much more easily.

The last example of this problem is a wife who feels responsible for her husband's behavior with their children and in social situations. The wife has described how she is on edge trying to discern what disturbs her husband lest he blow up.

T: If he blows up and makes an ass of himself, that's his responsibility. If he says something that's inappropriate, that's not your responsibility—that's up to him. He will have to stand or fall on his behavior and he knows that and he's responsible for what he does. To me it would be an enormous burden to have to walk on eggs for fear you'll do something that'll cause the eruption.

[The wife says it's not just his blowing up; sometimes her husband becomes silent and withdrawn and if they are with people, they will ask her what is wrong.]

W: I wish they'd ask you.

T: Why don't you suggest that to them? Say, "Why don't you ask Gene?" I mean, you're not his keeper. You're not responsible for every move. You're not his mother, either.

They don't have to check out Gene with you. They can check out Gene with Gene.

W: The kids do this—"What's wrong with daddy?"

T: Say, "Go ask Daddy—I can't read his mind." If they want to know what's wrong with Daddy, they should be able to go over there and approach him. That's an enormous responsibility for you—to carry Gene on your shoulders. . . . If he chooses to be silent or withdrawn, that's his choice.

W: I guess what I'm wanting for us is to be able to do congenial things together and I'll have a good time, [to husband] but I want you to have a good time too.

T: That's great—that's really good.

H: I've got no argument with that.

Another responsibility of the therapist is to recognize the importance of safeguarding the autonomy of each spouse. The therapist should work toward the goal of helping each spouse become less dependent on the other and better able to cope with reality problems. The therapist should usually refrain from presenting solutions and encourage the spouses to arrive at their own solutions. The following interchange demonstates this:

T: O.K., one of the things that is going to be hard probably for you, is to accept that it is your wife's responsibility to do or not to do. [This refers to what she does at home.]

H: That I've got to accept letting her take responsibility for it.

     [The therapist points out the contradiction of complaining that his wife acts like a child and taking over her responsibilities at the same time.]

H: I can't accuse her of being a child and things like that.

T: That's right. You see that's her responsibility [agreed-upon housework]. She may blow it, or she may do beautifully, but it's still something she should decide. "Am I going to blow my day and not do anything, or am I going to do it this way?" That's really her prerogative, that's not yours. Just like it's your prerogative to decide if you want to be in graduate school. You know, you would resent it if she told you you shouldn't be, it's really a rotten thing to do. It's really something that *you've* got to decide because it's the way you're going to spend your life.

H: What happens if I tell her, "It's your responsibility," and then I feel angry because I don't think [that she's done the work right.]

T: If you come home at night and the house is a pigsty, it's your responsibility to tell her, "This really upsets me." She may choose to do something about it or she may not. If she chooses to do nothing about it, then it is your responsibility to decide, "Can I live in a pigsty? Is she worth it?" And if you decide that she isn't, then it's your responsibility to do something about it. It's your responsibility to communicate your feelings about the hardship that it's putting upon you, and she has to decide, "Do I want to do something about it or don't I; does it fit my needs or doesn't it?" See, you may have some expectations like the house has to be utterly immaculate.

H: No.

T: I know you don't, but as soon as you did, she would have to decide, are you worth her sacrificing her life if that doesn't fit with her needs. She might decide you are, I don't know. She would have to make that decision. But you have a right to communicate that it's torture for you unless it's perfect, and if you have a right to communicate that, then she has a right to decide what she's willing to do. She may decide I can't "go it" no matter how much torture you have to go through, and you have to decide, "Can I live through torture?" I don't know if you're following what I'm trying to say. You see, I think each of you has a right to voice your complaint, like you [to husband] have a right to voice your complaints if you think she doesn't hold up on mutual agreements, and you [to wife] have the same right, but then it's up to the other person to

decide what to do about it. That's why I was a little bit
troubled by your wanting to mutually have him decide
what your day would be like. I heard your reason O.K.,
because you said he would know that you had done something the next day. I don't think that's up to you to check
on what your wife's done. I think if the house is a pigsty,
it's your right to say, "Damn it, I can't stand this, it really
upsets me," but I think that checking on whether she's
spent a fruitful day or whether she's done one chore or
six or how many hours it took, will only get you in trouble—that's her responsibility.

H: That's something I have definitely been doing.

T: O.K., well, it doesn't help her, I mean she's a person, it's
not going to help either one of you. She may choose to
goof off for twenty-four hours straight.

H: Well, part of it, I think, it's not really my feelings about
the house, because I've lived in pigsty places too. It's just
that I feel like, that she belittles herself because the house
is not the way she wants it to be, and then I feel like she's
not effectively accomplishing anything to change the
house, so then she's making herself feel worse.

T: Now what can you do about all that?

H: Nothing really, except that I . . .

T: You could ask her, "Can I be of any help in that, and
how?"

H: But you see, she'll tell me I can be of help by doing all of it.

T: But then you have to tell her that within the confines of
your responsibilities you can only do A, B, and C, and
therefore she has to struggle with that. See, that problem
you just announced that's hers *is* hers. You can't take that
over. If she feels lousy because she gets nothing accomplished, then she's doing something to herself. That is
her responsibility to struggle with that and do something
about it, and if it hurts you [to wife] enough you should
get some help, because that's for you to work on; that's
you, and you [to husband] can't take over whatever in-

ternal problem she has, assuming there is one, which I
don't know whether there is, but it's one your husband
labels. See that's hers—not yours.

As can be seen, the therapist is continually working to foster separateness, so that the wife could become more autonomous in her
decision-making and not have to check in with her husband. Their
relationship had become like one of parent to child; the therapist
hopes to make this more apparent to the couple and also to highlight
how this has worked against some of their stated goals.

In their communication breakdown and their focus on dissatisfactions, spouses often fail to tell each other things they have been
pleased with in one another over the years. When this has occurred,
the therapist should emphasize its importance. Indeed, this is a
major responsibility of a spouse: to communicate satisfactions as well
as dissatisfactions.

H: I think us being together and caring about each other has
    made a significant difference, and I don't think it has
    changed me so much as it has given me a lot of support to
    get through things, like graduate school, that, you know,
    I don't know how I would have done it without her.

W: Do you realize that you've never really said that to me. All
    those times I kept your dinner heated and you were at the
    lab and you'd come home from the library late and all
    you'd do would be eat and fall asleep.

H: I didn't have the energy to talk.

W: I know, but that's the first time you ever said I helped
    you through graduate school.

T: That's a very important thing to communicate to her. She
    needs to know that.

It is important in discussing responsibility with spouses that
both must make an effort to promote better communication. Often
spouses do not spontaneously communicate how they feel, but
equally often spouses desiring to know more about how their partner feels will fail to ask.

W: Like when we talked for a while and then we finally talked about children. It's the first time I really knew you cared about any children. You've got to admit I don't know what goes on in your head.

T: But you can also ask him.

W: Well, that's true.

T: It's both your responsibility if you're troubled . . . and his responsibility if he has something to say. But if he doesn't choose to [speak] spontaneously, because he doesn't feel like it, and it troubles you, then it's your responsibility to ask him. Say, "I have the feeling I don't matter, tell me, do I?" See, I'm trying to say you can ask for things. You may not get them, either of you, but you have a right to ask, and to communicate how important something is to you, and if the other person cares about you, he'll hear that.

Role of Blame and How To Deal With It

The need of a spouse to be allied with the therapist to place blame on the mate presents us with another major obstacle in helping couples learn to negotiate. Attempts to establish blame inevitably occur when marriages go awry; it is natural for people to perceive this in terms of what the other has done rather than what one's own contributions are. Interestingly, it often occurs that even when a spouse acknowledges some behavior is objectionable to the mate, he or she will continue to place blame on the mate—the objectionable behavior occurred because of what the partner did.

There are reasons for the tenacity with which spouses maintain their blaming stance. If they can succeed, the burden for changing will be removed from them, and they can deny any personal responsibility for what has happened. Since traces of guilt are present in all of us as residues of childhood transgressions and subsequent guilt-inducing punishments, we all have some desire not to acknowledge how we may be responsible. It is easier to accuse someone else and say, "It's them, out there—not me." The therapist will need to assess the extent to which this attitude is a fixed projective defense and thus less subject to change. Spouses who talk of their distress in terms of "I get upset when" rather then "he makes me" will be able to use help more readily.

The issue of blame becomes one of who is right and who is wrong, or who wins and who loses. What happens if the therapist allows the couple to continue behaviors reflecting this perspective when they begin therapy? Inevitably, as accusations are hurled, a counterattack (either active or passive) is launched, and a seesaw battle ensues. When a spouse feels attacked, he or she becomes defensive and then, out of anger, attacks back. Spouses do not need further exercise in this kind of interaction. Usually, by the time the couple come for help, they are experts at this combat; they know just what to say to each other that will hurt the most.

It is the therapist's responsibility to intervene—to interrupt, if necessary—and to redirect the interaction. Otherwise, the therapist is reinforcing a destructive pattern of behavior that should be changed. The important issue to focus on is not how bad a spouse is, or how much a given spouse's objectionable behavior has occurred, but what behaviors have occurred and how do they affect the partner—what specifically does the spouse have trouble accepting and what is the cost? In other words, the therapist wants to help couples differentiate confrontation from assault, the former identifying the behavior and its effect on the spouse, and the latter aimed at evaluating the behavior to the detriment and diminishment of the spouse.

There are many ways that the therapist can promote a shift from a blaming orientation. It is often helpful to remove behaviors from the context of blame by emphasizing the different styles of the spouses. Neither style need be viewed as necessarily bad; the difficulty arises when the two manners do not mesh. An example of this was a couple in which the husband was emotional and quick to become upset and the wife was distant and cool. The husband experienced his wife as not caring, whereas she experienced him as burdensome because of his emotionality. Both patterns of behavior were functional in other contexts, but they presented obstacles to some of the needs of each spouse.

To offset the harshness of a spouse's criticism of the mate, the therapist can make the point that both spouses no doubt have their gripes; where similarities are present and can be cited, this will make the accused spouse feel less singled out. In the following case, the wife has just finished a series of denigrating remarks, which concluded that the husband's trouble is that he doesn't know how to communicate logically:

> T: One of the reasons why I wanted you to start talking here together is so we can identify what it is that's going wrong that keeps you from being able to talk together. And I'm sure there are things that happen on both sides that make it difficult. See, I heard you both say the same thing about the other person—now you say he has kind of a one-track mind and sort of an insistence on his way and he says kind of the same thing about you. Things have to go your way.

One way the therapist can alert spouses to their tendency to blame is by emphasizing the importance of learning to send "I" rather than "you" messages.[3] Statements beginning with "you" are frequently followed by criticisms and complaints: "You are so lazy"; "You never take any responsibility around the house"; "You're never on time." One hopes to foster feeling and attitude communication by the use of "I" messages: "I am afraid I'll lose you"; "I feel lonely when you watch TV all evening." One must be alert for the you messages camouflaged by statements beginning with "I": "I think *you're* worthless"; "I feel all *you* care anything about is your work."

Below is an example of a wife who is having great difficulty tolerating aspects of her husband's behavior and departing from a blaming stance. The therapist works toward helping her learn to express her dissatisfactions in "I" terms rather than evaluative "you" terms.

> T: I do think that what Pete is saying is an important point. There are things that are going to be different about you and each of you is going to think the things you do maybe make more sense than the other person's, and that's probably going to be pretty much of a reality. You're not going to be able to change all those. You may not be able

[3]T. Gordon. *Parent Effectiveness Training.* New York: New American Library, 1970.

to change very many of them. And everybody is different. They have their own predilections to do things a certain way and again what's coming through from you [to wife] is sort of like damning those and saying those are wrong; they're silly, they don't make sense, I don't understand them or whatever. You may not understand them but they are a reality of each of you. That's something you have to learn how to deal with in some way. Otherwise, you . . . the reason I'm stressing this is I think it plays a large part in your criticalness.

W: Well, I do find it difficult to cater to, I guess that's the word, cater to some idiosyncracies that I find or think are totally foolish. I am intolerant. I am, and I find it very difficult. I find it almost impossible to do it agreeably and without coming on as "Oh, you're ridiculous."

T: I guess what would be helpful would be if you could come on honestly enough to say "I don't like them" or "It doesn't sit well with me" without having to add the additional value judgment of whether they're foolish or ridiculous or whatever. That's the part that hurts. It's when you damn him because of these things—that's gonna hurt. I'm sure from Pete's point of view they make sense for his total economy of functioning. There's some sense to why he does things the way he does, just as there is for why you do things the way you do. It's not that they're foolish. They make sense in terms of where you are, what you're struggling with, and what's the best way you can deal with it right now. I'm not trying to say that means you have to like them, but when you come across and say "It's ridiculous or foolish"—that's the part that makes it hurt.

W: Well, tell me again how to say it, because I find it hard to say anything except "That's really stupid—that's silly." I know you said it a minute ago but I lost it.

T: Well, anytime you can say it in terms of how it affects you and say with it, like "It's hard—I find it hard to take," that doesn't say "I find you're an ass for wanting to do that such and such a way." It's just that, "I find it hard to

take—I get upset in this circumstance" or whatever. Stay
with what your feelings are rather than trying to evaluate
Pete. You know if you say "Good Lord, nobody in his
right mind has to have that done that way."

W: That's about the way. [Husband laughs]

T: Those are the things that are going to get to him.

W: Well, there are many, many things like this and I'm sure
I don't handle them well, but I find it very difficult to be
tolerant of things that are so different from my nature.

T: I understand that.

[The therapist goes on to note an incident in which the
husband was displeased but withstood his irritation the
best he could without attacking his wife.]

In the process of helping spouses to become aware of the extent of their proneness to blame, the therapeutic goal of clarifying
the nature of individual pathology is advanced. As a spouse continues to use blame and cannot alter it, even with help, further diagnostic cues are provided as to the difficulty of the therapist in
helping to alter this behavior because of the fixity of the problem.
The comments below of a spouse give insight into the phenomonol-
ogy of blaming and its relation to anger. The blaming stance grows
out of experiencing grave vulnerability and threat to the individual—essentially a paranoid position. The therapist has been working with the spouse to substitute statements of feelings and needs
for blaming comments.

H: It's hard when you're angry. You feel the other person is
really out to get you.

T: I know it's very hard.

H: It's hard to make a statement that shows your vulnerability, like when you say "The pressure is too much. I feel
like I can't take it anymore." It feels like the other person
is going to give you the death wound right then. It's like
you have to protect yourself.

T: That's going to be an extremely difficult thing for you. It
will require a lot of courage.

An interesting phenomenon, which occurs occasionally, is that one spouse, instead of counterblaming, will assume all the blame. "I know it's me, she's right, I'm impossible to live with—always have been." Occasionally, this turns out to be a maneuver to avoid further accusations by the spouse, just as a beaten wolf offers his throat to his rival, who never takes advantage. If one confesses, then one can spare oneself the other's reproof. At such times, it is helpful to ask the other spouse if he or she agrees with the self-blaming statement—that the problem between the couple stems solely from the partner. Usually, the other spouse will not agree. This is very important, because now the therapist can state that both likely have complaints and that they should explore these grievances; the therapist should also attempt to stifle the issue of blame.

Another technique the therapist can employ to help the spouse lessen the use of a projective, blaming stance is to point out that a spouse's distortions of the therapist's remarks parallel distortions of the mate's. If the therapist can successfully use the self in this way, in a matter that occurs outside the marital relationship, self-awareness by the spouse may be increased. The hazard of this technique is that the spouse may view it as an alliance between the therapist and mate.

The excerpts from a session that appear below illustrate the pathology of the husband, who in his desperate attempt to seek gratification, remains fixated in his blaming stance. The therapist made numerous interventions to help the husband tone down his assault on the wife, since this was obviously making the wife less receptive. Despite efforts to hear the husband's frustration and to support him, the therapist was unable to redirect the interchange into a productive one.

> [The husband had been complaining to his wife that she had shut him out sexually and unleashed a prolonged attack.]
>
> H: You never used to be this way—you pick me to pieces on little things. No matter what I do you're going to find fault. All I get from you is total rejection.

In addition, the husband had been imputing motives, such as accusing his wife of deliberately belittling him. Therapeutic efforts to enable him to focus on his feelings and needs without the ac-

companying assault were unsuccessful. He would support his
contentions with detailed incidents that were almost impossible
to interrupt. The wife became increasingly unapproachable and
cold (counterattacks do not have to be overt) and would not respond to her husband's desperate pleas for affection. Since the
husband was unwilling to listen and modify his attack, the therapist attempted to redirect the flow toward having the wife state
her needs.

> T: What would it take from your husband to make you feel
>   more affectionate? Could you talk with him about that?
>
>   [This effort failed. The wife responded but began to
>   complain about her husband's demandingness. Before
>   the therapist could intercede, the husband resumed his
>   attack. The therapist tried again.]
>
> T: Let's get back to the point. Can you talk to your husband
>   about what he might do to help you feel more affection-
>   ate? Because I have the feeling that there must be some
>   things that get in the way of your wanting to be affec-
>   tionate. I mean, people are not absolutely either affec-
>   tionate or not affectionate; it has a lot to do with what is
>   going on between you that you are displeased with that
>   keeps you from feeling affectionate.
>
>   [The therapist is trying to encourage the wife to state her
>   unmet needs—so far the session has been overly domi-
>   nated by the husband.]
>
> W: Well, when I feel affectionate, he pushes me away.
>
>   [The wife now begins to give new information but is im-
>   mediately interrupted by her husband.]
>
> H: Well, I can remember that night . . .
>
>   [A rehash begins of the incident, in which the husband
>   resumes blaming his wife.]
>
> T: I didn't hear you responding to your wife's comment and
>   what your wife says is that sometimes when she feels af-
>   fectionate, you turn her off.

[The subsequent remarks of the husband make it clear that unless he can first feel accepted, he can not tune in to his wife's needs.]

T: If I hear things right, are you trying to tell your husband some things that would make you feel better, that you wouldn't feel so pushed away?

[The wife agrees and provides an illustration.]

T: So am I hearing that you are requesting something that he could do that you'd like to encourage him to do that might help you feel more affectionate?

W: Yes.

[The wife's request, a common one, is for more affection that does not lead to sex.]

T: [To husband] Why don't you just respond to that part of it?

The husband's response is that if he is rejected sometimes, he cannot be expected to be affectionate. What is clear here is that the husband is fixated at an early developmental level in which people exist only for his own gratification and do not have their own needs. The husband's inability to achieve mutuality is clear.

T: I hear your wife saying the same thing.

[The husband resumes attack on the wife, imputing many thoughts and motives; the therapist tries to help him with these.]

H: It doesn't make any difference if the thoughts are in her head or not, as long as that is the way I read them.

The husband is feeling desperate in his battle with the wife. The therapist has not been successful in redirecting from the tug-of-war, and the husband cannot hear the therapist or the wife. The therapist attempts to help the husband distinguish his feelings from the wife's thoughts. The husband becomes more desperate in his desire for affection.

H: I honestly feel . . . that subconsciously you hate me.

[The therapist invites the wife to comment on her husband's assumption, but her disclaimer does not convince
the husband. The therapist uses this example of mind
reading to illustrate to the husband how it fails to help
him.]

T: [To wife] What does that do to you when he says that?

W: Well, it makes me sad that he thinks that.

T: Does it make you more loving.

W: No.

T: [To husband] I'm trying to get across that mind reading
is not going to get you what you want from your wife . . .
because you want affection, not sadness.

[The husband does not respond to this. He immediately
begins to relate how something must have happened to
his wife to cause her problem—back to blaming and
attack. The therapist tried again.]

The above represents slightly less than half of the session. The
therapist was unsuccessful in helping this couple; two thirds of the
way through the session the wife was still asking for more affection
without sex, and the husband would not respond. The therapist was
still trying to help the husband feel understood and supported,
where possible, so that he could relax. He was still saying, "How can
I do [he could never clearly understand "do what," since he did not
really hear what his wife was requesting], when I don't get what I
want from you?"

T: I understand that you feel rejected, and it's going to be
hard for you, too, but right now you're both finding it
hard because each of you is feeling like you're not getting
what you want. It's not just you—she is just as strong in
her feelings over there. . . . She's saying, "I feel unloved,"
. . . and I think that when she feels more love, she'll feel
more like jumping in the bed.

[The husband resumes the argument; the therapist again
tries to tune into the hurt and disappointment behind the

husband's rigidity and anger, trying to support him. The husband is still accusing his wife. The session ends on this note.]

This hour is a good illustration of failure to help a couple where the paranoid, projective stance of blaming was pathologically entrenched. It was easy to predict that the couple would not return. They were unresponsive to therapeutic interventions, particularly the husband, who demanded his needs be met first and on his own terms. His wife, failing to serve his needs, was the target of continuous attack, and the husband was continuously angry and frustrated. The session provided much diagnostic information but failed to be helpful. It seems likely that beginning efforts to engage the husband in a therapeutic alliance would have had a better chance to succeed in individual therapy. However, the couple chose to come as a unit, and it is unlikely that the husband would have sought any individual help, so rigid were his projective defenses of externalizing blame. Fortunately, not many spouses who come to couple treatment are this difficult to help. The session is presented because it points out the therapist's efforts to deal with blame even under the most adverse circumstances. It may also illustrate that this approach is not magical and may fail.

In some cases, a spouse will feel singled out as being responsible for the marital problems, even when the partner has not unduly blamed them. Because at times therapy will focus on one of the spouses, the therapist must be alert to that spouse's sensitivity to feel blamed and work to counteract this, if necessary, lest he or she be discouraged from further therapy. In the next example, the husband has consistently felt blamed, even though his wife has genuinely acknowledged many times her part in their problems. In an effort to help the husband, the therapist responded as follows:

T: See, I don't see this as focused in any more on you than on your wife. It's not because you necessarily do or say the wrong thing; it's that some things are not going right between you. It may just as much have to do with how your wife is setting it up.

[The therapist is referring to a kind of interaction the couple have just discussed, in which the husband feels he is the one who causes the breakdown in communication.]

T: There's no way we can know that, unless we take a look at both parts, and sometimes it might be more what she's doing that pulls from you a response that makes for trouble, or it may be that you misread. It's going to vary from time to time. But we have to take a look if you're going to be able to [learn how] to be in ways that make things go better for you, and that's the point of this.

[The husband goes on to talk of being tired of having to look at what he's doing, and the therapist comments that she [the therapist] thinks it's partly because the husband puts what goes on in a context of what he's doing wrong rather than what's not working between them.]

T: The very things you do might work well with somebody else . . . but right now it's you and your wife trying to make it go, and it's not a right or wrong issue but what you two can work out between you to have some good things in life.

Anger and the Tug-of-War

Directly related to the blame issue previously discussed and a further deterrent to negotiating is that spouses often begin with many accumulated grievances and much anger. They are in no mood to negotiate; they feel they have been wronged and seek redress from the partner. One of the major therapeutic tasks is helping a spouse learn how to delay expressing anger, which is no small task. It is frequently necessary to interrupt a spouse whose outpourings begin to overwhelm the mate. In some cases, the therapist does this to protect the angry spouse as well as the partner; the uncontrolled venting of anger is often experienced as a threat to destroy both the self and others. Individuals who have not progressed beyond the symbiotic stage and whose self and object representations are relatively undifferentiated and negatively tinged are most subject to this condition.

One can acknowledge the depth of the spouse's feelings but should suggest restraint. It is hoped that by withholding the anger, the spouses can learn more modulated and functional ways of expressing themselves. Utilizing anger for assertiveness, initiative, and self-protection that are not damaging to others is constructive. Disagreements between spouses, that is, constructive aggression on a verbal level without assaults and insults, neutralizes the anger and promotes ego strengthening.

One way that couples may learn delay is by use of a "cooling-off" period when angers are mounting. In the case presented below the husband utilized this means of defusing the situation, although not without problems. It becomes clear in this example that a method of dealing with anger cannot be oriented exclusively for the individual; for the wife, the method chosen by the husband had ramifications that impeded success. This was revealed as the therapeutic work proceeded.

> [The husband has just described an incident between him and his wife in which they were both angry and were saying things to each other that were inflammatory. The husband said that he had decided that things were getting out of hand and left the scene to cool off.]
>
> H: Is this the wisest course or should we stay and hash it out?
>
> T: What usually happens when you two stick with it?
>
> W: Scream and yell and throw things—I throw things and he screams and yells. [Laughs]
>
> T: Are you able to get anything out of it or is it just both getting mad?
>
> H: Usually nothing comes of it.
>
> [The husband adds that they usually can sit down and talk about it later, but in the meantime there are hurt feelings.]
>
> T: Well, I think you've answered your question. Sometimes things get so hot that it's hard to do anything constructive. I think a cooling-off period is helpful to a lot of people. I think you've answered your question with regard to that. I guess the further question is how long before you talk about it.

The therapist makes a tactical error here in failing to consult the wife. This becomes obvious when the wife relates that she gets furious when her husband "walks out like that," and sometimes it takes her days to get over it. It is apparent that how the cooling off is done has important transactional aspects.

> T: Maybe, suppose instead of his just walking out in anger he could say to you "I'm so upset now that I feel like if I stay I won't be able to talk very rationally and we'll probably end up hurting each other. Would it be O.K. with you if you'd give me some time to cool off? And then I would like to get back to it."
>
> W: I don't know—that's certainly preferable to going out of the house and slamming the door.
>
> T: The way I hear you saying it is when that happens you feel like he's doing that to you.
>
> W: Uh huh.
>
> T: . . . rather than your both agreeing that, "If we get into it now, it's just going to lead to lot of hard feelings." Maybe you don't think that's true. I should have checked that out with you first. Do you think more comes out of it if you get into it hot and heavy? I'm trying to look at it from both sides.
>
> W: There have been times when we've agreed about it angrily and one or the other of us settles down. The thing that distresses me is that it's very disturbing to the children . . . [To husband] I do resent it, though, when you turn around and walk out the door. It's just like, "God damn it, I'm gonna leave you to take care of everything and I'm going to escape." That's what it says to me.
>
> [The husband replies that, at the time of the above incident, he did tell her that if he stayed he'd lose his temper, and that he was going to leave and cool off a while.]
>
> T: Did that still come through like he was just saying, "To hell with you"?
>
> W: Uh huh.

T: How could he have done it so that it wouldn't come through that way, assuming you both agree on a cooling-down period?

W: I don't know—I know I do react very badly when you walk out of the house 'cause it represents things that have happened before.

T: What if he didn't walk out of the house? Do you have a basement?

H: Yes.

T: Suppose he went to the basement?

H: O.K.

T: I'm just asking 'cause she's got that tied in with, like . . .

W: Leaving me with all the responsibilities.

[In the early years of their marriage, the husband was frequently gone from the home. The wife has remained resentful of this.]

T: Yeah, leaving her alone—I'm wondering if you [to husband] can get your cooling off without having to get out of the house. Would you [to wife] feel differently about it, maybe?

W: I think I would.

T: I think I understand what she's saying.

[The wife then describes how she had planned to get roaring drunk to get back at her husband after he left.]

T: See, she feels abandoned when you take off. It's like you're dumping her with everything, saying "To hell with you," and I hear your need for cooling off but can you find a way to cool off and say that to her without her feeling abandoned or contributing to it?

[The husband says his interest is not to abandon her—he plans to come back later when he cools off. He says he could go to the basement, or elsewhere in the house, but he can best get rid of his feelings when he is by himself.]

T: Can you ask for a hands-off period?

H: I do need a hands-off period and it would help me a great

deal if you could forget about the situation for the time
being and . . .

W: I can't make any promises about that.

H: . . . if there is any conversation between us, just not mention anything.

W: Well, I can *not talk* about it, but I cannot forget it.

H: I don't want you to forget it. I want you to remember it.
You might be able to use the same period to get your
thoughts straightened out about it, unless you think
they're already straight.

W: They generally are. [Much laughter]

H: O.K., all right then, yours are already straightened out.
Then, you don't need the time. Allow me the time. [Wife
laughs]

This interchange shows that although the cooling-off idea is generally functional, its effect on the spouse is very important. The necessity of checking out solutions with both spouses is stressed.

The next example illustrates how therapeutic efforts help a
couple learn how to deal with intense anger for each other better.
This was a difficult case, because their feelings were so intense and
their hurtful, assaultive way of dealing with their dissatisfactions
was so ingrained. During the first part of the session, the husband
had been complaining that he felt "left out" from the family, unappreciated, and unimportant.

T: And you feel somehow you're not included?

H: I'm not . . . I'm not.

T: O.K., so I hear you asking her for more recognition.

[The wife, rather than hearing this, goes on to complain
about how her husband's behavior annoys her intensely.]

T: Let me interrupt a minute, O.K.? I know you have a lot
of sources of irritation, and I know your husband has
sources, and we want to pay due attention to both, but let
me just stay with this for a moment, because I hear a thing

coming through from your husband constantly as if he's neglected. And what I'm asking you [to husband] now is would you like your wife to include you more in decision making—to pay more attention to you?

H: It doesn't make any difference because it won't be. [Note that the husband is ready to give up.]

T: Would you like it?

H: Yes!

[The husband complains again how this has not been the case.]

T: Would you ask her now what she is willing to do to help you with this?

H: Well, I can ask her, but it won't . . .

T: Well, ask and see what happens.

W: What are you willing to do—the checks? [This refers to making out checks to pay monthly bills.]

T: Not to help you [To wife] . . . I don't mean with chores— to help you [To husband] feel more a part of things and that you have some part in decision making. Ask her what she's willing to do to help you with those feelings.

H: I don't know how to put it in words.

T: Would you try?

[Long pause.]

T: Let me tell you the reason why I'm trying to help you this way—what's happened is that you've both built up all kinds of frustrations and anger, and you've got much you can say to the other about what you're doing bad. But what you haven't been doing probably for a long time is just, rather than accusing, blaming, attacking, or whatever, is just saying "I'm hurting," like, you know, I hear you saying "I'm hurting, can you help me with this?" . . . coming from both sides.

[The wife proceeds to talk of her husband's great anger, his fury with everybody, his accusations and continuous threats, and concludes, "It's not my fault."]

T: Could I go back a moment? You're amplifying on what I said I know is true, but what I still want to help you learn to do is for each of you to be able to speak up to the other person and say, "Look, I'm hurting in this way," and I want you to be able to say that to your wife 'cause I see that you're hurting.

H: Well, the thing is that I'd like to be given a vote on some things.

[The husband goes on to say that he provides the financial support but feels he plays no essential part in how things are run and that even his financial efforts are criticized. Then, a critical interchange erupts with the wife.]

T: Let me interrupt again. See, we haven't been able to get through with just one task. Now I hear you [to wife] saying more of your beefs, and those are things you're probably going to want to ask your husband for some changes on, but I want him to finish through this one thing. And I want you to answer that without coming back with your counterattacks about what he's not doing right. I just want to follow through with one thing. I want you [to husband] to have the experience of asking your wife . . .

W: [Interrupting] I hope you can do it. . . . [She then resumes criticism] And he flies off the handle—that's why we can't discuss it.

T: I want you to try to learn some new ways where you can talk.

H: All right, she has . . .

T: No, don't talk about her, I want you to say . . .

H: Well, I'd like for her to quit wasting so much time with her frivolous friends.

[The wife laughs sardonically at her husband's inability to comply with the therapeutic task.]

T: [To husband] I want you to say, "I'm hurting, yes, I am angry, frustrated a lot."

H: Yes!

T: "At times when I go through the house I'd like to blow it up. I'm hurting—what will you be willing to do to help me, 'cause I don't feel like I'm getting any recognition. I don't get what I need—what will you do to help me?" That's all I want you to do right now.

H: [To wife] Well, what *will* you do then?

[The husband and wife make several comments, each interrupting the other.]

T: First, tell her how you feel. I made those words up. I don't know as well as you do how you feel.

H: The reason why I'm frustrated is . . .

T: You don't have to tell her the reason—just tell her how you feel.

H: I feel furious! I feel pent-up! I feel like I can't move! I have no life! [To wife] You really want me to . . .

T: No wait, I don't want you to talk about what she does. This is one of the things I'm trying to help you with. You see as soon as you start asking for help and begin to talk about what the other person does wrong, it gets in the way of their hearing you—it goes both ways. . . . I'm trying to help you help her hear your pain, your anger, your frustration. I want her to hear that. She won't hear it if along with that you add, "You don't do this, and you do that, that's bad and you're this bad"; she won't hear you 'cause then she'll have to say, "Yeah, but you do this and that." I'm trying to get each of you to ask for something without accusing at the same time, because in a minute your wife is going to ask from you, "This is what I want," and I want her to say it without [criticism] 'cause you won't hear that either.

H: [To wife] I think I would like for you to accept me, the good things about me, and approve of them and not constantly knock everything.

This is a good effort by the husband.

T: Can you put that in a positive way—what would you like her to do?

H: Well she . . . I can't . . . you're never . . .

T: No—that's a statement you'll have to stop.

H: Well, I'd like for you to approve of some of the things I do well.

This is well put by the husband and deserves support by the therapist.

W: I do approve of all the things you do well.

H: I'd like for you to *say* it occasionally.

   [The husband is able to continue and to be even more specific, despite his wife's statement, which tends to negate his request.]

W: Fine.

T: Oh, now—wait. [To wife] Now one of the things that gets in the way of it—when a person asks for you to do something, is when you start to defend yourself in terms of how much you've already done.

W: Oh.

T: We don't want to do that here. I want you just to hear him and try to make some commitment to him.

W: Could he be more specific?

T: O.K., that's a good question. Give her some idea of how she could make you feel better. [To wife] See, if he feels better and does more for you, then you're going to feel better and do more for him, and with time you'll get something going different. [To husband] She's asked you a good question.

H: Well, almost in every area from her I'd like more support.

T: Can you be more specific? That's quite general. Can you tell her how you could feel that support, what she might do or say?

H: Well, she could just not be so critical.

T: Oh, now put it in the positive. I want you to be kind of specific to help her see the ways in which she could get across some feeling of complimenting you—of making you feel good. And you're the only one who can tell her how it would make you feel good—what kinds of things she could do or say. Now I don't know if she's willing to do them, but I'm just asking you to ask her. See, she'll have to make some decisions about what she is willing to do and what she's not, but that decision is going to have to hinge partially on what you [to wife] can get him to agree to do for you.

The husband begins to detail some specific requests and to stand up for his rights. However, this soon succumbs to counterpressure of the wife, and much disagreement follows. Much effort is required by the therapist to help the wife recognize the issue of the husband's not feeling approved and accepted by her.

The above sequence illustrates the hard struggle the therapist had in trying to help the spouses rechannel their anger into more constructive behavior and eliminate their characteristic pattern of attacking each other. Although this is the first session and does show promise of success, one can also identify the unyielding stance of the wife and her need to be in control as major problems in promoting any give-and-take. Also, she suppresses her husband with her righteousness. It will be difficult to support the husband sufficiently to help him become more forceful in getting his needs met without alienating the wife by appearing to take sides.

The therapist who works with couples must be ready to deal with raw, intense expressions of angry feelings. At times, they may be abruptly directed at the therapist for his or her failure to side with a spouse. It is important that the therapist not experience this anger personally, since this will render the therapist less effective. Ideally, the therapist should maintain his objective stance, attempting to help the spouses harness their aggressions for the purpose of asserting their rights to separateness and for the gratification of needs.

It is important to recognize the reason for the aggression, lest it serve only to hurt and threaten the partner or the therapist. If

a spouse's outburst can be understood as being related to an experienced threat, it may soften the effect on the partner.

Although spouses usually experience hurt in angry interchanges, every so often a spouse will show disdain for negotiating
and even state that he or she wants to hurt the partner. Although in
the long run this will bring back more grief on the spouse, it is unlikely that explaining this will change the spouse's stance. One must
work with the spouse to increase awareness of the hurt that lies
behind the vindictiveness, the frustrations and disappointments
that must have been experienced to lead to the desire for revenge.
This may be difficult to do in the couple session, but if it can be
done (and we have seen it), the awareness and expression of the hurt
often dissipates the anger. In turn, this invites a much more sympathetic position from the spouse, who may now seek ways to alleviate
the pain or at least acknowledge concern for it.

Even if one can get each spouse to accept that objectionable behavior of the mate would not have occurred if the spouse had not
behaved in some way to provoke it, one often encounters stiff resistance from both, which results from their competitive tug-of-war.
Neither wants to be the first to change, which is often viewed as
accepting all the blame. One strategy for dealing with this tug-of-
war is to say, "It seems to me that there are some changes that you
want to make that will make things a lot better for both of you. As
I see it, the best chance you both have for getting some of these
changes you want is to decide what you personally are willing to
do for your spouse which will meet some of the needs your spouse
feels are important. This will then give you better odds on the possibility of your spouse's effecting the changes which you want. This
is something each of you will have to decide—what you can and are
willing to do [assuming that the couple have already discussed what
changes they want]. Now there is no guarantee that even if you make
a serious effort to do some of the things your spouse wishes, that
you will get everything or even anything in return. Your efforts may
net you nothing. But I can guarantee you from this vantage point
that you will have increased your odds considerably. I can also guarantee both of you that what you are doing now [present behavior
patterns that are grievances to each] is absolutely guaranteed to fail.
What I am stressing is that a certain amount and kind of risk taking
is necessary."

appel à la responsabilité individuelle dans le couple,

The therapist speaks to each spouse addressing them jointly to review carefully what they stand to lose or gain, referring to their present untenable patterns of behavior and the ensuing pain, and hoping to mobilize in them some decision-making as to what efforts they are willing to extend. To this extent the work is toward fostering separateness of the couple, weakening the binding dependence, and facilitating autonomous decision making.

What one wants to avoid is a stalemate, each spouse waiting for the other to go first. Spouses often state their willingness to do something, but, at the same time, they are secretly assuming that if their mate does what he or she should, then the problem will be solved and the spouse will not have to do anything. This problem can be met by saying, "Up until this point both of you are very unhappy with the way things have been going. There are some things you want different which seem imperative to you. You say in so many words that you just cannot go on any longer the way things are. What I am suggesting is that once each of you has decided what you are willing to do to make things go better [again, these should be *contract* spelled out behaviorally rather than in vague, abstract terms], that you give it your all. Then you will be better able to decide what you will want to do from that point on. In other words, as a result of your efforts, either some things will improve a little, moderately, or a lot, or perhaps not at all. Then you will be in a better position to make the kinds of decisions you have been wrestling with as to whether or not you are willing to continue in the relationship. You will know, relatively speaking, what the limits are of what you can do personally to influence your spouse toward change. You may be up against tremendous odds because of certain fairly ingrained problems your spouse may well have had before your marriage that will continue no matter what you do. On the other hand, you may find that if you change some of your behaviors, some of the spouse's behaviors which are so irritating to you are less likely to occur. Less frequent occurrence of such behaviors may change the tolerability of the situation for you. Whatever happens, I contend that you will have a clearer perspective on how your life is likely to be and will be better able to decide if you are willing to accept it or try for a better life, perhaps with someone else." This sounds like a long-winded lecture. It would rarely be delivered all in one piece, but hopefully, the ideas will be conveyed as the therapist works on the issues at hand.

One assumption in the above is that change is subject to volun-
tary control. It is obvious that for some spouses this is only partially
so, and the points mentioned may not have the impact desired. The
therapist should recognize and accept this but not overlook the
value of this stance—promoting separateness and mutual responsibility for decision making. In the meantime, through other therapeutic efforts, one will be working to facilitate the experience of
being more able to make choices for oneself.

Much has been written on the problems emanating from a
person's resistance to change—the fear of the unknown, the willingness to accept a familiar although uncomfortable position rather
than face the anticipated perils of being different. Change is hard to
come by for all of us and for very adaptive reasons inherent in the
nature of things. There is almost an ingrained attitude that things
will get better only when the external changes, in contrast to when
we personally take responsibility for altering our behavior, feelings, or attitudes. To the extent possible the therapist needs to put
his weight behind the value of change for self-gratification and self-
enhancement, not discounting that this feels risky.

Compliance and Deadlocks

Often a disagreement, despite an exploration of the spouses'
feelings, may remain deadlocked. If the issue is one of beliefs or
attitudes, this is easier to deal with. One can stress to the couple that
for them to expect to see eye to eye on everything is folly. If they are
aware that they are going to argue when they discuss certain issues,
perhaps they can avoid these issues. Although it would be ideal for
both spouses to hold similar views on politics, religion, and friends,
this is unlikely. If an issue requires no action, couples can learn to
respect or at least to accept differences and to avoid provoking arguments. Indeed, in healthy marriages, many learn to negotiate their
differences into strengths for themselves and their children. It is
helpful to emphasize that with regard to values, there is no right or
wrong, only how people feel about the issues. If one can remove the
issue from a right/wrong context, then spouses may feel less need
to fight.

Problems arise when possible resolutions to an issue are mutually exclusive (for example, whether to go to a movie). If by explor-

ing the positions there is no solution, one might comment to the couple that there will inevitably be impasses and encourage them to come up with ways to deal with them. Hopefully, they will decide on a compromise such as flipping a coin or taking turns deciding; at this point, little else remains. However, if they can agree on even a superficial solution, it may save many hard feelings in the future.

In some cases, rather than deadlocking, one spouse will renounce his or her own desires and seek to gratify the mate's, or the spouse may feel that not agreeing to a seemingly rational, obvious solution offered by the mate would put him or her in a bad light. Thus, the spouse agrees to avoid discord or to save face, but there is little chance of this kind of resolution succeeding. The therapist should not be surprised when this occurs and should immediately suspect that some important, unidentified wish was not recognized by either the therapist or the spouses, and that the resolution has not met at least one spouse's needs.

At times, a spouse will return to therapy and report desirable changes made by the mate as a result of previous negotiating. If both spouses are satisfied, the spouse who modified his or her behavior should have all this fully acknowledged and receive positive reinforcement. However, to determine how satisfactory the solution is, it is extremely important to ask this spouse about the change. What was the degree of struggle? What was the personal cost? Was it reasonably comfortable or not? A solution that works well for one spouse but not the other, even though he or she complies, is no real solution.

For example, in one therapy session, the husband had complained bitterly that he and his wife could not discuss anything without a fight because of their differences of opinion. In the next session, the husband happily reported that his wife was no longer hassling him and that things had improved. Exploration of how the wife felt, however, revealed that inhibiting her views was extremely difficult, for her; in addition, she felt shut off from her husband and consequently withdrew. Although she talked about efforts to reach out to other people to whom she could talk as a substitute, it was clear that the solution irritated her. Probably extensive work would be necessary to help them learn how to talk together and accept differences without shutting off communication. As a start, the therapist might encourage them to engage in a here-and-now discussion in which they knew disagreements would arise, so that the therapist could help them recognize how their communication leads to arguing.

As stated above, the therapist must be careful not to accept reports of improvement without checking them out with both spouses. As in the above example, although the husband felt pleased because a desire of his was met, the effort required for the wife to behave desirably was contrary to one of her frequently expressed desires—to get more attention from him. Her behavior was a withdrawal out of anger and frustration, and she did not see how she could go on doing this. It was only a temporary compliance to relieve some tension but hardly an adaptive solution, ultimately comfortable to both. Such temporary holding measures may do more harm than good as the accommodating spouse harbors increasing resentments.

Resistance to Change

Inevitably, when a spouse begins to state some of his or her wishes for more gratification, the partner will experience this as a demand for personal change. To an extent, this is quite true, although the partner often overreacts to the requests as a demand for total personality change. However, these wishes will be less threatening and better understood if the therapist aids in their expression. Typically, spouses view themselves as a single identity "I" rather than as an "I" who thinks, feels, and behaves in many different ways, some of which are seen quite positively, and some which are not. When they hear needs expressed that require them to change, it is as if the single entity "I" must cease to exist and some new model be put in its place. This is not only unwarranted and resented, but also is and feels impossible. One spouse expressed this view well: "I guess because I felt in the past in order for us to make it, before we came here, I thought I'd just have to be somebody else, and I got to the point where I felt I just couldn't do it." Because spouses feel that their mates want them to change into a new person, they feel rejected for what they are. In defense, the spouses often offer stiff resistance, assuming a stance that says, "I am what I am, me, and I'm not going to change."

The therapist can agree that the spouse will always be basically himself or herself; it would be unrealistic for the partner to expect otherwise. However, one can go on to say that this does not preclude the spouse doing some things differently that would make things work better for both partners. At this point, the therapist can refocus on the kinds of behaviors that each may attempt to change.

In one example, the husband felt the wife was critical because of his lack of self-confidence. As long as the problem was discussed as a personality characteristic, not much improvement was likely. The unconfident spouse felt unable to change and rejected. It was important for the therapist to separate the personality trait from the behavioral manifestations that interfered with the wife's desires. It was not the lack of self-confidence itself that created the problem but the fact that the husband did not want as much social life as the wife.

By separating the personality traits of the partner from its behavioral manifestations, the spouse can express a need without demeaning the partner's character. In turn, the partner, feeling less criticized and more accepted, will be more likely to change a behavior that is frustrating to the spouse. In the above instance, more social life would decrease the wife's desire to accuse her husband of lacking self-confidence. Obviously here the issue was not just a disagreement on socializing, which can be resolved simply, but a more complex one that requires several stages of unraveling before the couple can achieve resolution. The process whereby they move from their initial positions toward resolution is as important as the solution itself—they are learning to resolve differences.

Frequently in therapy, a spouse will state with finality to his or her partner that he or she will not change in the ways the partner is pressing for. This may result from many different situations. It may reflect a mature conclusion resulting from years of attempting to change, with some success, and discovering one's limits for further change. In other cases, this may arise out of a stubborn, self-protective position in which the individual refuses to accept any deficiencies in the self and sees others at fault. As an example, one wife commented to her husband, "You have said it yourself, '*I am* this way, . . . I'm not going to change; the children must change to suit me,' and that holds true with me and that's fine up to a point, but it creates great tension." Where the defensive structure is rigid yet fairly functional in other contexts, one may have to recognize the slim chance of change and look for other ways to help the couple (for example, working primarily with the other spouse or individual therapy).

Sometimes a refusal to change is a way to shirk responsibility and to avoid the anxiety and frustration involved in responding to the spouse's desires. If the other partner accepts this stance, then he or she will likely feel frustrated and defeated, since any change in the relationship must come only from this partner's efforts.

In some cases resistance to change arises out of the felt limits of one's power to do any more than one has. It is felt as if the self has already been extended to the limit, and further efforts to comply threaten the very economy of an already shaky equilibrium. Negotation is experienced as further hassle in a context of a life already beset with hassles almost beyond the level of endurance. With individuals demonstrating such fragility, the marital focus, because of its demands upon each, may well be contraindicated, and individual therapy recommended.

Occasionally a spouse fears that if he or she concedes on a point, it will lead to a string of demands that would violate his or her selfhood. As one wife said, "I've changed; I can continue to change. I think I've demonstrated that over the past year. But it seems like if I change a little bit, then you demand more change from me. What is the end point?" In these cases, the therapist can encourage exploration of the spouse's underlying feelings; perhaps the spouse will then feel less threatened. At the same time, it would also be important to help both spouses understand the implications of the statement in terms of the couple relationship, the kind of effects it might have, and the feelings it might engender. This might be best handled by asking the partner wanting change to verbalize the acceptability of the spouse's hesitation to change, what it entails, how much discomfort the partner experiences, and how not changing may translate into counterpressure for the spouse.

One often finds that an intense rivalry can develop around the issue of change over whose needs will be met. With great anger a wife said to her husband, "Even though it was against my needs,

I again gave up my needs for your needs. . . . But when the situation came up again, it was your needs rather than my needs—your needs to have a life outside of work and home—you know 'cause you said it to me—you just couldn't do it—you had to have it outside the house." Inevitably, the argument centers on who has the greatest freedom to do as he or she pleases. It is not uncommon for spouses to detail with envy what they perceive as their partners' advantages: in the case of the husband, the wife's freedom from work, to run around, shop, have lunch out; in the case of the wife, her perception of her husband's envious position of having adult conversation, attractive females around, interesting activities, freedom from crying children or dull housework. Husbands remark on how fantastic it must be to sleep late and stay home all day. By contrast, wives who feel caught in the dull, monotonous, unrewarding duties of housework and children point out what a privilege it would be to be involved in other activities. The resentments are likely to be equally keen on both parts. As phrased by one husband, "I was resentful that you had the freedom to enjoy yourself and you didn't have the responsibilities I did . . . I'm also resentful of you because you have the luxury that you can pick and choose whether you want to work or not, and I don't have that same option!" Feelings probably originating in sibling rivalry problems are easily called into play, with one spouse citing the other's enviable position to buttress the argument of why the other should have to change.

Problems with change can also result from one spouse imposing his or her standards and ideals upon the other. This is especially difficult to deal with when an individual has very high standards, a compulsive mode of operation, a low tolerance level for perceived failures and inefficiency. As one wife told her husband, "You have very high ideals for yourself, and you don't tolerate any imperfection in anyone else. You cannot accept them as they are, and no one can meet the standard." Although one may consider this behavior defensively functional, the therapist will still need to help him or her see the effects on the mate and the price to be paid for such inflexibility. The best way to do this is by having the partner describe his or her personal discomfort and how this will in turn generate problems for the spouse.

The Heavyweight versus the Lightweight

A major stumbling block to negotiating is when one spouse is easily intimidated by the partner as the work of stating needs begins. Bach refers to this as "the heavyweight versus the lightweight."[4] We have found that it is imperative to support the lightweight in efforts at self-assertion but in a way that the partner does not experience as taking sides. One way to minimize this is by pointing out that the heavyweight will not be given to as long as the mate is prevented from satisfying his or her own needs. This requires encouraging the lightweight spouse to express the experience of intimidation as he or she begins to state desires. One will need to show the heavyweight spouse what behaviors are experienced as intimidating; then, different ways of behaving that would facilitate freer expression by the lightweight spouse can be explored.

Many spouses have great difficulty in clearly defining for their mates what they need and would like. The most uncommon words in many marriages are "I want." This seems to be especially true for individuals who are shy, lacking self-confidence, and prone to feel guilty for what goes wrong; they require particular encouragement to express their needs.

In the example below, the husband began by saying somewhat hesitantly that he would like to have more sex with his wife. He was particularly discouraged, and it was difficult for him to talk with his wife about what he wanted.

> H: I don't know, it's really hard to say, I guess, a lot of times I feel like I'm just not close to you and different things. You really have a lot on your mind, you know, with the new baby—that's a different story and that just has some problems. But even before that and you know, basing things on and when . . . I don't know . . . I try to be affectionate or something . . . I want too much from you I guess.

Notice the blocked, hesitant style and the difficulty that this husband has in asking more of his wife.

[4]G. Bach and P. Wyden. *The Intimate Enemy: How to Fight Fair in Love and Marriage*. New York: Morrow, 1969.

W: Yeah, but what do you expect me to do?

H: Just hold me sometimes.

W: Well, I do that pretty often, I . . .

H: Yes, you do.

T: [To husband] What you're saying is not just lovemaking; [to wife] that if he could just get more loving or feel more loved, maybe then the actual physical sex wouldn't have to be as frequent.

H: Yes, we have discussed that before.

W: Yes, but I don't know how to do any more than I do.

T: Can you help her with that? It sounds like you're wanting and needing a little bit more than where she is when she says, "I don't know how to do it anymore," so something is amiss here.

H: I guess . . .

W: [Interrupting] I can't have my arms around you all the time, with the baby.

H: No, I don't want your arms around me all the time.

W: That's what it sound like to me. That's what it seems like, it would be that if I give you more than I already do.

T: [To husband] It may be some things more than the arms around you. [To wife] You may need to help him in other ways. Perhaps through messages which come across from you that make him feel loved or not loved. Maybe you need to help him know more about what's in these messages.

H: I guess, oh, what am I trying to say?

W: Well, you have to tell me, because I don't know. You have to tell me what you expect me to do because I don't know.

[The husband then goes on to say that he feels that when his wife is unhappy, he is very concerned and wants to help but that his wife does not share with him.]

H: I guess a lot of times when I talk to you, you really are discouraged about things and really in a bad mood, and I really want to make you feel better. I don't feel like I can do that . . . and I really feel distant from you a whole lot of times . . . and sometimes I just want to talk to you so bad, and that's really selfish of me.

W: Don't feel like that.

H: Well I do, you're always so busy with the baby and I don't like to bug you.

W: When you call me in the day it's bad, because I can't just drop what I'm doing and talk on the phone for an hour, that's impossible.

H: I know that.

T: I hear your husband saying two things. One is that he wants more from you, of whatever, you know, that would make him feel close enough, and the other one is that he is not sure how you are receiving some of his giving to you, like he doesn't know how his behavior is coming across to you. Whether he is trying to talk to you to make you feel better or whatever, he's not sure how you are receiving this. . . . . And it might be worthwhile to talk with him a little bit about these, like what he can do for you. For example, like when you are frustrated.

[The wife states that all she needs is to know that he's there behind her, but that it does not help her to sit down and talk about things; that is not her way. The wife then contrasts herself with her husband, saying that she prefers to keep things to herself, whereas he likes to share.]

T: But people are very different and they have learned different ways of handling problems . . . maybe your wife has chosen a different way; perhaps it's not a sharing way. Perhaps it's keeping things to herself. I don't know if it's the best way, but it's her way. Is this something you can accept without feeling excluded? That's the problem.

H: I know, because I think that's how I feel.

Another fear of the lightweight is to speak up in the therapy session because he or she will "get it" when the couple get home. Again, one tries to minimize this by encouraging both spouses to state their grievances openly, in a way that neither spouse is embarrassed. A spouse is less likely to be angry and punish the mate at home if he or she has not suffered in the hands of the partner during the sessions. It is important for the therapist whenever possible to offset particularly hurtful or denigrating remarks by reinterpreting them more positively. Spouses often belittle themselves as well as their mates; for example, one wife described her husband as "having it all together" and herself as "empty-headed" and "Always scurrying around." The therapist will discourage spouses from downgrading themselves, perhaps by calling attention to their strengths and assets lest they fail to work for self-gratification.

Separating Issues

One problem that prevents spouses from being heard is an inability to work on one issue without mixing in related issues. For example, one husband complained bitterly that when company came, the wife took great pains to clean the house and to dress appealingly, but she made no such efforts just for him.

The therapist pointed out that the husband's complaint essentially was, "I feel as if you don't pay sufficient attention to me. I'd like you to make more effort with yourself and with the house so that I feel you really care when I come home." The inclusion of the addendum of comparison (to when company comes in this case) inevitably invites trouble and yet it is one of the most common ways that complaints are expressed. After the wife is faulted for her behavior when company comes, her energy would be directed to defending this as appropriate, which, in fact, it may well be. Thus, she will feel unjustly criticized and fail to hear the main message—the husband's wanting her to show more appreciation of him, not less for company. The therapist should be alert to the comparison context in which complaints are presented, so that one can help spouses separate issues appropriately.

When the Cognitive Negotiating Approach Fails

Although the therapeutic comments on helping spouses learn to negotiate are addressed to each spouse's ego, many unconscious factors may defeat these efforts. What may appear as a superficial problem may be rooted in deep, inner conflicts which prevent the spouse from altering his original position. By way of example, a common problem presented more and more by couples is the dispute over who is to assume how many and which household tasks. Although the wife may be operating from a vantage point of equality and symmetry, neither she nor her husband may recognize that a shaky sense of masculine identity underlies his stubborn resistance to sharing the household duties. The therapist must keep in mind that any adequate solution must consider both spouses' positions.

Negotiating cannot be a simple matter of working out percentages of time or availability of each. Since unconscious feelings play a part in creating the problem, a purely cognitive negotiating approach is doomed to failure. Absolutely essential is that at least the therapist have some awareness of the contributing problems. Without necessarily working toward greater awareness of the threat posed to the husband by his wife's requests, the therapist may guide them toward some resolution wherein more feminine related duties are undertaken by the wife and those less feminine by the husband. In this way the therapist, through added awareness, can prevent the negotiating approach from completely failing.

The following example is one which on the surface would appear open to negotiating but where initially it failed completely. In one session the spouses were disputing the wife's opening of her husband's mail. Because of the intensity of their convictions, these seemed like irreconcilable differences not open for compromise since each spouse remained fixed in the "rightness" of his or her position.

Any simple and immediately obvious compromise solution, such as the husband agreeing to let his wife see his mail after *he* had opened it, was no solution for either. The wife felt she had a right to share her husband's mail; he felt she was intruding on his rights. Obviously, reality negotiations concerning how to deal with the letter-opening disagreements were not going to work. Much more was necessary for the spouses to understand what their disagreement was all about. It is axiomatic, when obvious solutions are not grasped, that the therapist must point the couple toward the task of understanding why not.

The therapist began by encouraging both to discuss their feelings and thoughts with respect to the problem. After some time and effort both spouses began to better understand reasons for the intensity of each other's feelings, and each became less entrenched in maintaining his or her own view. The husband's reluctance was expressed as feeling like a child again with "mother" snooping into his affairs. Once his wife viewed his protest from this context, her own attitude and stance changed; she had previously interpreted the behavior as her husband's wish not to share things with her. Being able to understand his behavior as not aimed at her allowed her to feel less need to press for "inclusion" in this way. At the same time it opened up an opportunity for them to discuss her feelings of "being left out" more than she wished, and allowed them to explore more acceptable ways to both of alleviating these feelings. Examples like these stress how superficial the therapeutic work *may* be if it stays with and focuses only on a solution to the surface problem without promoting an understanding of what needs are served by the resistances to negotiating.

Sometimes, when working at a cognitive level, the couple become unwilling to alter their respective positions. The therapist may then need to work at a different level. One technique used to break this bind, borrowed from gestalt therapists, is to suggest that a spouse say a sentence to the partner that is believed to be at the heart of the matter. This may facilitate the flow of feelings, so that new material may emerge that can be worked on.

In one instance, a couple were hotly disagreeing over an issue that ostensibly could have been solved cognitively; the husband was adamantly refusing to include in a dinner-party guest list a man of whom he was jealous and to whom the wife had showed some attention. His wife was incensed at being told what to do and of being unjustly accused. Efforts at compromise had been fruitless. Though angry feelings were implied, none were directly expressed.

The therapist's first attempted solution was to suggest to the husband that he say to his wife, "I am very angry at you." The husband repeated this several times, but apparently his defenses against acknowledging his anger did not allow him to become aware of it. Shifting to a less threatening statement, the therapist suggested he say to his wife, "I feel shut off from you." He was able to say this more convincingly. Then, he began to express to his wife his hurt, which was that if she cared sufficiently, she would understand his position. A meaningful interchange became possible without dwelling on the disagreement over the dinner guest.

In this example, we are trying to illustrate several points: that cognitive problem-solving can fail; that impasses may be broken by shifting to a different level of transaction; that the therapist's assumption of a feeling state may be correct, but the spouse may not be ready to get in touch with this feeling; that if this occurs, the therapist can promote awareness of a less threatening feeling; and finally, that spouses repeating appropriate statements several times, as convincingly as possible, may mobilize feelings and facilitate more meaningful communication. In short, working at the feeling level is useful for breaking up impasses reached at the cognitive negotiating level. It facilitates individual awareness, which, in turn, may ease the tension between the couple.

In another example, the husband, who was controlled, periodically depressed, and well defended against experiencing his anger, had been trying to control his wife's behavior, using constant jibes and implied criticisms. Although she had not been a model of decorous behavior, the wife seemed to be genuinely trying to please her husband. Intermittently she would become discouraged, convinced that no matter what she did, it would be fruitless. There was much resentment and tension between them; although this had been expressed verbally, there was no resolution. The husband voiced resentment for being dependent on the wife, yet he held on to his anger tightly and wielded it like a weapon.

With the wife's approval, the therapist instructed the husband to say to her that he hated her and to hit her with a paper bat on her leg. Acting out anger is generally not encouraged, but was used here as a therapeutic assist to facilitate awareness of feelings. The husband found this extremely difficult to do but did manage one weak blow. With gentle pressure and encouragement by both the wife and the therapist, several things ensued. The husband turned on the therapist in an outburst of anger. He feared being left alone with "no one there to pick up the pieces." He continued in this vein, emotionally repeating that he would end up being totally alone. As the statement released more anxiety of abandonment, he said, "I must be the meanest man in the world." In this small piece of behavior, the client briefly got in touch not only with his anger, but, more importantly, with the fear that prevented its expression. His archaic feelings of being bad were juxtaposed with a fear of abandonment. This clearly stated diagnostic information shows a developmental deficit at the separation-individuation period which helps the therapist become aware of the severity of the husband's problem. Part of the therapeutic task through this period was to support the husband, reassuring him of continual help and availability. The experience, while valuable, was also stressful and frightening for the husband, raising vague fears and anxieties. Individual sessions were held with the wife's encouragement to help him work on these fears.

Sample Session

The previous section was included to emphasize that a cognitive orientation has limited effectiveness. Ordinarily, couple therapy is not neatly divided into cognitive and noncognitive interventions. The therapist is usually working in many different ways, shifting from overt behaviors to feelings and resistances to change. The edited session below is a typical effort to help a couple negotiate on a specific problem and illustrates varying points of focus and interventions. The spouses' problem was not important in itself, but it served as a vehicle for expressing much of the nature of their interaction, which allowed the therapist to increase the couple's awareness of the factors contributing to the surface conflict.

The husband was defending himself against the wife's criticism of his choice of clothes. He had just agreed that she ought to talk about something if it bothered her, but "I think you should be a little more selective in what bothers you and not let insignificant things bother you." The problem here, of course, is that what is insignificant to one person may not be to another. The therapist saw this as an example of the husband saying that the wife should not have certain feelings, and responded accordingly.

> T: That's a difficult thing to try to legislate—feelings. It might be more helpful to talk about what she could do that would be more acceptable to you.

This comment stresses individuals' rights to their own feelings and the importance of accepting these, which redirected the interchange toward what behaviors might be changed:

H: Yes, there are some things she could, [to wife] you could
do that would be acceptable to me, rather than outright
criticism.

[The husband suggests how his wife could have talked
with him differently.]

W: Well, I don't think that would have solved the problem.

[Further comments promote more arguing.]

T: Well, let's get back maybe to a more basic issue for the
moment. Do you want her to help you with your clothes?

H: Yes, I would like for her to.

T: Okay, *how* would you like her to help you?

The therapist attempts to guide the interchange that follows to help
the couple work out some clear understandings. The wife states
she is not sure that her suggestions are appreciated and gives instances to support this. The therapist suggests to the husband that
he must help her know more clearly when and how he wants to be
helped and what suggestions are welcomed. A long discussion ensues as the husband tries to clarify these points. Part of the therapist's goal here is to support the husband's rights to make his own
choices and for autonomy, but in a way that will not alienate the
wife; at the same time, the therapist acknowledges the wife's right
to her feelings.

T: [To wife] That doesn't mean you have to like it [referring
to the husband's choice of clothes—laughter]. He can't
decide that you're going to like it.

The therapist is working to promote separateness. The husband
then gives a long list of his preferences.

T: [To wife] Does that help you?

W: Yes, that does, but . . .

[The wife has more questions; a long discussion of further negotiating follows with some disagreements, annoyance, and humor. The therapist intervenes at a point
of disagreement.]

T: And what I hear you suggesting to her, she doesn't accept. Maybe you would like a counterproposal on that.

The therapist is working toward the couples arriving at a mutually satisfactory solution.

[The wife expresses annoyance at the husband for being angry when she makes a suggestion.]

T: Can you explain to your wife why you get so mad, what that's all about, before we get back to settling the issue?

Since there is much anger in the interchange, the therapeutic goal is not just that the couple learn how the husband can accept comments from his wife regarding his manner of dress, but to help them understand more about their continual tug-of-war, of which the clothes issue is one example. This intervention is not productive initially; the couple stay with the clothes issue until the husband, in repeating what his wife had said to him, mimics her tone of voice, which implied ridicule.

H: Well, your tone of voice rather than your words is what carries the implication to me.

T: And the implication is?

H: The implication is that it looked pretty awful, and "if you expect to go anywhere with me, you're either going to change or I'm not going to like it."

T: It was *critical*.

The therapist sums up the emotional impact of that statement.

H: Yes, I think it was critical.

T: Very critical. It wasn't the words *per se*. He heard criticism and put-down.

W: [Defensively] Well, I don't really remember how it was said.

T: I know you don't. I'm saying, I don't know how you said it either. It could have been your husband's oversensitiv-

ity or it could have been that it was a vehicle for expressing irritation for you, but I think he is right in pointing
out that it's not just words, it's how they're said. You
could say it in a very kind, loving fashion—that same
message. Like you care so much that you want to help
him or you could say it in a "Damn it, you look like some
idiot!" tone. I don't know either what your tone was, but
I think that's something you have to tune into—what
he's hearing over there, and that's consistent with what
he's hearing in lots of ways. He's not feeling cared for;
he's feeling criticized and condemned. And that's something we talked about last time, too. It comes through in
so many little different bits of behavior. I think I heard
Sam [the husband] say last time that it was very important for him to feel like you cared for him. That doesn't
mean you have to like everything he does or wears—because you're two different people—but it's what you then
do about it that leads to a source of difficulty.

W: I understand what's being said here, but . . .

[The wife suggests that the husband's manner of dress is
sometimes done deliberately to irritate her. She is not
amenable to responding to his needs as expressed above
because she has her own discontents. He denies the al-
legation and further disagreement ensues.]

W: And I consider it a reflection upon my ability to take care
of your clothes.

A new issue has been introduced.

T: Wait a minute, that's quite different than what you said,
that's not the same thing.

[She goes back to the original point of the husband deliberately looking bad to annoy her.]

T: Now, wait just a minute, let's make sure we get the issues
straight here. If he looks bad, et cetera, who's that a reflection on?

W: Well, it probably shouldn't be a reflection on me, but I
take it as being one.

T: Yeah, you're going to have to be very clear to separate this out, because if he chooses to look bad, et cetera, he's an adult, and that's his choice . . . and that could only reflect on him. So I see you taking over a responsibility you can very well give up. You are *not* responsible for how he dresses . . . that doesn't mean if he asks for help you can't give him suggestions, I don't mean that. Now it seems like maybe that issue has colored your perception to the point where you feel like he deliberately chooses things to get at you by being in some way a reflection on you, like you say.

[The wife does not respond to this. She continues with the original emphasis on the husband's deliberately dressing to annoy her. The therapist tries a new approach.]

T: Well, what could he say . . . to convince you [that he does not deliberately dress badly]?

W: He did a pretty effective job when he says he didn't pick it [a tie] out to please me, so he didn't pick it out to bug me, either, so . . .

T: Do you believe him?

W: Yes, I do.

T: O.K. . . . where does that leave you?

W: With no argument. [Laughs]

T: See, you've got to put it in terms of something to continue the argument, and I'm trying to get away from the need for argument and help you see the difference between what's your responsibility and what's his responsibility.

W: O.K., that leaves me with only . . . my opinions are only welcomed at the particular occasion that you [to husband] mentioned, and other than that I shouldn't have to feel responsible for what you wear.

T: That's true.

W: Well, it would be easier if I didn't, it really would be, if I didn't have to feel responsible, I don't know why it bugs me, but it does!

T: Well, you don't have to like it if he [wears such and such]
     . . . but it's not your responsibility. If he wants help . . .

W: I can go along with those techniques. I can't promise how
     much it won't bother me, but I'll make a conscious effort
     not to.

It is obvious that the wife's feelings are ingrained and that she cannot
readily forego them just because she cognitively understands that
how her husband dresses is not her responsibility.

T: No, I don't think you can make any promises that it won't
     bother you. It probably will bother you.

     [The therapist goes on to say that the wife can communi-
     cate the bother when it gets excessive, but that if it is com-
     municated in a caring and not critical way, she will have
     a better chance of influencing her husband. She essen-
     tially agrees but wants to continue the issue of her need
     for her husband to change his angry response.]

W: No doubt my tone of voice needs some help with it, but
     no doubt your reaction needs some improvement too.

     [The husband begins to defend himself, saying he does
     not always "stomp off mad," and an argument ensues.]

T: [Redirecting] It might be worthwhile to work on with you
     [the husband] some, how you express your anger toward
     your wife when you get angry, what you do character-
     istically?

H: Turn my back, figuratively speaking, and grit my teeth.

T: So you don't engage—you try not to engage.

H: Generally.

T: I think perhaps, because that's a characteristic way you
     have, it's easier for her to read into things anger when it
     may not be there. As in the case of the clothes, she's read-
     ing that you're doing something to get at her, because it
     seems like when you have anger, you don't express it di-
     rectly—you might use some indirect way to express it.
     I'm not saying that's the case, but frequently when people

have trouble coming out straight with anger, they find other ways of getting their anger expressed.

H: Yeah.

T: So if, in fact, that is true, which I don't know for a fact that it is, it might suggest that it would be helpful for you to learn some ways of being more direct. In other words, if something comes up that annoys you, you just say it straight out, you know, whatever it is. For example, like with the clothes, if she says something that you interpret as critical you might just say, "Get off my back, they're my clothes and I'll wear what I want; I have good reason for doing so."

H: O.K.

T: If you, in fact, feel annoyed; now if you don't, I'm not suggesting you do that, but if it hits you and you find some rising anger, say, "Get off my back, those are my clothes and my selection. I know what I'm doing and I've got good reason," rather than avoiding. You know, I have the feeling that you avoid because you think you will get into more arguments, but I feel like in the long run you will get into more that way than you would if you came out straight with it.

H: You're probably right, because I don't think we've managed to avoid many arguments using that way of doing it.

T: And furthermore, I think they [angry feelings] come out sideways [indirectly], and then they start contaminating many ways in which you operate together, and that makes it easier for her to read anything, you know, in the way of a withdrawal, you're not participating, as really your anger.

H: O.K.

T: You're doing that to get back at her in a way. I don't know how comfortable that [direct expression of anger] will be for you. It's easy to say O.K., but . . .

H: Yes, I realize that.

T: It's not going to be that simple.

H: I'm saying O.K. in that I understand what you're saying.

T: Right. Can you see some merit, perhaps, if you try it?

H: Yes.

T: Why not, just for practice, tell June [the wife] to get off your back.

H: Get off my back, June. [Laughs nervously]

W: You did do this the other morning, you know, when you had on your pink pants and red shirt, and I said, "God!" and you said, "I don't feel like being bugged about my clothes this morning so just hush" and I did.

T: [To wife] How does this sit with you when he says that?

W: That does better, it really does. Because I don't know when you're going to explode if you stomp off and do it, and the next minute I ask you if I can have my grocery check and you fly off like that, you know. It does make me feel a little bit more secure to know exactly in proportion, you know, what the anger is all about.

H: All right, I will try. I'll make an effort to be more open with my anger, with my disgust, [laughs] and with my annoyance.

T: O.K., let's hear a little bit more about your disgust. I'm not sure what that's all about.

H: All right, in essence, this whole bit is about my . . . her having more of an influence on my mode of dress because of my feeling about the importance of clothes in the first place, and the whole thing . . . it seems picky and it's disgusting that an argument or discussion should ever come up about clothes. It's not disgusting in that it's a distasteful subject; it is not disgusting like sewage or something like this; it's disgusting that it should ever be elevated to the plane where it's worth an argument.

T: O.K., maybe it might be helpful for the moment, if you would let Sam know why that's important to you, because you see it's not just the clothes. It obviously has much more meaning, just as your reaction is not just to what she says, it's how she says it, the feeling of being criticized, and she doesn't approve of you and therefore is not as caring, and this is loaded with all kinds of meaning. I'm sure there must be some kind of meaning here. That's why it bugs you so much.

[The interchange continues, the wife emphasizing the husband's lack of pride in himself, which bugs her.]

T: [To wife] What does that mean in terms of you, if he doesn't have much pride in himself?

W: Well, maybe I feel like I've fallen down on my job to inspire pride in you [the husband]. I don't know whether that makes any sense or not.

T: You mean, you're responsible for him having pride in himself?

W: I think in some ways I might be. Maybe I don't have enough confidence and don't build up your confiin yourself and don't do my part in some ways. I do consider it a reflection on the way I have treated you.

The therapist continues with the responsibility issue; discussing the wife's guilt would also have been helpful.

T: I wouldn't be willing to accept that responsibility. I don't think you can be responsible for Sam's pride or lack of it or degree of it or whatever. This is not to say that you can't help him.

W: Well, all right, it does bother me when he does these kinds of things, and I've looked at him and tried to analyze it, and I feel like you don't have very much pride in yourself.

T: Well, I know it bothers you—there's no question about that.

W: I know, and I'm trying to give you the reason why it bothers me and that's the only reason I can come up with and I've thought about it, I really have. Maybe I'm not responsible for the amount of pride he has in himself.

T: Well, if people saw your husband walking by and he

smelled, and had on a dirty shirt, and his shoes unbuckled, and he's not shaved, now what would they say?

W: "God, what a slob she's married to." [Laughs.]

T: Now what would they say about you? What would that
mean? I guess, you couldn't do any better?

W: Yeah [laughs], that's what I would think—"Can't she do
something with him"—maybe—maybe not in this day
and time.

T: No, what I think you would come back to is that you'd
think people would think that you didn't "do so hot" and
therefore, obviously, there must be something wrong
with you; you couldn't catch anything better than that.

W: Oh, I don't really think so because, [to husband] basically
I'm very pleased, you know, for people to know that I'm
married to you.

T: Not when he smells and has his shoes unbuckled, looks
unshaven, and doesn't have pride in himself. [Wife
laughs.] It sounds like . . .

W: Tell me, because I don't really know.

T: No, it sounds like you're not that secure in yourself, because over here if he topples off from looking like that
great image, [you think] that's going to reflect on you—
you get shaken up. He's got to always look the perfect
part.

W: [Softer] I really hadn't thought about it that way. I have
attempted to look at it and analyze it, but it never . . .
that didn't occur to me.

T: You see, I know it's important to you. I know that, and I
think it's important for your husband to know it's not
just all about trying to knock you [to husband] down and
criticize you. You see, she's struggling in terms of feeling
good about herself, and to an extent that's not firmed up
as much as it might be, and anything that you do becomes
of more importance. You know, if you smell, that shakes
her up even more—or whatever—something that so-
cially might reflect negatively. She is going to feel it more

in terms of herself; it's not just in the service of criticizing
you. That's not to say that each of you may not use these
same areas to get some of your anger across for other reasons. That's certainly going to come in too. [To wife] But
I'm just struck by the degree to which this is important
to you.

In the process of negotiating the problem about the husband's
clothes, the couple were able to generalize the disagreement into a
different context that could spare them future arguing. Of course,
this understanding might also aid in resolving the clothes-choice
problem itself, as it became separated from the underlying needs it
reflected. This is not presented as successfully completed therapy.
Much more work is needed to resolve such pervasive underlying
problems as the husband's difficulty in expressing anger directly
and the wife's negative sense of self-worth. However, this sample
illustrates well the work necessary to help spouses become more
aware of what interferes with negotiation.

5

Facilitating
Couple Communication:
Problems and Methods

Talking and Learning to Listen

Beyond the reasons previously mentioned, there are other reasons to help the couple avoid talking to the therapist about each other. We believe that if one spouse has something to say to the other, then this should be said directly to that spouse, not to the therapist. The therapist should not be used as a go-between. If the comments are worth saying, they should be said to the person for whom they are meant. If a spouse says to the therapist, "He/she's never home on time," we encourage direct communication as opposed to talking about the spouse. One must work hard to help spouses talk directly *to* each other, not *about* each other.

When a spouse talks directly to the partner with a complaint, the feelings accompanying the statement are more readily mobi-

136

lized and directly communicated. Thus, the communication is fuller and has a greater chance for constructive impact. One of the goals of therapy is to help spouses communicate directly both content and feelings.

We encourage couples to talk with each other in the belief that whatever happens in the therapy sessions will result from their interchange, with the therapist's help. This does not mean that the therapist never talks directly to the spouses nor they to the therapist. Obviously, many comments will be made to both spouses as the therapist makes suggestions, gives encouragement, and directs them interactionally. There may even be a one-to-one focus when this is warranted, for instance, to recognize with a spouse the extent to which a particular individual problem is bothersome, to encourage individual therapy, to focus on the implications of an individual problem for the other spouse. This last is less likely to be useful unless the other spouse has gained some appreciation for how the partner is encumbered with the particular problem.

One way of working is the use of what we call "therapist processing." By this we mean that the therapist interprets for a spouse what the partner has said. Occasionally, some degree of processing is both important and helpful. For example, the therapist may be able to state more succinctly a rambling group of comments by a spouse, the point of which may have been lost on the mate. Checking out the accuracy of the therapist's summary with the spouse is also important, lest the therapist process incorrectly. If correct, the therapist might facilitate the continuation of the spouses' communication efforts by suggesting that the partner respond to the spouse as interpreted.

Another kind of therapeutic processing is helping spouses to expand upon incomplete communications. For example, in one session the husband reported that some of his reluctance in coming had to do with "feeling on the spot." The therapist then asked the wife if she thought she could help her husband with this. Although this would have been a good comment for follow-up, one intervening step was left out—asking the husband to detail how he felt on the spot; that is, what was transpiring in the session to produce this. It may have been the way of speaking and the comments of the wife or the therapist; this would be important to know.

Therapeutic processing may also present problems. It is often unnecessary, it disrupts the interchange, and it may foster overdependence on the therapist to interpret the spouses' messages. One wants to aid them in talking directly to each other so that they can eventually be understood without help.

One of the most common errors by beginning couple therapists is the tendency for too little intervention in directing and structuring how the couple are to work. If one listens to tapes of beginning therapists, one usually hears the couple flooding each other with complaints while the therapist is left behind. It is the therapist's task to slow down the interchange and to help the couple focus on a particular issue. With experienced therapists, often half or even all of a session may center on one or two major issues.

When the therapist makes his interventions, it is important to maintain a slow pace—the couple need time to hear and assimilate. If too many points are made and the therapist works too rapidly, the couple will have difficulty in making use of the comments. It is most helpful to focus on one aspect of behavior or principle at a time, with appropriate pacing of comments and supplying sufficient behavioral referents for any major points or interpretations.

Often not listening is also a problem of the therapist. Sometimes the therapist is so tied to an internal agenda that he or she fails to maintain a focus on where the spouses' attention is. We have had many a chuckle over taped sessions where the therapist, oblivious to the forceful expression of a concern by a spouse, has continued with an unrelated point. The therapist and spouse are so intent on their own thoughts that they are both unaware of each other's points. This does not model good communication for the couple.

Spouses frequently complain that their partners do not listen to them, and in fact, interruptions are common phenomena. This often arises when a partner, hearing the spouse begin to criticize and attack, interrupts with a counterattack, thus justifying the spouse's complaint of not being listened to. Helping spouses hear each other is an important therapeutic goal. In the case of the interruptions, work will need to be done to help spouses talk without sending not-O.K. messages. Recognizing that this will take some time, the therapist can have couples practice taking turns at com-

depister les obstacles `a la Commn.

pleting communications with no interruptions allowed, in order to give each the experience of being "heard out."

Below we see a therapist's attempts to help a couple with their communication problems. The therapist focused on having the spouses acknowledge communications received and on feeding back their understanding. What often happens in discussions between spouses is that a spouse feels that the partner has never really heard what was said because of his or her reply. Thus, acknowledging having heard what the spouse says and communicating back one's understanding of it can eliminate this problem in communication.

T: [To husband] What you're doing right this minute might be representative of what's happening. When you say you don't think both of you are listening to each other, maybe we could do something about that; if when you say something, you try to respond to her by first saying, "I understand what you're saying is . . ." and then respond to that, which would give her a chance to correct it, correct you, and you [to wife] try to do the same thing with him. Go back one step now, can you respond to, I asked him to tell you some way that you could feel more comfortable and he said to you, if you would respond to what he said and try to understand it rather than shifting to something else? O.K., could you respond to him on that?

[The therapist goes on to say, "The first problem is that you have to be receiving each other's messages correctly." Several interchanges take place.]

T: Just for practice, why don't you tell him what you think he just said, what he wants from you—check it out with him.

W: You want me to listen to whatever it is you're saying and try to understand it?

H: Your trying to understand what I'm saying rather than picking and running off with it. That I can say something, and you'll take it.

A spouse may also be reluctant to state a point because of fearful anticipation of what may follow. In the next example, we see a failure to communicate for fear of criticism (not-O.K. messages) and the emotional reaction of the listening spouse. The wife has been expressing a desire for more communication and closeness. The husband related his fear that if he does share feelings, his wife might not understand.

T: By understand, you mean judge you?

H: Yeah, judgmental kind of thing—and it's easier to sit on top of them [feelings] and work them out myself.

T: [To wife] Do you hear that part about judging him? That's getting in the way of his being more open with you.

[The husband relates his fear that if he confides his feelings, his wife will get upset and "down," and more hassle will result. Then he will feel guilty and confused.]

T: Let me underline the second thing he said that gets in the way of sharing. The first one was that you'd be judgmental, and the second thing is that you will take it upon yourself such that it weighs you down. And then he feels a double burden—he'll feel guilty because he's weighted you with something. Now that puts a real task on you. It's always true when you hear a spouse talking about their problems; it's hard to keep yourself out because they affect you; there's no way it can be otherwise. On the other hand, if you take over all that and react in the same way they do, there's no way you can be of help to them. If you can in some way keep your distance, even though granted whatever happens to him does have an impact on you . . . but at some point he's wanting you to be able to hear it without you then having to stew about and be burdened down with it. Because obviously he won't want to come to you anymore—because rather than getting relief, he's gotten more trouble, having burdened you . . . and that's a hard thing for any spouse when they're sharing their difficulties. In some way you have to manage to keep some distance—so it doesn't become your burden, and I know that's easier said than done.

Another common problem, particularly when one spouse wishes to share with the partner feelings of frustration, disappointment, or anger, is the "solution-response turn-off." Many times the spouse is not seeking help but wishes to share feelings with someone who can be sympathetic. When the reply is primarily confined to suggestions on how one could have avoided or better handled the particular problem, it engenders feelings of being misunderstood and criticized. As a result, the spouse becomes angry or feels let down; consequently, there is hopelessness with regard to getting close and sharing. In this example of the solution-response turn-off, the wife has just been talking about her difficulty in being as independent as she would like.

H: It's your problem and if you need to talk to somebody about it, it's no burden to listen to you and you have to realize that.

W: Well, I really don't ever want it to be.

H: Well, it's not, and I don't feel that it is. My way of getting over my problems is working on my problems on my own. But if that's not your way and your way is talking to me, then do it; it's no burden to me.

T: Would you let her know if it is a burden?

H: Yes, she knows that I would.

T: If he would let you know that you don't have to worry about it, you can just stop worrying about being a burden.

Apparently, there is more to the issue than has emerged so far; the wife is still hesitant about approaching her husband. Finally, she is able to communicate more clearly what the problem is:

W: Well, sometimes I feel like I can't just say I'm having this problem of being independent, because I feel like you would say, "Just go on and do something," you know, "Go on and do something; be an independent person." And just to go to do something to be doing something isn't that great.

H: No, you have to want to do it before you can do it.

W: I know it.

T: I hear something else she is saying . . . that if she opens up, somehow you really won't hear how hard it is for her, and you will give her solutions that she can't follow, and that will make it worse.

It becomes clear that what blocked the wife's sharing her concerns with her husband was her anticipation that he would tell her what to do and not appreciate that what appeared like an obvious solution to him was a complex problem for her.

In the comments below, we can see the perspective of a spouse who struggles with wanting to solve the mate's problem:

H: Once I got over feeling . . . I usually felt, "I know the solution to that." Once I got over that wanting to tell her the solution, it was more tolerable, but it was frustrating to think that I could know the solution and I might tell her the solution, and, you know, since I think I was actively responsible for it.

T: Yeah, well, that's assuming responsibility. Your solution might not work for her anyway; what would seem a rational solution to you might not have made any sense to her.

H: Of course, and my similar need to present a solution stopped.

T: That's the thing we talked about last time—being able to listen and hear somebody's discomfort without feeling you have to give them solutions or feel responsible.

Below is another illustration of a couple struggling with the problem of communicating successfully. In addition to giving solutions, there are other problems in the interchange. One is the wife's becoming so indignant and angry (over-identification) at the mistreatment of her husband by others that she could not respond to his feelings; another is that the wife is prone to interpret her husband's not wanting her to solve his problem as a reflection of her personal inadequacy.

> T: What gets in your way of being able to talk with your wife about your down feelings? Maybe you can talk with her about that.
>
> H: I think one of the things that happens is that I think you [the wife] do a lot of things that you criticize me for. You try to give me solutions.
>
>   [The husband gives an example of an incident at work that upset him, which he had related to his wife.]
>
> H: I think what you did then is you really overreacted and got really angry also at what they had done, and I had to defend them. I didn't view it as helpful to me.
>
> W: You don't like if I react that way—you don't like if I just sit there quietly—then I'm not showing any interest. I don't know what to say . . . [to therapist] then I think when he comes to me like this maybe he's asking me for what I see, or asking me to toss out some of my ideas, [to husband] but it's not what you want. Then you take it as my giving you advice.
>
> T: What would be helpful?
>
> H: I guess the way it is more with me is trying to let you know more where I am.
>
> W: I want you to let me in on things so I know where you are, but I don't know what you want me to do with that, and I get real self-conscious about that. It's not that I don't want you to say anything—it's awkwardness—so what would be helpful?

The wife sincerely wants to respond helpfully to her husband but is genuinely at a loss as to how to react. She then worries that maybe her husband doesn't feel that she was qualified to offer advice; her problems with self-worth interfere with her attending to her husband's feelings.

> T: I can see one danger that may happen here is that you're so easily pulled to weighing things in the direction of whether you're O.K. or not O.K. that I'm afraid you may too easily misperceive his wanting something different than advice as a reflection on you—but so many times what most of us want is to share some feelings and not necessarily come for any problem solution. The danger for you is if he doesn't want to hear any opinion, you'll probably take that as you're not O.K. Maybe he just wants to share some feelings, some things that grated on him that made him feel bad . . . none of which requires any great problem solution of any kind.

The therapist tried to point out how the wife's own concerns impede her hearing what her husband needs.

> W: But the thing that's happened if I don't say anything or give any . . .

It is noteworthy that the problem is perceived dichotomously— either giving advice or saying nothing.

> T: I'm not suggesting that you not say anything.
> W: What do I say?

Spouses sometimes need to develop empathic listening.

> T: How can you stay with him without giving him problem solutions? How can you let a person know that you hear them and care about what they say and understand some of what they're struggling with?
>
>   [The therapist posed this as a problem for the wife to consider. The wife comments that on some occasions she

would say, "That's too bad," but her husband then would get disgusted and think she was not interested.]

T: That kind of remark could sound like a dismissal—it may not be that.

W: I can see that. I really don't know.

[The therapist suggests that the husband bring up the recent issue at work as if it were new so that they could work on the communication problem. The husband complies, telling his wife in the present tense of his discomfort and how it really bothered him.]

H: I got angry—then I started getting depressed.

T: [To wife] Can you respond to this?

[The wife has difficulty replying, saying it was presented differently than before. The therapist encourages her, repeating that the wife's interest in wanting to know what to do in this situation, however artificial, could provide an opportunity for learning. A long pause follows.]

W: Should I say what I said then?

T: I don't know—what can you say that will help your husband know you care, you're interested, but won't turn him off? If you don't know, ask him to help you. What would be helpful for him to hear?

[The wife comments on her similar feelings of disgust and upset at what had happened.]

W: And I'm sorry it happened . . . I fully understand how frustrating a situation it was.

This is a good effort, but notice how difficult it is for spouses, even when they are trying, to stay with their mate's feelings and experiencing of the problem.

Often it is assumed by a spouse that the mate is looking for a solution to a problem. This may place a burden on the spouse who feels unequal to the task, as in the following:

W: Most of the time I feel I can't give him the solution.

T: Most people can't give people solutions—that's the thing, but you can let them know you care . . . and understand.

Learning that solution giving is not needed can relieve the spouse who feels that he or she should but is unable to do so. A helpful therapeutic intervention for a spouse who assumes unnecessary responsibility is to ask the partner to clarify what he or she is seeking.

The inveterate problem solver will need much work in order to respond appropriately. The logically-oriented individual not particularly attuned to feelings has difficulty discerning understanding from problem-solving. In such cases, it is particularly important to alert the other spouse to the need to communicate clearly what is desired. One wife told the husband, "If I want advice, I'll ask for it—then you'll know."

A different communication problem is the spouse who responds with a lecture. As one wife put it, "He talks *at* me, not *with* me." She went on to say that even in the most mundane conversation, her husband replies with highly academic, intellectual comments.

T: I think she's saying, "I'm looking for some kind of emotional response—not necessarily an intellectual or even very rational one—but more an emotional, empathic type of one."

W: I think that says it very well—much better than I did.

A spouse may also be frustrated with a partner who literally does not listen and gives no response. One can encourage the spouse to relate to the partner the importance of knowing that one can have an audience when one really needs it. The therapist can suggest that comments be preceded with such remarks as, "Hey, I really need to talk to you"; in other words, the importance of the desire may have to be specifically stated. Although this may not resolve all problems, it is at least an active effort to achieve one's end.

Stating Needs and Expectations

Since couples are inevitably well practiced in voicing negative comments, stringent therapeutic efforts are necessary to help spouses voice their wants without adding put-downs (criticisms, complaints, or unfavorable comparisons). It is often helpful to attenuate a spouse's desire to criticize the partner by quickly intervening with, "How would you like things to be different? Maybe you can talk with your spouse about what you want and what you think it would take to make things go better between you." Although this is simple to say, to help spouses eliminate using put-downs is a formidable task. Requests for gratifications are usually veiled by insults, belittlement, and all the other ways that not-O.K. messages can be sent. The more a spouse joins desires and expectations with positive messages, the better the chance of being decoded and responded to. (However, in early therapy sessions, where anger is likely to be more intense, this is often not possible.)

In the following interchange, the husband does a good job of expressing his needs and wants to his wife, spelling them out in behavioral terms:

H: [To wife] I want you to help me and not hinder me.

T: How would she do that?

H: [To wife] I want you to encourage me.

[The husband goes on to say that a lot of times his wife does not listen to his program on TV and that he wants her to listen to it and to tell him what he has done wrong and what he might do to improve it. He communicates that he does not feel that she pays sufficient attention to what he is doing.]

H: I'll try to tell you exactly what you're to listen for, and I would appreciate it if you'd listen to that. And if it sounds good to you, I've done a good job, and if it doesn't sound good, then I'm not doing a good job. And if it doesn't sound good to you, then somebody else will likely be displeased by it as well.

T: Are you trying to tell her you want her to be a sounding board for you, for her to tell you what her responses are to what you're doing?

H: Yeah, to a certain extent.

W: O.K., I'll try.

The interchange is good because the husband for the most part remains task oriented in communicating specifically what he wants from the wife, rather than complaining about what she has done wrong or has not done.

In the next example, the wife has more difficulty stating her needs without put-downs. She has just been commenting on the resentment she feels for assuming more than her share of the responsibility for the kids. In the context of having been working on the importance of spouses' stating their needs by beginning with a description of their feelings and wants, the therapist asks:

> T: If that comes up, how will you communicate that?
>
> W: Well, I hope I will communicate it by saying I need you to take the children . . . I probably . . . well . . .
>
> H: You should state your needs and let me answer.
>
> T: I think he's right. I think you should start off by saying, "I'm really feeling pressured."
>
> W: O.K., what did I say?
>
> T: "I need you to take the children today." That's O.K., but it would be better if you could start by telling him where you are. I'm really feeling . . .
>
> W: I'm really beat. I don't feel like taking Peter to the baseball game tonight. I know you've got a lot to do, too—if you can—I really need a break. I've taken the kids places several nights this week.
>
> H: No, don't say that. [Laughter by all]
>
> T: He's right—that's the kind of thing that hooks—who's done the most—it hooks that measuring-stick thing of trying to weigh things.
>
> W: That's true.
>
> H: I've done this much; now you've got to do that much.
>
> T: Now it's your turn.
>
> W: That's true.
>
> T: It really hooks it. [To husband] That's great you picked that up. That's exactly what I've been saying. If you can just stay with—"Look, right now, tonight, I'm so beat, I

really need this break. One more thing and I feel I've really had it."

H: When you were saying that, when you were telling me the pressure you were under and, you know, your feelings—that was making me feel like, well, I'll take Peter tonight, 'cause I know I would like to do this for my wife, or I'd like to do this so she won't have any more on her. But when you said, "I've taken him for two nights already," it made me feel like, "Well, I've taken care of them also. Two nights doesn't mean that much."

T: Tremendous! See, as soon as you can start identifying the things that hook the bad stuff, you really start learning what to say that doesn't get you in trouble.

W: Yeah, I can see where it did that. That wasn't what I was saying. What I was saying was I've been out three nights in a row, and I'd like a break. I wasn't saying you hadn't done anything.

H: I know. Well, I understand your saying that, but it made me feel that way.

T: It's measuring and weighing who's done the most.

H: I didn't realize how important it is that you just state your own needs. I never thought of that before.

T: It's much less likely that the person will hear it as accusations if you're talking about your desire than if you're talking about what they haven't done or what they should do. That's what gets you into trouble. And hopefully each of you will decide for yourselves what you can do. If you're not feeling attacked and so forth, hopefully you'll both want to do things to help each other when you can.

H: Feel like doing more.

T: Yeah, I mean if you hear her as hurting, hopefully it will elicit some desire to want to help her, and hopefully vice versa. But if you hear it as a criticism, like "You haven't been doing as much as I have," what that's going to elicit is a tendency to say, "Oh yeah? Last week I did it six days," and then nobody's gonna get their needs met.

H: I have to work hard on that.

T: It sounds simple, but it is very hard.

H: It really is.

T: It's really hard. It's your old problem when the feelings get in there.

H: Yeah, because that's a part of the feelings. You feel, "Well, damn, I've done it three nights in a row—let her— she hasn't done it at all." Then it's hard to keep that part out of it. It really is as if that is there.

T: And in fact, that may be really true—it's just that it won't get you what you're trying to get, which is a break and some help. Now there's another thing you can do with that feeling, which is better not done when you're angry—better if you're feeling anger over something like, "I feel like I'm getting too much of the responsibility" to wait till you're in a more tempered mood and say, "I really would like to talk with you about how we're managing the children and the time. I am feeling a lot of pressure and what I would like is some more help from you to take Peter to the baseball game." It's a different way of going about the same thing. Maybe you really are feeling like you're doing too much, but if it's put in terms of "You're not doing enough," it doesn't get you anywhere. The other person will tend to rally to the occasion and then tell you . . . I'm sure you can come up with thousands of things he never knew that you did, you know. It makes each of you feel unappreciated. It may be that in the process of trying to have his needs met he'll want more from you than you'll want to give, and to try to meet every one of these needs would stifle you. There has to be room for some expectancies over there— some of these things she'll have to have—when people are together, certain things will need to be done.

In the last example, a wife points out to her husband how she experiences a certain way that he talks as a put-down.

W: Well, we discussed a little bit of this . . . you used the tone of voice that came on like a parent talking to a child, and I think this has something to do with the way you respond in something like that. It comes from a level that's not just two people discussing something that shouldn't be so emotionally laden. I really think you come on with this parental-type forcefulness, and I feel it as a put-down, "No, you cannot" . . . if there's a way of saying things to me that doesn't come on like a parent putting a child down, I think I could accept it.

T: Have you heard that kind of tone in your voice or can you have some kind of feeling for what she's talking about?

H: Yes, I do have a feeling for what she's talking about, and I'm sure that I do come on like that.

T: Is that something you're willing to make some effort to do something about?

H: Yes.

T: O.K. I know when you say that, you're sincere, but it kept going through my head, "What's going to get in the way of that?" I know that it isn't easy.

H: Yes, it's going to mean a lot of changes.

T: Feelings creep in and kind of mold the way you say things. . . . I wonder if you could work with her on what might get in the way of that for you—'cause it probably has something to do with her and what's going on between you.

Occasionally, a spouse will indicate that, "If I have to spend so much time trying to decide what to say and how to say it, it's not worth it." The claim is made that it will stifle spontaneity. The therapist can agree that it is a lot of trouble in that change will require a lot of effort on the individual's part; only the individual can decide if it is worth the effort. One can also agree that it may curb complete spontaneity but indicate that the outcome is a desirable one. An illustration of this point follows:

The husband has just objected to the task of constantly analyzing every move and thinking it through to see if it is the right approach.

H: How can you get to the point that you can just live so
     you don't have to mull over every action?

T: If everything you do spontaneously works beautifully
     between you, that's really great and ideal, but it rarely
     works that way with people. For a lot of the things each
     of you would do spontaneously won't hit it off well with
     the other person. That's the trouble. I understand your
     wanting to just live and be and not have to analyze, and
     that would be the ideal if you could get there. Right now
     the process may not be "being completely spontaneous."
     It's the opposite. It's taking a look and analyzing, hope-
     fully to get to a state where that won't be as important
     or necessary. But it is part of what you're going to have
     to do now, if you want to take a look at the things that
     are making things not work well between you. I don't
     see any way around that.

Spontaneity used in this way is an escape; it only means that
this is the state of one's current hierarchy of preferred defensive
behaviors. If complete spontaneity means freedom to hurt, violate, or assault because it comes naturally, then it can only lead to
disaster. Unless one learns to control feelings and take others into
consideration, complete spontaneity will likely do harm not only to
oneself but also to one's partner, since it invites anger, retaliation,
and alienation. These points must be conveyed to the spouses; with
practice the stumbling, new behaviors will become smooth and
habitual. Although spontaneity and honesty in the expression of
feelings are to be valued, how feelings are expressed will have everything to do with how they are perceived. Efforts at control and
moderation are unavoidable if any kind of harmony is to exist in
relationships.

Expression of Feelings

We are including this section lest the reader say (as spouses
frequently do), "Oh, you want me to be a Goody Two Shoes, a panty-
waist." The above section does not mean that any feelings are to be

left out, especially angry ones. A spouse should communicate loud and clear all feelings which are present and why. Our main constraint is that they not be expressed at the expense of the spouse; spouses need to learn how to use their anger to fight, but (as George Bach details[1]) to fight fairly. A statement of anger within the context of expressing needs and frustrations can help communication. For example, "I really get angry when you don't help me. I feel that I am left to assume all of the discipline of the children, and I don't like it one bit. I want you to help." This is quite different from a statement like: "All you ever do is sit on your butt in front of the TV and read, and I am left with everything to do; you're just like your father, a lazy, no good bum." In the former case, at least the possibility is open (and if this takes place in therapy, the therapist can help assure that this happens) for the listening spouse to appreciate the significance of the expressed desires. The spouse may inquire as to how he or she may help, or the therapist may assist the objecting spouse to specify what kind of help is needed and why.

It is only by acknowledging feelings and their intensity that spouses can indicate to their mates the importance of issues and their need for change. Helping spouses to be aware of and to communicate their anger, hurt, dissatisfaction, frustrations, sadness, or whatever emotion they are feeling is a crucial part of the communication process. The purpose is not for catharsis *per se,* although there may be some therapeutic benefit in this, but rather to communicate the seriousness of their need to be heard, in the service of working on improving relations. But an equally important task is for spouses to learn how to express their feelings in a different way than they customarily have. Feelings should be communicated as resulting from a frustrated need and accompanied by a statement of the changes desired with the emphasis on the latter. Considerable attention should be given to having spouses reflect on feelings, the reasons for their occurrence, and their consequences, both to improve the cognitive control of the objecting spouse and to increase the possibility of a different reaction from the partner.

[1]G. Bach and P. Wyden. *The Intimate Enemy: How to Fight Fair in Love and Marriage.* New York: Morrow, 1969.

It is also the therapist's task to aid spouses in learning to modulate and find better ways to deal with their feelings. Anger, especially if intense, seems to be the most difficult feeling for spouses to express when they put into operation what they have learned with regard to communication skills. The therapist will want to encourage their learning to delay expressing anger, recognize the choices of what to do with it, and assume responsibility for the choices made. There is no question that for many people who have not learned to experience feelings without being overwhelmed by them, that learning to tolerate one's feelings and to control one's actions will be an enormous task.

The excerpt below illustrates some of the above points. The husband is reporting an incident of being at a party with a man in whom his wife had previously shown some interest. He comments on feeling very angry at him.

T: So when you were in contact with him, at some point, you experienced anger?

H: Yeah.

T: But apparently you chose not to act on your feelings?

H: Right.

T: I think that's real important. One of the questions you've said in here many times is, "What can I do? I can't make feelings go away." Feelings may not go away immediately, but you don't have to act on them. That's a choice.

W: Yeah.

T: In that situation you chose not to act. You could have ripped him up one side and down the other because you were feeling angry in remembering things of the past, or you can . . . there are many courses of action.

H: That's getting a little easier for me. Only problem is when I get mad—really angry.

T: That's when everybody has problems.

H: I forget all the rules.

T: That's understandable. You have to make special effort when you're getting extremely angry—because that's the time when you'll want to hit back—not just you, but all people. But it's a time you'll most likely mess up things for yourself.

As a first step, it is helpful to remind people who are overwhelmed by anger that they are responsible for the anger, not the stimulus. If they can accept this responsibility, then they can more readily find ways of dealing with anger.

Priorities in Feeling Issues

Many annoyances and dissatisfactions occur between any two individuals living together, and we can assume that this is intensified when children are present, due to the fact that there are more people whose needs must be met. A spouse cannot assume that the partner knows the relative extent of different dissatisfactions. One helpful function that the therapist can serve is to educate spouses to communicate to the partners where in the hierarchy of annoyance a given item falls. It is interesting to observe how often grievances are all lumped together as if they are all equal. For example, if leaving the top off the toothpaste is a mild annoyance, it should be distinguished from feelings about the partner being gone from home three nights a week.

It is important to set up hierarchies of annoyance, because communications are often confused when spouses blow up in a way disproportionate to the event (the "straw that broke the camel's back"). Consequently, spouses are unclear where their partner stands on many issues. Frequently heard is, "Well, you never said anything about that. I didn't know it was that important to you." It is imperative to convince couples, if they are to work toward improving their relationship, of the importance of communicating where they stand on issues. Irritations should be sorted out in terms of which ones are mildly annoying and can be lived with, which ones they feel some pressure to change, and which ones are so intolerable that negative consequences are already occurring. (For example, a spouse may continually experience tension or be thinking about breaking up the marriage.) Once each spouse knows the importance attached to specific grievances, then he or she is in a

much better position to decide which ones require serious attention and what the consequences will be if no efforts are made to
accommodate the partner.

Ongoing Communication of Dissatisfactions

Many spouses store their grievances until they explode. Bach[2]
has referred to this as "gunnysacking." The therapist will want to
encourage the spouse to express grievances as they occur in order
to avoid this phenomenon. The therapist's efforts will often be more
effective if the partner indicates that ongoing communication is
preferable to gunnysacking. A spouse may experience difficulty
in accomplishing this feat or even find it impossible. An overdetermined fear of retaliatory anger may prevent an attempt to
be open about an annoyance. In some cases, a spouse may need
individual help with the problem. As much as possible, the therapist and the other partner together should encourage the spouse.
This may be facilitating since the spouse as well as the therapist is
frequently perceived in a parental role.

T: Well, let me go back just for a moment, and see if you
    can maybe talk with Anne [the wife] about why or what
    goes on, that maybe things do build up a long time before
    maybe the whole thing snaps, and you have a reaction. Is
    there something you can get from that which will be
    helpful for you, if you discuss it with Anne? Maybe you
    figure if you said something early, she'll take a swipe at
    you because she'd be displeased with you. You know say-
    ing what you feel does run some risk 'cause you [to wife]
    might have to say, "No, I don't want you to do that," or
    "No, I don't like it," or something. I don't know what
    you're anticipating. There may be reasons why that
    has to do with anticipations.

H: Yeah.

T: That you need to check out with Anne, [to husband]

[2]G. Bach and P. Wyden. *The Intimate Enemy: How to Fight Fair in Love and
Marriage.* New York: Morrow, 1969.

because if he's got that all figured out in his head of how you're going to respond, you know, he probably prefers to avoid it. Now he may not be correct in his anticipations. I don't know that, but I think it's something you ought to talk about together.

Ironing out grievances as they occur prevents a build-up of angry feelings and a block in communications, but equally important, it allows for the resolution of problems as they occur.

In the session below, the therapist is trying to help the wife learn how to express her ongoing dissatisfactions more readily; the wife has difficulty modulating anger and is often depressed. The wife says that when someone is "on her," she feels defeated. She tells her husband that as a result, she turns him off or behaves in a negative way and says things she later regrets.

T: I think that's a feeling you would like to avoid, so you don't feel backed into a corner. You explode and say things that maybe later you wished you hadn't.

W: Well, anytime that someone loses their temper and says things, they're going to suffer guilt . . . and I think the thing I'm going to have to learn to do is to say, "I don't like this right now, so please don't say it."

T: Can you do that without . . . can you tell him to get off your back?

W: Well, yes.

[The wife says this with no conviction.]

T: He's a pretty strong person; he may not get off. What are you going to do?

The therapist wants the wife to deal with the difficulty of the task.

W: I know it.

T: What are you going to do?

W: Well, keep trying.

T: O.K.—the next time, while we're talking together, if you feel that your husband is being critical of you, I want you to do that. Are you game?

W: In a nice way.

The wife needs support; this is why the therapist is trying to help her practice in the session.

T: [To husband] That's what I want to help her do is for her to be able to tell you to get off her back, but not do it in a destructive way.

     [The wife tries to change the subject and the therapist redirects.]

T: Wait a minute, now, let's not get diverted from something that I really want to work on, and that's your being able to tell your husband to get off your back when you experience him as being critical. [To husband] Is that O.K. with you if we work on this?

It is important to include the husband lest he feel the therapist is allying with the wife against him. Needless to say, a relatively solidified therapeutic alliance would have to be achieved before this could occur successfully.

H: Sure.

The therapist explains to the husband that if his wife can do this better, her resentments will not accumulate to the point where he gets clobbered with them, about which he has complained. The therapist tries to make clear that this will be in both of their best interests, again so the husband does not feel that the therapist has sided with the wife.

In this last example, the wife graphically describes the toll she pays as she senses mounting tension in her husband, who does not fully communicate the source of his annoyance.

W: What the kind of position that this puts me in is, it puts me in this edgy position that I talked about before. I've

got to constantly be keeping one eye on you to check it
out with you to see if this is O.K. and how far can we go
in this situation without . . . before you reach the breaking point. I mean you do communicate with me when
things are irritating; you don't communicate what it is.
I know that something is bothering you, and I sift
through my mind, "What is it? What is it? Is it this, that,
or the other?" It puts me in a very uncomfortable position where I have to constantly watch things to see that
they don't get to you, especially if we're in public—and
I guess more in public than at home. I guess if we're at
home, if you blow up or things go wrong, the people
there are used to it and can take it, but when we're in
public and little irritations are building up on you—none
of which along the way you have let go of and said anything about—I have to be in a constant state of awareness
to be sure things don't get to you so that you explode, or
that you do or say something that's embarrassing to me
or distressing to the relationship we may have with
other people. And it does put me in an edgy position, and
I guess this is one of the reasons I would prefer that you
be able to express it along the way rather than have it
build up. Am I making any sense to you at all?

H: Yes, yes, you are, and I agree with what you're saying.

T: [To wife] How about when you begin to sense that, you
ask Steve [the husband] if he hasn't said anything to you,
say "I'm beginning to feel uneasy, I get the notion you're
not in good sorts" or whatever, rather than your letting
it continually build up so you have to walk on eggs. What
would happen? Would that suit you if she asked you?

H: I think in a large number of cases, Mary [the wife], just
the mere fact that you let me know that you're irritated
would do a tremendous amount. The fact that somebody else recognizes that there was something in the
situation that's irritating me.

[The wife responds that she has asked the husband what
was bothering him and that it only irritates him.]

T: The same question can mean . . . like, "*Now* what's wrong?" can be a condemnation, or wanting really to help, "What's wrong?"

[The therapist changes voice inflection to illustrate the differences in the way the same question is asked.]

W: Oh.

T: It can show concern or it can show like, "Oh, here we go again."

W: Well, maybe if I don't wait too long, maybe if I do it earlier.

T: If you can pick up on it earlier . . . I guess really what I'm trying to say is that the burden is on both of you to try to sense and pick up early—not just Steve but both of you. And the reason I was concentrating on Mary is that she might sense it before it really jelled in your [the husband's] mind. You might not even be aware of it as early as she is—that happens.

H: Yeah, I'm sure that it does.

T: So that if it did, she could go ahead and communicate to you about something that's going on.

W: This has been a big problem.

Note that, in this session, the therapist tries to get both spouses to assume responsibility for avoiding a build-up of dissatisfactions.

Positive Strokes

When improvement has occurred and is acknowledged by the couple, it is useful to encourage the spouses to relay their pleasure at the changes and to detail what changes they experience as positive. Specific behaviors that are reinforced verbally are more likely to recur. Initially, the therapist may have to facilitate a description of the positive changes. These therapeutic efforts are highlighted in the session below. In the second part of the session, the therapist works specifically to teach the spouses how to pay compliments without undoing them (that is, adding negative comments to the positive ones). The couple have had several weekly sessions.

W: Well, I think you've been much easier to get along with—
     very sweet and very comforting.

     [The ensuing interchange does not relate to this com-
     ment, so the therapist redirects the interchange.]

T: I think it would be worthwhile to underline what you
     said about your husband being very sweet.

     [The therapist attempts to reinforce the positive expres-
     sions of one spouse toward the other.]

H: I don't think I've been any different.

A frequent reaction is for the praised partner to disclaim being
different, since this would imply responsibility for change and possible guilt; otherwise, why the need for change?

W: Well, I can tell you—you have been.

     [The wife details how.]

T: She experienced you as being different, which is really
     good.

     [The husband responds by saying all the things his wife
     did that were improvements in her behavior. He con-
     cludes that if he has been less critical, it's because his
     wife didn't do the usual things that required criticism.]

W: Well, the fact is that it's worked well.

     [Interchange follows.]

T: Well, I think it's important to take credit where credit
     is due, and I imagine there have been some things maybe
     that have been different . . . she has experienced some-
     thing that is different. I think it is important to identify
     what it is you're doing differently so you can maintain
     it or whatever . . . I'm talking to both of you. What ef-
     forts you've made, you could be aware of what they were
     so you could continue. Because it seems to ease up some
     of the tension and make things more pleasant.

The therapist hopes to reinforce changes by helping the couple
become aware that the improvement is their doing, and to assist

them in identifying the specific behavioral changes that have made things better.

T: We started off with kind of saying things were better, and I wanted to focus maybe on what each of you had done to make things go better.

[The husband now lists several things his wife has done differently.]

T: [To wife, after acknowledging the husband's comments] He feels like he hasn't done much different, but apparently you perceive him as being different, as behaving differently.

W: Well, I do think he has.

T: Could you tell him how?

[The wife, who starts to talk to the therapist instead of the husband, is encouraged to talk to him.]

W: I think you've been more careful not to lose your temper.

[The husband explains that several external sources of irritation for the wife have been eliminated; he has difficulty accepting his wife's comments and rationalizes any changes he may have made. His positive comments to her are mixed with negative ones.]

T: O.K., I was trying to get at something that seems important; I don't know how it seems to you. It seems to me that you people have trouble saying nice things to each other; maybe when we listen back to the tape you can hear that. There are always phrases such that you get negative, also; it kind of takes away from, and I was wondering if you would be willing . . . maybe just to see if you could say something good that stops there and doesn't some way or another have the other creep in with it also.

W: Uh huh.

T: If you could just strengthen it—just have it be a positive, straight, clean comment.

H: Uh huh.

T: Would you be willing to try that each to the other?

W: I'm not quite sure I understand what you mean, you mean just . . .

H: I understand exactly what you mean.

T: Could you [to husband] go first, and maybe you could illustrate to your wife the principle?

H: Is it like . . . for instance, you always plan good menus for dinner—without qualification.

W: Well, that makes me feel *very* good.

H: That's what she [the therapist] is talking about.

T: That's what I'm saying.

W: Oh, you didn't mean it.

H: No . . . but . . . it was true.

T: But if he had said dinner was very good tonight, but usually it's barely edible . . . see, that's a compliment, but you give it and then take it away. I mean, I know you each have dissatisfactions; I know you both have some things that are irking you, and those things aren't going to go away, but I'm just trying to help you get the spirit of maybe, just sometime, for you to say something that's just a clean, straight compliment that's positive or something, that would make a person feel good.

W: Well, I'll tell you I'm very proud of you, because you have done a marvelous job in your work . . . and sometimes, oh, I'm about to . . . [Laughs]

    [The wife recognizes that she is about to utter a negative remark. She then says positive remarks without any qualifications and begins to talk of some events that she participated in that pleased her husband. Her husband, in turn, acknowledges her effort and commends her for it.]

T: So, you were really making an effort?

W: Yes.

T: You knew that was something that would make your husband feel good.

[Interchange follows.]

T: It sounds like you've been going out of your way to do some kinds of things to make things go better. Were you aware of why you felt differently and were more willing to do this?

W: Well, I just—I can't—it's hard to explain, but I felt better about myself being able to do that. Now I don't know . . . because I haven't felt that I was being torn down and . . .

T: [To husband] So, in some ways, she got some support?

The therapist is trying to help the husband see that he will have greater success in getting from the wife what he wants if she feels less criticized, and that he is in part responsible for the positive changes in the wife. The conversation moves on to the subject of the husband (who is an upper-level executive) wanting his wife to socialize with his associates more. The therapist tries to help him understand how this is difficult for the wife, the difference between his outgoing nature and her reticence; then, the therapist brings the issue back to the wife's feelings about herself.

T: [To wife] Maybe it relates to how you feel about yourself. . .

W: Oh, that's true.

T: . . . being more willing to venture out.

W: Yes . . . if you have confidence in yourself or have been supported.

T: [To husband] The importance of that to me is the role that you play in that, because you want her very much to extend herself more, and you very much play a part in whether she does or not, because when she feels better about herself, she's freer and more willing to do so.

[The husband is reluctant to accept this; more interchange ensues.]

T: [To husband] Even if you don't think that out, you don't
even have to say, "I'm deliberately not going to do it," it's
got to be there. So I think you're not giving yourself
credit and maybe you're not aware of having gone out
of your way to do things differently. She did feel that
you were different. I'm not trying to say what caused
that; there's a whole chain of things going on, but, in
some way or another, she felt less attacked, and then she
felt better about herself; and the result was something
that brought pleasure to you because you [to wife] felt
better about yourself, and it made you [to husband]
feel better, because it was functional for business and
other reasons.

In another session, the therapeutic task was for each spouse
to tell the partner something that the partner had done that made
the spouse feel good. The husband had been telling his wife how
pleased he was that she had continued to make breakfast, even
though she was no longer working and did not have to get up.
However, as he went on talking, he referred to the fact that he had
been getting up and making breakfast for the kids for years. The
wife responded angrily, saying this was not so, that she had been
doing it.

At this point, the therapist asked the husband to reflect on
how he had communicated his positive stroke so that it led to a fight.
The husband had difficulty understanding what had transpired,
so the therapist asked the wife if she could help him. She stated
clearly that what she had heard was criticism, not a compliment.
The therapist tried to amplify this by reviewing the kinds of remarks
that communicated criticisms and asked the husband to attempt
the task again, limiting himself only to positive remarks. The therapist suggested that he might include more about his feelings. The
husband then did quite a good job. He related that when he gets
up, he knows he has to go to work and face a day that often is troublesome and has many difficult problems to resolve, that he is not
enthusiastic about leaving and facing these hurdles. It makes him
feel good to know that there is some reason for him to do this,
that his efforts are appreciated—and that his wife's getting up and
making breakfast is responsible for his better attitude.

It was then easy for the husband to understand the wife's consequent nonargumentative response, since she did not hear criticism but only need and appreciation; her reply was appreciative and did not lead to an argument. In fact, her husband's sharing his feelings was very touching to her and probably added a perspective on the husband that she had lacked before.

Another way the therapist can work for positive reinforcement is when the spouses refer to better relations in the past. It is important to remind the spouses of these successful modes of relating, because they provide hope for the future.

W: We used to be able to talk all the time.

T: That sounds very good . . . so that means something's happened in your way of communicating that's gone astray—which means if you could do it before, hopefully you can do it again. But you see, I need to have you start here, so sitting here as a third person I can help you see what you're doing that creates distance between you and makes you feel it's hopeless, and "I can't talk and I can't be heard," and that's what I want to help you with.

If while one spouse is harshly criticizing the other, something is said that allows the therapist to point out a positive aspect of their interaction, it is helpful to do so. It reminds the spouses that although all they now see is negative, there are also positive aspects to their relationship which for the moment may be obscured. In the following example, after a barrage of criticism from her husband, the wife pointed out that when things are really going rough in the family, that she is the one to whom the others turn for help.

T: Do you feel like you can turn to your wife when you're really down and hurting—that she's there and will stand by you?

H: Yes, I guess I do.

T: So that's a real positive thing you have going for you.

H: Yes, I do.

Avoidance of Abstractions

Couples are generally prone to state their grievances in vague, abstract terms: "The problem is that he doesn't love me"; "We just don't seem to agree on anything"; or "We're just too different." Although these comments do communicate feelings, to begin therapy by tackling these abstractions directly is putting the cart before the horse. After hearing these statements, the therapist should try to get the couple to specify what causes some of the feelings. The therapist may then say, "Much of what we feel is determined by how things are going between us—how much we are getting our needs met, one by the other; I assume from what you are saying that you have developed some ways of being with each other which are not satisfactory and are even stressful to you, which you would like changed. Otherwise, you would not have come. Consequently, maybe the best way we can begin is to take a look at what some of the ways are of your being together which are not working. What I am trying to do here is to find a wedge, an opening we can begin to work on." The therapist could then comment, "Maybe you can begin talking together about what is happening between you that has led to these feelings which you now describe."

Complaints like "she doesn't love me enough" are not only abstract, but also push the accused into a defensive stance. After all, how much is enough—who can measure love? And even if one could, the spouse that complains is not really complaining about some relative amount. The spouse is saying that there are not sufficient instances of loving behavior. What the therapist must help the spouse do is to translate the abstraction into ways the mate could behave that would contribute to feeling loved and convey the importance of the need. The mate may not have been aware how important this is to the partner or may have honestly thought that the partner knew that he or she was loved. One often hears a spouse say to the other, "Well, you know I love you." But what is sufficient will have to be worked out by them both; it cannot be defined unilaterally. Obviously, for many people, the words "I love you," if occurring without supporting behavior, will by no means suffice.

Below is an illustration of a couple who are dealing with the problem of whether they love each other. The husband has been telling his wife that he does love her.

H: See, I can see in your eyes now that you don't believe me.

W: No, I'm not disbelieving you. Now, when you say, "I love you," I'm looking at it from my view of what I consider love. And what you consider love and what I consider love are two different things, and I've got to see what you're talking about when you say, "I love you"—what you really mean . . . I really don't know what you're talking about. I'm not saying I doubt you. I'm just saying I don't know exactly what you mean.

Notice that the discussion is still at a rather abstract level. With further interventions, the wife begins to detail what she is attempting to communicate.

W: Well, you used to say you loved me, and you'd do things, and you'd say things, and you don't do these things and you don't say these things anymore, but that doesn't mean you're not showing it in a different way.

T: [To husband] Do you understand what she's saying? If I were in your position, I would want to check out specific things she's talking about. [To wife] You're using a lot of abstract things.

W: O.K., like you always seemed like you used to want to be around me a lot, and now you want to be around me sometimes. O.K., I can understand that, but I don't know if that means your love has changed, or the depth of it has changed. There used to be certain ways I could know that you liked me by the way you treated me and the way you talked to me, but we don't talk that much anymore, and when we see each other, it's late and we are both tired. O.K., well, I don't know if the situation is now that we still love each other, we're just different people, or we don't love each other.

Note that the wife has made some effort to discuss the change in her experience of love in terms of the way her husband talks with her and treats her. It would have been helpful at this point for the therapist to pursue what she meant specifically. We only know that she is complaining about a lack of time together compared with their previous relationship.

In the example below, the therapist focuses on the wife's abstract statement that she lacks self-confidence. In the part of the session detailed, the therapist supports the wife in asserting and specifically communicating her needs and feelings.

> W: My major problem right now is my self-confidence. I'm not particularly worried, but . . .
>
>   [Several interchanges take place.]
>
> T: Are there some things that you would like to ask of your husband that could help you in this area?
>
> W: Well, I could ask that, since we are understanding that one, that I am this way, that I don't have confidence . . . that complicates matters more.

Note that the wife is unable to make any requests of her husband, and her needs remain obscure.

> H: It would be more helpful if I had something more specific to go on, though—understanding is just a term.

The husband refocuses on the interaction.

> W: I suppose in some things, right now, I'm afraid of you.

This was a major step for the wife—to translate her lack of self-confidence into a fear of the husband—something that can now be worked with.

> H: Afraid of me?
>
> W: Of you.
>
> H: That's ridiculous.
>
> W: I'm not afraid in the sense of . . .
>
> H: My doing you physical harm?
>
> W: No, right.

H: How in heavens name did you get to the point that you were afraid of me?

W: I don't know.

T: It might be more helpful if you could talk about what it is you're afraid of, what he might do or say, rather than worrying about how you got here.

The therapist does not want the focus to shift away from the present.

W: I don't know whether I'm just afraid of you or of being insecure, that I'm almost hesitant to approach you.

The wife describes her feelings without connecting them to anything her husband does.

T: To approach him?

W: Not really approaching you, [but] making love, because I've got myself to the point where I am now. Because of the past, I am completely unsure of myself.

T: What could your husband do?

W: I don't know how to approach that.

T: What could your husband do to help you, make you feel less afraid?

W: I am really serious, I don't know how not to feel, if I knew how to ask you, I would, and I really don't. I don't know what to say, so . . .

The wife is having great difficulty making any requests of the husband.

T: I know it's hard for you to know how not to feel this way, but could you try to focus on what your husband could do in relation to you to help you feel better? What kinds of things?

W: Well, I guess if you're getting down to specific things, I

know there is a feeling of warmth between us, which to
me is *not* there.

Now the wife identifies something concrete.

H: This has changed . . . and is this what you're saying to
me, that you feel it's lacking now?

W: Well, it can't be that or any more of it, there's a feeling
that you're almost distant from me. I don't know whether
it's tied up now, I suspect part of it is, at least where it
started, and that's the realization that was the case.

[A long silence follows.]

H: Well, I know that we can't go back there, so, you know,
what can I do now?

W: Well, I think, I don't know, probably one of the things
in terms of . . . let's say I'm making you unhappy now,
I feel the failure, there's something that is going to push
us further and further away from each other; and until
I get that idea out of my mind, it will present difficult
problems. Right now I feel that way, it seems.

The wife again is focusing on her concern that she does not please
her husband.

H: Well, there are feelings that I naturally am going to have
as a result of this; are you asking me to conceal these?

[The husband is referring to when his wife's concerns
interfere with his sexual satisfaction.]

W: No, don't conceal them.

[The therapist intervenes unsuccessfully.]

H: I don't think it's going to help you for me to say, "There
baby, it's O.K." if it's not O.K.

T: I was thinking more in terms of not requesting certain
feelings, but what he might do, because it's very hard
now for either one of you to request that the other not
feel a certain way; it's always hard. I was thinking you're

entitled to your feelings and they are going to be there whether or not, you know . . . [To wife] you're saying, "I feel insecure, I'm afraid to approach him, I'm afraid if it's a failure, then I will feel worse." I know you would like for him not to have certain kinds of feelings, because they will upset you. Let's not try to work on these at the moment. I was suggesting that maybe you might be more specific about things he might *do* that you think would help your situation, not how he feels—but things that he might do when he may be upset, frustrated, disappointed, or any of these.

[The wife makes some unclear statements, suggesting that sex is over too quickly. This seems important, and the therapist attempts to focus on this.]

T: I'm not sure whether you're requesting something specific of him or suggesting something you would like to try; are you clear on what she is asking of you or telling you?

H: Not really.

T: [To wife] Can you be more specific?

W: Just the feeling of being touched and loved physically more.

Again, the wife is not able to specify what she would like her husband to do.

T: Are you saying, "I want more touching, more foreplay, more embracing, more hugging, that's what I'm trying to get"?

The therapist is working to help the wife to tune in to her concerns, her feelings, and what she wants from her husband. This is much different from the original concept of her lack of self-confidence.

T: Are you suggesting something new that you would like to try on for size to see if it might help you with this?

W: Well, yes, I'm suggesting, I'm groping toward this, because I don't know and I'm looking for something.

The wife was unusually halting and vague in her communications, and the therapist had to guess what she was attempting to say. As the session continued, it became clearer that her lack of self-confidence related to her fear of not pleasing her husband and her own frustrations in wanting sex to occur in a loving context so that she could feel closer to and more loved by the husband. As this was spelled out, the therapist was able to communicate that if the wife could feel more loved, she would more likely behave in bed more agreeably to her husband, thus gratifying the husband as well.

Avoidance of "Why" Questions

We have already detailed how understanding "why" may be helpful in the therapeutic work. We are referring to "why" questions that do not elicit further understanding, but are, in fact, camouflaged statements of blame; for example, "Why did you do that?" often means, "How in the world could you have been so cruel as to have done that to me?" Spouses frequently use the "why" stance in such variations as, "I can't understand why you would do such a thing; you know better." These comments should be revealed as disguised, angry protests, which will usually evoke a defense and argument. If one can use these comments to explore the spouse's feelings, some gains may be made. However, as statements of blame, they are best avoided.

In agreement with gestalt principles, we frequently interrupt and ask a spouse to rephrase a question in the form of a statement, whether of needs or of feelings. The following excerpt illustrates these points:

H: In many ways, obviously, I'm not the same person that I was twenty years ago, although I'm more like the person I was then than you're like the person you were.

W: Do you resent that so much?

H: No, I don't resent it. I . . .

T: Wait a minute. Don't answer that. [To wife] Could you put that question into a statement?

[The therapist should have added, "of your feelings."]

W: Could I put that question into a statement? You're wanting me to say that you [the husband] resent me?

T: I'm wanting you to state what's behind the question, by
     asking him the question.

W: Oh, all right. You resent the fact that I am not . . .

T: Could you put that into a form of feelings. Your feel-
     ings aren't his feelings. I don't know what he does.

The therapist is trying to help the spouse, not too successfully, to
acknowledge her feelings: "I *feel* you resent my changing." (Tech-
nically, these are thoughts rather than feelings.)

W: Oh, all right. I think any time I make a statement like
     that, he realizes that it's my feelings and not that I'm just
     saying he resents the fact.

T: I'm not sure what he thinks, but I'm convinced it's your
     thoughts and feelings.

W: Right.

T: I don't know the reality of that . . . I wanted you to make
     clear that you were making a statement that has to do
     with your position and what you think.

At this point the issue was diverted. It would have been helpful
to have suggested to the wife to check out with her husband her
assumption of his resentment.

Red Flags

It is useful to help spouses become aware of ways in which
they communicate that set the partner off. Although these "red
flags" vary from spouse to spouse, the two that are discussed here
are almost universal. One is what we can call *labeling*, that is, using
some negative adjective or noun in referring to the spouse when
complaining about his or her behavior, such as calling a spouse
"lazy" or "good-for-nothing." Spouses are much more willing to listen to a detailing of a given behavior judged objectionable, for example, "This house frequently is a wreck when I get home, and I can't
walk for stepping on toys." Labels are always character assassina-
tions, which direct attention away from the desired behavior change.
In the interchange below, the wife has been complaining about those

aspects of her husband's behavior that she finds exasperating. The therapist has been trying to help her explore what she might do.

H: What she does do is she'll say, "Do you realize you're being childish?" and things like that, which when I'm already irrational and angry, then that makes me angry at her.

T: One of the things you both probably have done, because most couples do to some extent or another, is use labels, and these are very unhelpful—adjectives like "childish," or "immature," and so forth.

W: Or "hysterical."

T: Or "hysterical." . . . These are things that you are going to have to start working on, to get them out of your vocabulary, because they are accusations.

W: A lot of labels we use . . . we hurt each other with.

T: I think it would be helpful if you would try to work on identifying behaviors that bother you, not labeling what the other person is. Do you see the difference?

Much practice is often necessary for spouses to retrain themselves. They frequently use their anger to justify labeling. But it is especially when spouses are angry that they need to restrain themselves if they wish to alter their unsatisfactory relationship.

The second red flag is a critical statement including the phrase "you always" or "you never." It is likely that the accused will not hear the request for change and will feel fully justified in defending the self, since exceptions can always be mustered up to dispute the statement. For example, "You never take me out," can be countered with, "Why that's not so; only last month, when your mother was here, we all went out to dinner." Alerting spouses to the self-defeating aspects of these phrases, using examples as they occur, can aid them in becoming aware of how these phrases harm their relationship.

Mind Reading and Vengeance

A frequent occurrence in therapy is for a spouse to say "We feel . . ." or "Jack thinks I am a real slouch because I don't have any sensitivity." To establish separateness, we make an active effort for each spouse to speak for the self only and not to make assumptions about what the other thinks or feels. We stress that none of us are mind readers and encourage spouses to ask directly how the partner feels or thinks. We point out the possible dangers of assumptions which are not validated and try to use examples from the process of therapy to illustrate this. We want to encourage the communication process and negatively reinforce the tendency for spouses to infer thoughts and feelings of the partner because they know them so well. Granted, spouses often do know each other well, but this fact plus the usual emotional involvement with a spouse frequently leads to erroneous conclusions, as well as valid ones.

Spouses quite often object to the assumption of their feelings, thoughts, or intentions, and one can detect in their replies their opposition to what may be interpreted as a violation of their autonomy. The following interchange illustrates the therapeutic handling of this problem:

H: I think Shirley is more bothered, too, because her best friend just got a divorce, and . . . I really think that bothered her more than she realized.

W: I don't feel particularly bothered by it.

T: [To husband] Well, I think the kind of thing you're doing now, which is what you objected to in your wife's psychologizing with you, is telling her what her feelings are. That's probably one thing you both will have to watch. She's in a better position to tell what her feelings are. That kind of statement sometimes gets you into trouble; it's like her telling you what *your* problems are.

An excerpt from a beginning therapy session further shows the above points. In this case the assumptions may be correct, but the therapist chooses to use the comments to foster separateness:

H: We both feel that we have a definite need for each other; there's no question about that. Neither one of us feel that we can get along without each other.

T: I notice that you both from time to time are speaking for each other. [To husband] You just said, "we need each other." I think maybe for our purposes here it would be helpful if you both speak for yourself, so we can be clear on each person's feelings, so maybe like instead of saying "we both feel," you can say how you feel. Then if your wife wants to, she can make clear her position, and sometimes it might not be quite the same. I would like to know that, and more importantly, you should know that. Maybe there is some slight variation in what she feels. Now I think you were trying to tell your wife, if I understand you correctly, that she is very important to you—so maybe you can tell her plainly.

H: [To therapist] She is, very . . .

T: I mean, don't tell me, tell your wife that.

Reading the intention of a spouse's behavior is much more disruptive if the perceived intention is malevolent. For example, in one session a spouse insisted that her husband's "bitching" about his nights of baby-sitting, when the wife was gone, was done deliberately to get back at her for what he perceived as her chronic bitching about the day's problems with the children. Although he disclaimed this and said that he was merely recounting some of the problems in handling the children, the wife still felt he was punishing her. Another wife insisted that her husband's attentions to another woman were done deliberately: "He can't tear me down other ways, so this is one way he can fight back, so I'm helpless." This distrustfulness and resentment indicates a marriage fraught with disharmony and may, in some cases, represent projection by the spouse.

An interesting occurrence is that once couples learn to identify mind reading, they begin to use its detection as a further weapon, which, in turn, increases defensiveness and furthers counterattack; they delight in "catching" their spouses. It is necessary to help each spouse recognize mind reading without creating a new problem. If a spouse can learn to express the negative feelings of being labeled or of having thoughts or intentions misread rather than catching their spouse, it will help to alleviate undesirable behaviors.

One of the factors that plays into this is the couple's proneness when angry to attack each other with the most devastating comment that they can hurl. Often, they do not fully believe the comments, although there may be a kernel of truth to them. People often remember exaggerated criticisms and forget positive comments made at other times. For example, in the heat of an argument, one wife told her husband that he was the worst lover she had ever had, and in another case the husband told his wife she was the worst housekeeper in the world. As a result, spouses often misjudge many behaviors and readily make false assumptions about their mate's feelings and thoughts. In sorting out beliefs based on these exaggerated statements from actual convictions, it is helpful to point out that the remarks are intended to hurt rather than convey fixed judgment. One can aid a spouse in determining what is actually believed by the mate by asking the mate about its validity. Many times couples will acknowledge their proneness to exaggerate and will state that, in fact, they really do not believe the comment but were trying to hurt the spouse.

Modeling

Many ways have been presented for the therapist to help the couple improve communication. One additional way is through the use of modeling by the therapist. Helpful comments are, "Now let me get this straight, what I hear you saying is . . . ," or "If I understand you correctly—you can check me out on this—I hear you saying . . . ," or "I'm not sure I understand what you're saying; perhaps you could restate it."

Since couples often do not readily learn to communicate clearly even with modeling, something more is needed. Whenever a communication from one spouse to another seems unclear, the therapist can comment on this and ask the partner to whom it was directed if he or she is similarly perplexed. If the answer is yes, then one can encourage this partner to ask the other to restate the comment. Note the emphasis here is not on the therapist's confusion, but rather to use this difficulty in understanding as a clue that the partner might not be understanding either. The therapist then redirects the flow back to the couple interchange.

Modeling may be used in another way to help couples. When attempting to have spouses reenact an encounter and one of the spouses is having difficulty, the therapist can play the role of that spouse. It is advisable to do this at a time when expression of feeling is stymied. One hopes by modeling forcefulness, directness, and an obvious display of feeling that the observing spouse will be able to eliminate constraints in self-expression.

Nonverbal Communication

Efforts must be made to point out to couples how they communicate nonverbally. Whenever nonverbal communication is observed, one should call attention to it and ask the spouse if this could be communicated to the partner more directly. If there is difficulty, one may ask the partner if the behavior was noted and what meaning it had. One may even add, "The way I read it was such-and-such; I am not sure that this was the way that you were feeling and wonder just how you were feeling."

The purposes of identifying nonverbal communication are: to help spouses identify their characteristic ways of communicating feelings, which they may not be aware of; to encourage the couple to become aware of nonverbal communications and to reflect on their meaning; and to encourage the comparison of their interpretations to see if they are being decoded correctly.

Unconscious nonverbal cues can be powerful stimuli for unwanted responses; for example, a spouse will respond angrily to a specific facial expression. Once greater awareness of such stimuli has occurred, the spouse may understand better the reactions of the mate, previously attributed solely to verbal stimuli. Knowledge of these cues allows better control of communication both by the sender and the receiver.

Working in the Here-and-Now

One of the most time-consuming and counterproductive events in therapy is going over a previous argument or past event, in which each spouse tries to establish how much objectionable behavior occurred and how often. Inevitably, this leads to more disagreement over what actually happened. Rather than shedding any new light on the dissatisfactions between the couple, it only serves to generate heat.

If one does not intervene, these interchanges can consume vast quantities of time and negate the possibility of therapeutic change. This should be communicated to a couple very early in therapy. One can state that there is no way to establish what actually happened, because each perceived and experienced things differently, and even if it were possible, it would not be helpful. One can also suggest that what might be useful would be to talk about the problems that they have and see what they can do about them now. One can then extract from the previous argument what appears to have been the primary subject of conflict (often a complaint about a spouse) and focus on this, redirecting the discussion to the present. One might also check out if they have frequent difficulty with this subject (as for example, how the couple spend their money, or how they deal with their in-laws). If a particular problem is discussed often, the therapist can suggest that they talk about it, but in a different way. They can be discouraged from "rehashing" the past; instead, they can talk together about how they see this as a problem now, how they feel about it, and explore what they can do about it. Once the therapist has identified this tendency to replay a past event and has labeled it for the couple, one can use the term *rehash* to quickly indicate what is occurring in order to halt the process.

Working in the here-and-now has other functions than avoiding rehash. As has been indicated, it is often helpful to work on specific problems. One of the main reasons spouses prefer to avoid the here-and-now is that it implies direct confrontation, and it may generate discomfort from doing something new rather than rehashing old, familiar programs. One can suggest that the spouses select one grievance and direct it to the partner, so that both can practice doing something contrary to their usual style. Hopefully, the couple will find the new experience unexpectedly constructive.

In one example of bringing the past into the present, a wife related that while visiting her mother out of state, she had called her husband back home to tell him she had felt hurt by her mother's reaction. She felt "let down" by her husband, who did not say the things that would have reassured her. It was suggested that they reenact the event in the session. Several interesting things happened. The wife found that as she related the event to her husband, she sounded quite cool and not at all hurt. When she began to get in touch with hurt feelings, choked up, and began to cry, her husband spontaneously moved toward her, held her hand, and teared up in sympathy. The wife was able to move from her initial position of blaming her husband for not being more giving to seeing how she had concealed her pain. This led her to acknowledge two things: This pattern of behavior was to avoid being vulnerable, and she expected that she would not be given to and helped to make it so. It also allowed her to experience her husband as giving. Her husband further added that in her usual way of relating painful things, he concludes that they are of no consequence and thus dismisses them. Thus, both spouses learned valuable things about each other that could lead to changes by both.

The transcript of the therapy session that follows illustrates the therapist using the here-and-now to increase understanding, particularly by having the couple focus on listening to feelings. The couple have just been discussing the wife's complaint about the husband's not helping her when she comes to him with a problem. What she is hoping to get is some listening to her feelings, but instead he very quickly offers practical suggestions, often telling her what she should or should not do (the solution-response turn-off). She goes on to say that this gets her "back up" and an argument ensues. She wants her husband to be less volatile, more empathic, and able to hear her when she wrestles with a difficult issue, rather than telling her what she should do. Her husband struggles to understand her. As he puts it, "You want me to listen and then say, 'Uh huh, uh huh, O.K., yeah, well, and what else,' and so forth, and perhaps ask questions." His wife then says that he does not even hear out the situation before he reacts. The wife then asks the husband if he understands her, and he says, "Some of the time, yes, I can understand that. It makes good sense, but.'. . ." The husband admits to some of the wife's accusations but still seems to be protesting.

T: [To husband] What's wrong with it for you?

H: Wrong when—wrong with?

T: Well, I keep hearing you say, "Yes, I understand it,

but"—and I know there's something, another part of it. [Husband goes on to say he cannot see this as an overriding problem and feels criticized.]

H: I'm trying to find out what the basis of the criticism is. I realize I may have done these things on several occasions, but . . . there are even more occasions when I didn't react this way.

T: Well, if we could get away from counting up, can you hear what she is asking for?

H: Yes, and I think it's reasonable.

T: What troubles me in your response is the way you describe what you're "supposed" to do . . . it doesn't get across [that] you're tuning in to where she really is.

H: Yes, and this is the point I'm trying to get clarified. I'm not sure exactly what I am supposed to do. I can empathize, and I can just sit and just listen and give noncommittal answers in a sympathetic tone, and I can relegate myself to this or I can converse about the situation as it's going along, and I realize that conversation doesn't mean pointing out opposite sides or different sides for what you apparently are looking for in the situation, but sometimes that does come into the picture.

[The therapist acknowledges the problem for the husband of not just saying "uh huh" and his uncertainty about how to communicate; then the therapist alerts him to the undesirable problem-solution (solution-response turn-off) approach. Because it is difficult for the husband to grasp what goes wrong in an abstract discussion, the therapist tries to reenact an interchange to see what they can learn.]

T: I'm not sure it's that easy to put into practice. [To wife] I thought it might be helpful right now if you'd just pick something you'd like to tell Arnie [the husband] that's important and tell him, and you [to husband] see if you can find a way of talking that isn't sterile but in a meaningful way, but one that doesn't set her off. Can you [to wife] pick something?

W: Yes, I can pick something that has been a problem to me.

T: Just go ahead as if you were at home.

W: I really hesitate . . . [to husband] I guess because I don't
     know your reaction. I don't know what you will do. I sort
     of sense about one thing that you will do, but I won't say
     it ahead of time, and I guess that's the reason I'm hesi-
     tating. You know how close Arlene and I have been in
     recent weeks and months. I have really had my feelings
     hurt, because she and I were such very good friends, and
     I haven't communicated much with her, and I miss her
     as a very good, close friend. It does cause some hurt to
     me, and I haven't said anything to her, you know, but I
     have wanted to say something to you. I guess I was look-
     ing for someone to [whom I could] say, "Something's
     upsetting me," and just wanted to talk it over with you.
     And the times that I go and play tennis twice a week, of
     course, I don't get much opportunity to talk with her,
     and she and I communicated so much for so long. I feel
     that since I'm not working over there in the office, that
     our friendship is not as close as it was once and I do feel
     in some way hurt by this.

H: Well, uh . . . you feel like she's pulling away from you or
     do you feel like that simply the situation of not being
     able to see each other on a day-to-day basis is . . .

W: I guess I feel like she's pulling away from me.

H: You know, on a number of occasions when the time
     permitted you have made a special effort to see her, and
     I guess on occasions she did come over to the house,
     especially to see you and talk to you. Maybe, it's diffi-
     cult—it seems if you don't see each other. Well, have
     you thought about staying a few minutes after the tennis
     game? I know that you have been taking one of the chil-
     dren with you. I'm not quite sure why this is—just maybe
     because they wanted to go, because you felt like three of
     them was just too much, I don't know. But maybe if you
     could after the game, it would be possible to spend a little
     time with her then—I don't know, if you want to do that.
     Because you know if you get back at 8:30 as opposed to

9:15, it doesn't make much difference about how things are set up in the morning. I can put the children to bed; putting three of them to bed is no more difficult than putting two to bed. Have you given any thought to maybe leaving the children at home and just making some time? Whatever is convenient for her; some nights would be, some nights wouldn't, perhaps.

W: Well, I've thought about that, but what I'm trying to say is that it's not that I haven't got time to see her. It's just that she doesn't have time to see me, and my feelings are hurt, and I really just wanted to talk with you.

T: Can you hold it a minute? Can you see that you [to husband] launched into problem-solution?

H: Yes.

T: Now that may or may not be helpful. I'm not saying that it isn't helpful, but it may not be. But what frequently happens when someone tells you something about a hurt is pretty soon all the effort goes into problem-solution, and then they begin to feel like they're not . . . the part they really wanted tended to, which was their hurt, kind of gets lost in the shuffle. That's especially true because, with this kind of thing, there's probably very little in the way of problem-solution that Lois [the wife] couldn't come up with on her own. Now I think you wanted to do something additional, which was a good thing to do. You wanted to say, "I would be willing to do something for you if I could help you," you know, when you were offering to put the kids to bed, and I think that was a good part of it. In the process of listening, you know, you could have said, "Is there anything I could do to help you?" But again, you see, that's not a problem-solution. That's not sending solutions. That's respecting the right that she probably thought of all the external ways of getting more time, seeing her, meeting her, or whatever. She is fully prepared to do all that, but it does offer her some support for something, you know, that does matter to her. There's a difference there.

H: Yeah.

T: And the big point I'm trying to make is that a good part of the time when people communicate something to you about a problem, they're not seeking a problem-solution. Now, sometimes they are. She might come in and say, "Now look, I have had it with this budget. I've sat down and I have done it twenty ways, and I just can't find a solution. Can you help me?" That's different—she's really looking for problem-solutions. But frequently, in the realm of feelings, when someone starts sharing something with you, they are not looking for a problem-solution, because there is no one solution, and if you get hung up on trying to tune in just from that angle, you're going to miss the other angle, which is she wants just to talk about it. The end result of which will be that *no* solutions will have been arrived at probably. Maybe she'll come to some in her own mind. I don't know, maybe not. [To wife] Now am I doing a disservice to anything in your point of view?

W: No, absolutely not. You interpreted exactly what I was talking about.

T: [To husband] So, I wanted you to note how soon . . . it didn't take you very long before you got into a problem-solution. So that's something when you play the tape back over you can listen to, and listen to what you said. And you were doing fine for a while, you kind of asked her questions and you showed her you were interested, and then very quickly you began to formulate problem-solutions. Now this may be because that's what you do a lot. Maybe your work is such that that's constantly what you have to do, solve problems.

H: Well, it is. [Laughs]

T: Well, I understand that, and see, it's an asset at work. It's a real strength, and maybe it's one of your best strengths. But here it could work at a disadvantage. I'm not saying it's a bad thing; it's a good thing, depending on wherein you use it.

H: You've got to use it properly.

T: Yes, but I wanted you to hear a little part.

W: [To husband] I know your motive behind it is an attempt
     to help. I can see that. I can see you thinking, "Maybe
     this will work"; I do realize that. I do see it, but I begin
     to sense in myself a closing up when you begin launching
     into all these damn practical things. I sense a closing up of
     my feelings, and then I'm ready to end the conversation.

T: See, that's very important to hear. What you would in-
     tend to be helpful turns out to close her off, which sort
     of ends it. It's not your intention. You're trying to do
     something good for her, but it just doesn't work that
     way for her.

H: O.K., I think I've got it now. It's going to take some work
     in applying it. [Laughs]

T: Because it goes against something that is probably a nat-
     ural thing for you, which is solving problems all day long
     at work.

H: O.K.

     [The couple then apply the above understanding to the
     husband's way of talking to the children and how he turns
     them off.]

H: The way to play that then is to sit and listen without giv-
     ing comments or directions.

W: I guess you could say, accept the person, the things
     they've said and done.

   In the final example of working in the here-and-now, the therapist tries to help a couple "relive" in the present a previous incident
that went badly. The husband, frustrated at feeling overburdened
and not sufficiently supported by his wife had angrily threatened to
leave. The therapist's goal is to help the husband state his feelings
and frustrated needs behind the anger instead of making threats.

T: Why don't we see if you can get yourself back into some of
     the feelings that you were into? Let's see if we can re-do
     that incident now and see if you can tell her how you're
     feeling—what's going on inside of you.

H: Well, I was feeling a lot of depression—from work.

T: See if you can act as if it's now.

H: O.K.

T: Put it in the present.

H: "Oh, I'm feeling a lot of pressure from work and from being sick—prospects of all the work I have to do this weekend—not knowing if I'm going to be able to handle it. You're getting angry at me about . . . and also I was . . ."

T: "I am . . ."

[The therapist suggests a beginning of a sentence in the present tense.]

H: "I am feeling some negative feelings because when . . ."
[The husband then begins to blame his wife, commenting on what she should and should not have done. The therapist tries to help the husband tune into how he has shifted away from the task set for him—communicating his feelings—to blaming his wife.]

H: What I was feeling was that she wasn't . . .

T: What are you doing now when you're saying, "You should have done this"?

H: She was saying I should have known that, and I should have realized that, and what I'm feeling is that she didn't understand anything or even care or take thought or effort to understand what was going on with me.

Note the difficulty the husband has in staying focused on his feelings of depression and pressure. The last sentence starting with "I'm feeling" is not a feeling at all but a thought containing a blaming criticism of his wife. After several more interchanges, the therapist again directs the husband to talking of the incident as though it were in the present.

T: Oh, let's go back to the point where you said you sat down and here comes Jamie—why don't you just take it from there and put it in the present. Tell her . . . what you need and how you feel.

H: And do it the way I should do it?

T: Just try it again for size. I don't know about "should."

H: What would be best?

T: What might make things go better between you.

H: O.K.

[The husband makes an attempt, leaving out feelings.]

T: Have you let her know how really badly you feel?

H: Well, I haven't gone into any details.

T: Well, now, if it's really important . . . now she may be pre-
    occupied with many other things, and unless she hears
    this as a real, tremendous plea, she may make a choice
    that will leave you hanging dry and hurting more. If
    you're really hurting bad, you're going to have to let her
    know because she'll have to weigh that along with other
    pressures to make a decision. You were saying you need
    help, you feel like you just can't manage, I presume.

H: Well, you know, like if she could just say, you know . . .

T: I want to work on what *you* can say first—get it across to
    her, the extent of your need. I don't know what it is; I'm
    not trying to shade it in either direction—I don't know.

H: Okay, my need . . .

    [To therapist]

T: O.K., tell her.

H: Oh . . . my need is that . . .

    [The husband again details specifics in terms of what his
    wife "should" be doing.]

T: You're concentrating a lot on what she's "supposed"
    to do.

H: No, I'm saying I'm not expecting . . . [such and such]

T: I don't want you to worry about that. Were you really
    feeling up-tight—I mean, was it a pretty shaky feeling for
    that to happen?

H: Yes, it was, but I didn't expect anything if she had really
    important things to do for her . . .

T: Don't worry about what to expect. I want her to take care
of that. And see, that messes up what you're getting
across. When you listen to this again, listen to yourself.
Let me be you a minute and say . . .

The therapist is trying to get the husband to state his needs so that
the wife can respond to them. It will be up to her to decide the extent
to which she is willing to meet them, but first she must know their degree of importance to her husband. Because the husband is having
difficulty, the therapist decides to role-play the husband as to how he
might have felt at the time he angrily threatened to leave, substituting feelings and needs for threats.

T: "God, am I glad to see you. You don't know what a day it's
been . . . I'm feeling horrible, and I really need you . . .
will you help me?" See, what I want you to do is just tell
her where you really are—don't get all that worry about
what she's going to do.

The therapist continues in this vein, trying to help the husband express to his wife his frustration and need for help. This proves a
very difficult task, and efforts are largely unsuccessful in this session.

Another way of working in the present is illustrated by a
method suggested by a colleague for helping break up the polarity
of disagreements.[3] One spouse plays the role of befriending the
partner; then, speaking to the partner as to a friend, the spouse
talks about an imaginary person seated in a third chair, who represents the partner. In the process of talking to the friend (the actual
partner), the spouse voices complaints about the "mate." The roles
should then be exchanged between the spouses. In addition to
breaking up polarities, this technique should also encourage empathy for the spouse's position.

[3] E. Maggard, personal communication, 1975.

6

Reeducation:
Altering Attitudes,
Perceptions, and
Misconceptions

"The Real Problem"

A prevalent misconception of couples which will need correction is that there is one big problem that must be detected in order to restore marital harmony. The therapist needs to convey that there is not just a single problem, except that they are both feeling ungratified and unhappy in their relationship. This lack of gratification (feeling unloved, discontent, or frustrated) is actually a result of what goes on between the couple, and there are innumerable interchanges occurring that convey meanings and generate feelings, satisfactions, and dissatisfactions. In the therapeutic work together, one goal will be

190

to examine the kinds of behaviors that have played an important part in their disharmony.

For many spouses, this focus is truly a baffling and alien approach. Often, their conception of therapy is to give detailed histories of their lives separately and together, and then, as one spouse phrased it, the therapist will be able "to get to the bottom of this." Again the assumption is that there is a single underlying factor that comprises the "real problem" and which the therapist will be attempting to uncover; the responsibility is placed on the therapist for this work. The following comments leave little doubt as to the husband's conviction that some primary cause is responsible for his years of grief with his wife, and he appears to be searching to find it.

> H: Well, I know somewhere along the line that something happened, and I used to beg her to tell me what made her change; and you [to wife] said you didn't know what it was, but I know something did happen and I don't know what it is. But I believe something happened after the birth of Jack, and our relationship has never been the same since . . . I don't know what it was. I just know that something came that made the change, but what it was I don't know.

On occasion, a spouse even has an idea about what the big problem is, like the husband who tried to convince the therapist that the root of the problem was his wife's frigidity and her puritanical upbringing. Although such an individual problem and its psychogenesis may exist and play an important part in the marital disharmony, focusing on this exclusively will hinder the necessary perspective on present transactions. Assuming the discord results from a single, external cause is often a way for spouses to avoid looking at their own parts in the ongoing transactions.

In these situations, one can agree that there may have been one very important thing that has happened, which has played a part in the present problems. But one should go even further and say that there are probably many more such things, some of them known and some not. However, the therapeutic task will not be so

much to go back and identify these, as to take a better look at what
is happening now between the two with which they are dissatisfied.
One can add that as this is done, all will get a better perspective
on how things came to be, but that this will not be the major thrust
of the work. In other words, the emphasis is not on why things came
to be the way they are, but rather identifying how things are now
and determining *what* can be done to change this situation by working together. A major danger with a "why" orientation is the belief
that if one could just understand why, then the solution will become obvious and things will automatically fall into place. One
needs to communicate early that the work will involve more doing
than understanding, although the latter is certainly important. The
understanding that occurs is usually a by-product of focusing on
current transactions, feelings, and dissatisfactions.

Interaction of Individual with Marital Problems

It is usually helpful to clarify, where necessary, the spouses'
understanding of both the individual and transactional parts of
their problems. In some cases, an individual problem may be exaggerated by the marital friction, and in that sense, it may be symptomatic of the spouses' disharmony. Often, spouses need help in
untangling their personal problem from their marriage problems.
As one husband said, "Are things really not as bad with us—is it just
in my head—is it a personal kind of thing with me or are there really
dissatisfactions?" He goes on to contrast his reaction with that of
his wife, who sees their situation as less dire. In an attempt to bring
the situation into a more realistic perspective and to undermine unrealistic wishes, the therapist replied, "Well, I think, as you both
know, there are dissatisfactions, but it's possible you might have
attached too much weight to them and expected things which are
unrealistic to expect. Maybe it would be helpful if you would talk
with your wife about what's been going on with her, because through
her eyes things have looked different." The therapist redirected
the flow to the couple interchange.

Whatever the case, how the therapist focuses on the individual
problem is crucial. An individual with a diagnosed problem must

be ready to acknowledge this without feeling overly defensive for the therapist to focus successfully on the individual aspects. We prefer to explore the nature of the individual problem in the context of its contribution to marital friction rather than to analyze its origin. The individual spouse can be encouraged to reflect on his or her behavior towards either the spouse or the therapist in terms of the understandings of the past events. Although the emphasis is in part individual, one still is working from the relationship framework, hoping to help the couple improve their interaction. Whatever is functional for this purpose is legitimate. If individual focus becomes too dominant, then the goals toward which the triad are working will not be reached.

When appropriate, it is helpful to illustrate how individual problems of both spouses interact to produce difficulties. In the following case, the therapist tried to relate this after work that focused on the issues of interpersonal control:

> T: I think you [to husband] probably have a predilection to feel controlled already built in that is independent of your wife, and you [to wife] have a predilection to feel that your emotional supplies are always in danger of being cut off, independent of your husband, and just these two things rubbing together are causing a lot of friction . . . things you had independently that together make for problems.

When one begins to focus on one individual, it is important to remember that both spouses are present. The partner may be able to appreciate the spouse's problem in a helpful, empathic way; however, on the other hand, the partner may use it as more ammunition for blaming the spouse. Such knowledge may be employed to exonerate oneself at the detriment of one's mate as well as oneself.

Some examples will illustrate the attempts to clarify individual and marital problems in the process of improving spouses' abilities to negotiate. One husband continuously felt unjustly accused by his mate. The therapist tried to aid the husband to see how his behavior might contribute to this perception and attempted to clarify the wife's part in this. In this case, the husband, through repeated behavioral examples, became aware that he was set to read reproof. In addition, he became more aware of what he did that caused his wife to behave in a way that would appear unfair to him. At the same time, with his feedback, the wife was able to see how her behavior reinforced his set. Although this part of therapy did not alter the husband's set, he was encouraged to stop and think when he began to feel this way. This seemed to lessen his anger at times, although it was a continual struggle for him. At least as helpful was the fact that his wife now felt less need to defend herself and could identify some of her husband's misperceptions, which made her less likely to precipitate a quarrel. Thus, although the husband's set to hear accusation was not altered, helping them distinguish their respective contributions to the problem promoted separateness and individual responsibility. In some cases, when an individual becomes more aware of how marriage has been used for projection of an intense, individualized conflict, he or she will seek individual therapy.

In another example, the therapist was attempting to enable the husband to listen to his wife's feelings, since they seemed extremely relevant to the couple's sexual problems. The husband experienced his wife's sexual behavior, both compliance and avoidance, as distasteful. Although the wife admitted that she had always had problems with sex, it seemed clear that her present behavior was aggravated by experiencing her husband as overbearing in his demands for sexual contact and in his inability to respect her feelings or needs. The wife attempted to tell her husband why she avoided sex. The therapist hoped that by dealing with the wife's feelings, it would enable the husband to understand her plight and alter his behavior.

> W: Because I know that there are times when I get very nervous. I don't know why I get upset, because if I know you are going to be there and I'm going to be under you and I'm going to be smothered, I just get this feeling, and I want to be alone, and I don't want somebody over top of me bothering me, and I know if I . . .
>
> [The husband interrupts and talks at length.]

W: But I can't help it—it's the way I feel. And I know I have to go ahead with this [sex].

Because the husband cannot attend to any aspect of his wife's communication, there is much extraneous dialogue before the subject is resumed. The husband is intent on talking about his own hurts and blaming his wife.

T: I heard your wife say something that made me think it is important for you to tune in—that maybe a special concern of hers that plays a part in this [their sexual problem] is this fear of smothering and fear of closed places, and like you being on top. I don't know how much of a concern this is, but it may be something you need to hear and help her with, because it may make things worse if you don't tune into it. [To wife] I don't know whether he understands clearly the panicky feelings you probably get.

H: You didn't used to have these panicky . . .

T: That's not relevant now. The fact is that she has them now. We're not really trying to deal with what used to be. Things have changed. You are not the same people you were when you were courting, but I think more important than what she didn't used to be, is her being able to tell you something about her panicky feelings, so that you know about them, because you could be involved in helping her not feel these anymore. I think it's important [in order] for you to get what you want to hear her. I would like you [to wife] to talk with him about that, because I'm not sure he's heard that too clearly.

[The wife begins by talking about the size of the bed.]

T: Talk about your feelings—not so much the bed, but talk about what it does to you. I think that's more important.

[The husband interrupts to say the wife's sexual behavior is the same no matter where she is.]

T: No, you're getting off the subject. I want you to talk about this specific thing for a moment.

W: It's a panicky feeling. Well, I just don't like to be down and can't get up.

T: Where you feel that you don't have freedom to control what happens to you.

W: Yes.

H: Well, I don't think . . .

T: [Interrupting] Do I hear you [to wife] as making a request that he hear that carefully, that that makes things worse? [To husband] For whatever reasons right now, it's very important for her to feel like she has some control over what happens to her and if she is blocked from movement, it will make her feel very anxious and afraid. It will make things worse.

     [Several interchanges follow.]

W: So many times when we do make love, I asked you if I could get on top and you never, never want me on top. You always want to smother me, and I can't breathe down there.

T: You're asking for a change of positions? That might make things better?

W: [To therapist] Yes, I've mentioned this to him before.

T: [To husband] You should hear that very carefully, because it's probably important to your wife. I don't think I'm overestimating the importance of this.

     [The therapist refers to the fear and anxiety in the wife's face as she speaks. The husband will not hear and continues with protests, emphasizing that his wife has the problem.]

In the above session, the therapist chose to focus on what was probably an overdetermined problem of the wife's hoping to help the husband appreciate how his wife's feelings about this problem were a major difficulty in their sexual relationship. At this point, the goal was the simple one of helping the husband to be aware and to acknowledge the distress of the wife; the more complicated goal of enabling the husband to become aware of his excessive neediness and his overdemanding behavior would have been more difficult to achieve because of his defensiveness. So, the therapist chose in this first session to try to help the husband to hear his wife's feelings. In this case, even this small goal was unsuccessful. Another goal could have been to work with the wife's overdetermined feelings, but this would have destroyed the couple focus and reinforced the husband's entrenched blaming position.

In contrast to this case, at times one spouse will assume the blame for the marital problems. Here, one must assist the spouses to appreciate their respective parts in the frictional interaction without one spouse assuming all the responsibility. In the example below, the husband had just said that he would like to have sex with his wife more often. He commented, "I don't know why . . . I really feel like it is my fault." Apparently, his wife's efforts to assure him that this was not so had been unsuccessful, even though his wife had told him that she herself was not sure why she wanted little sex. She related that she just was not interested in sex and felt that this was the case not just with her husband but with anyone. Even with these comments the husband still assumed that there must be something wrong with him.

> H: Well, I just feel that I should be able to make you feel more interested.

He goes on to tell her that he really cares about her, and his wife reassures him that she also loves him, which the husband acknowledges. Since the husband seems anxious to assume more than his share of the responsibility for the breakdown in sexual relations, the therapist intervenes to see if this can be corrected.

> T: Let me break in here for a minute. Your husband said he felt he should be able to make you feel more interested. Could you just respond to that part of it and tell him whether or not there are some things that he could do that might turn you on a little more, if there are?
>
> [The wife's reply is that she can't think of anything other than that her husband might be a bit more aggressive and that it is hard for her to tell how he feels about sex.]

T: How would you like for him to let you know?

W: [To husband] I would just like for you to be a little more aggressive sometimes.

T: Do you understand what she means?

[The husband replies to his wife that he had tried doing this, but it did not seem successful; either she was not in the mood or he would feel no response. In the end, this made things even worse, since he felt like he was imposing. So after that he quit being aggressive.]

T: Do you want him to quit?

W: Want him to quit?

T: Doing anything.

W: No, I don't want him to quit doing anything.

T: I think that he is very discouraged, . . .

W: I know.

T: . . . and he feels like he has made efforts, and he has been put off, and he is discouraged, and I think maybe if you are sincere in saying that you don't want him to quit, you should try to help him with that now.

[The wife again tells her husband that she does not want him to stop being aggressive, but that there are many times when it is a bad time for her because of fatigue or other reasons. She also says, however, that she cannot remember her husband being aggressive very often.]

T: O.K., it might be that your memory is not accurate, or it may be that you're [to husband] not getting your messages across.

H: That's probably it.

Note again the husband's overreadiness to blame himself.

T: I don't know what it is, but I think that it is something maybe you should look at. You might need to look at your messages, because maybe they are not coming across. Maybe you think they are, but maybe you stop too quickly. You feel discouraged when they are not received the first time and then you give up. Maybe she thinks you're really not interested. I don't know that, but maybe that may be operating. But your wife says, "I don't want you to stop, I want you to want me." Is that correct?

W: You're right. I don't want you to feel that I hate you, I don't want you to feel discouraged, because it's not you. I don't think it has anything to do with you; it's just that, I don't know, I'm just not interested.

Although the husband may play some part in the problem by being readily discouraged and unconfident, as the session continues it becomes apparent that the lack of sexual interest is, as the wife says, primarily her problem. The therapist helps the husband to see the extent to which the problem is his wife's, so that he will not blame himself unduly; and at the same time, the therapist attempts to help him with his discouragement and to do what he can to arouse his wife's interest.

W: Well, sometimes I don't tell him the whole way I feel, because I think he will think, "My God, that's my fault too."

T: I see. [To husband] So you can see a thing that's probably getting in the way of your wife's sharing with you, and that's your tendency to take blame for it. That is, she may be censoring what she tells, because she doesn't want you to say, "Oh, what have I done now," or "You wouldn't feel that bad if I weren't so and so."

Sometimes, without specific efforts to uncover how unresolved conflicts from the past are contributing to their present disharmony, spouses will become aware of how this is so by themselves. It is as if previous memories and experiences emerge with new "felt" meanings and impact, allowing for meaningful connections between the past and present. The following comments illustrate how new perspectives emerged for a husband after many months of couple treatment. As the patient unfolds his new understand-

ings, the therapist tries to relate these previous experiences to past
and present marital problems.

H: A couple of weeks ago, Peg and I were driving home after
a session here and started talking about various things.
One thing led to another and I was probably trying to
figure out why I was ill at ease with Peg and John [their
son] when John was very little, and I attempted to solve
that problem many times before. I knew I was ill at ease
and I think that last Saturday I finally was able to put
my finger on at least part of it. And I guess from the time
I was seven or eight years old—I'm going to set the stage
here a little bit—my father died when I was seven, and it
was during World War II. And my mother's younger sister, who had just been married for a year or two, and
whose husband was sent overseas to France . . . the sister
came to live at our house and during that time my mother
was teaching and she was away, and so a good deal of
the care of my sister and myself fell to this aunt, who was
pregnant and who was worried about her husband being
overseas, and who was essentially a very unstable person
at that time. And the whole household came eventually
to revolve around this aunt and her needs and the needs
of the child when it came, and I suppose I felt very dis-
placed. But anyway, I can remember thinking about this
aunt and my cousin, that since they came, there has been
nothing but trouble—there's been no time for me. There
I was, seven or eight years old, and this went on for about
three years, and she stayed with us for about three years.

T: When you say "cousin"—do you mean the birth of the
baby?

H: Yeah, the baby—this whole . . . but at any rate, pregnant
women and babies were nothing but trouble. They gave
you no time for yourself and no attention to yourself.
They were nothing but trouble and that attitude—until
last Saturday when I put my finger on it—I don't know
why I was able to then—but anyway that's the way I
viewed children—young children and pregnant women

and new mothers, and I'm sure, I'm sure unconsciously this is the way I viewed the birth of John—[to wife]I told you this—and you and your needs and your involvement with him and I know that that feeling colored my initial views and my actions with you and with John. And because of that I couldn't view him as being entirely pleasing and at least emotionally pleasing, an addition to you and I.

T: Apparently this was something really that was extremely of importance to you—making this connection was a meaningful thing. [To wife] Is this something you had understood before?

W: I hadn't . . . believe it or not in all of my armchair psychiatry, I had never come up with anything like this, and I'm bad about analyzing Gary [the husband], and I think it makes him mad when I do it, but I had never made that kind of connection, but it does make awfully good sense to me; it's better for me to hear that than to think there was really something wrong with me or in which there was some way the two of us did not please you.

H: Well, I told you for years there was nothing personal in the way I was being. I objected to John—I didn't hate him—and now I know he was just a symbol of something, and this trouble . . . this having no time for me. Now, you had time for me, that's beside the point, really. The reality of you and John and me, I wasn't paying much attention to . . . couldn't mean anything but trouble.

W: You said to me last week, on top of that, when you got off the plane you saw me there standing with the baby and you said, "Oh Lord, there's another Daisy [the husband's aunt]," and she has the same color of hair that I do.

H: That's right, same color hair, the same, I mean, I didn't say that, I mean I didn't even think that, but that was there—that picture was there. On top of Peg's coloring, Peg's hair, there was quite a similarity between my cousin [and John]. When she was just born, she was a big child—a nice-looking baby. John was a big child; he was a nice-looking baby. I guess it was too much to accept. [Laughs]

T: Yes, plus, of course, the reality of a new baby—it does take a lot on mother's part, and it had to take some away from you. So you've got that old hurt going over that intruder who took so much, and then here comes this little baby that does take some time.

H: Well, on the surface, in thinking, I knew that children take a lot of care, but I never made this connection until a couple of weeks ago, when I was coming home. And I can see that a lot of my attitudes, a lot of my views, a lot of my spontaneous reactions to things that John has done, that Richard [their second son] had done, that Mary [their daughter] has done, has been . . . well, what else can you expect—a kid is nothing but trouble. And that's been a spontaneous reaction to what I would do— that was there—that sparked any kind of spontaneous reaction towards a knock on the head [of the children] or a vicious answer to something they have done or to some question they have asked. Like when I'm involved in doing something else and they break in and want some attention of one kind or another, it's been there. I'm afraid over the years I've formed some kind of pattern of being . . . thinking of them as being trouble. Rationally, I've realized they're no more trouble than any other child and probably better than most, but still things that they did that was less than, let's say, what an adult could do, or cause more trouble than an adult would cause, that was just another fact of my original view of pregnant women and children—they're nothing but trouble.

T: I'm wondering, you've elaborated on it pretty clearly how it affected you with the kids, you know. I'm wondering how you think it played into your relationship with Peg. Maybe you and she could talk about that, 'cause you've both talked about those early years—things not going too well. I'm sure it must have had some spin-off with her, too, you know; you keep saying pregnant women, as part of that scene—that bad picture, "Oh God, here it comes again," and of course, you've [to wife] been pregnant three times and a new baby came, so in your life you've had to face that now.

H: Well, when I married you and you married me, I wanted someone whose life was centered around me, and I intended to make my life center around you. But when John came, of course, there no longer could be the total attention, the total attention to the wants and needs of mine to you and you to me, and the couple of weeks we had before I went overseas was not enough for me to get used to you, much less the idea of having a child. . . . Well, and the fact that John was already there when I came back and you, as you have mentioned many times, you were so obviously proud of him, like "Look what I've done; look at what we have; see how well I have taken care of him." This was your feeling and it was . . . I just didn't, I could not feel that that was good, because it showed, it was evident that here was something, that here was somebody who was taking your attention, somebody that you were proud of besides me. Someone except me that you devoted your time and attention to. And I know very well that had to be done; I knew at the time that that had to be done, but not withstanding all those rational things that I knew and that you knew, John still was trouble. I know my action then hurt you terribly, while the very presence of John hurt me. It's nothing towards him, there was nothing towards you. I had animosity towards the situation.

W: Well, I sort of rationalized in my mind that I had nine months to get used to it, being a mother, having a baby, and then five months to take care of it. I guess the six months after you came home from overseas I put the blame on the fact that you were still unhappy because you were still having to remain in the service, and they had told you you would get out, but when you came back, they gave you another six months. That and the fact that two months after you were home, I was pregnant again, and I decided that all of that responsibility on your shoulders was more than you could take. I guess I accepted that initial disappointment right there and figured when you got out of the army and into a regular job, that maybe things would be better; and I suppose I was more disappointed at that point than I was earlier. I know it had some very bad effects on us.

H: Even later when I didn't take the other job. To let again my whole household revolve around the needs of a pregnant woman and a child was more than I could face, and I suppose that's one reason I would not change jobs. I wasn't going to let that happen again, and I know how this affected you.

W: You wouldn't change jobs. Not only that, you wouldn't even read the want ads in the paper when I would open them up and lay them in front of you—you refused and closed your eyes.

H: That's right.

In this case, a profound reaction to the early loss of the father and the experienced displacement of the boy who felt his aunt and her infant received more of his mother's attention played a crucial role in shaping the husband's attitudes towards children and anyone, especially his pregnant wife, who reminded him of this. To protect himself, he steeled himself in his marriage against intruders, which interfered both with his parenting and his relating with his wife. The significance of this understanding, not only for the husband but also for the wife, is revealed in the wife's remark that it was better for her to hear her husband's explanation, which made good sense to her, than to think something was wrong with her or the son.

Separating Feelings and Intentions from Behavior and Outcomes

In the process of altering ways of thinking that inhibit negotiation, it is important to help spouses learn to separate feelings and intentions from behavior and outcomes. A spouse often assumes that because he or she feels angry, the behavior that provoked this was done intentionally, for example: "You deliberately talked to that other woman to make me jealous!" It is crucial to recognize that feelings often distort the logical process and the interpretations of behavior, which cause the spouse to assume erroneously that a certain behavior was intentional. Using the example above, the husband may have talked to the other woman for many reasons besides trying to make the partner jealous. The therapist must be diligent in making spouses more critical of their assumptions about their partners' intentions, especially when strong feelings are involved.

One of the most commonly encountered examples is the spouse who insists that the partner deliberately withholds sex as punishment. Although in some cases this may be true, more often there is so much tension between the couple that the partner does not want to engage in sex. It is hard to feel stimulated when one feels angry, distant, depressed, or afraid to become involved lest one be hurt again. A spouse is likely to feel even greater pain and harbor more resentments if behavior by the partner is considered deliberate, as the following interchange illustrates:

> [The husband has just told the wife that he believes she tries to punish him for his inadequacies.]
>
> H: I'm trying to work that through, and it compounds it when you toss in the cruel disapproval—something that really hurts.
>
> [The wife denies that she has any intention of hurting him, but her husband is disbelieving.]
>
> H: How do I believe that?
>
> W: I agree with you that there are a lot of things about you that I've not accepted and I realize it, but I've never intentionally tried to do anything to hurt you.
>
> [To substantiate his point, the husband recounts the many times his wife was inconsiderate of his needs.]
>
> T: There's a difference in her doing that intentionally to hurt you and your not liking it, and it being inconsiderate.

H: I thought it was intentional, because I always just let her
     know how I just thought it was highly inconsiderate.

W: It was immature; I regret it like hell now. I guess that's
     where we disagree—I never once said I'm going to stay
     out tonight not because I really want to but because this
     is a way of making you feel bad.

H: Was there never an emphasis on, "I'm going to stay out
     'cause I don't want to . . . go home to him"?

T: Even if that were there, it wouldn't still be under the
     heading you're putting it under—she was doing it to
     hurt you. It may have been she was reacting to some ten-
     sions, but that still is not the same as doing it deliberately
     to hurt you.

H: But I disagree because it kept happening over and over
     again, over and over.

T: What do you disagree with?

H: That it wasn't intentional.

T: I think what you're saying is you couldn't get through to
     her how important it was to you for her to hear *your*
     needs and see what that [her behavior] was doing.

H: Right! Which means I was a nobody—I didn't count . . .
     it didn't matter what I thought or felt.

Because of the intensity of the hurt, it was difficult for the husband to understand that each spouse, albeit in different ways, may
hurt the other—not on purpose, but out of their own frustrations
and unmet needs. Although this does not justify such behavior or
make it less painful, if a spouse can begin to view it as an attempt at
problem-solving, it may lessen the hurt and make the spouse less
prone to interpret the behavior as intentional and related to an
inadequacy of the spouse.

A variation of this is that a spouse thinks that because he or
she feels a particular way in response to the partner, the partner
should change his or her own behavior. For example, a husband was
angry with the wife over some past extramarital relations and was
attempting to control her behavior with his hurt and angry feelings.

The therapist said that he had a right to fully inform his wife of his feelings, but that efforts to dictate what she should and should not do would only compound the problem. In other words he was justified in letting her know his pain, anger, and degree of tolerance for such behavior, but that was as far as he could constructively go. It was up to his wife to decide what she would do as a result. The husband's response was, "But how can I get rid of these feelings?" This is a very difficult task to help a spouse accomplish. The only way he could conceive of not having these feelings was to insure that the behavior that caused the pain did not occur. And to insure this, he resorted to various controlling and coercive measures as attempting to decide choice of friends and how time away from home was spent. Although this behavior is understandable, in these situations the spouse must be helped to see that he cannot control the other's behavior and therefore through this means eliminate his pain (in fact, controlling efforts may bring on more pain), and to be responsible for himself for working through the pain. There is no immediate or external escape from the feelings, and the spouse needs to know that the discomfort can be endured and eventually overcome. In this case, the therapist must also challenge the assumption that there is only one way to deal with such feelings and help the husband see that forcing the wife to behave as he wanted neither eliminated the feelings nor altered his wife's behavior; in fact, it increased marital friction and the probability of the undesired outcome. The paradox is that in striving to avoid something, people often increase its likelihood.

Feelings do not dictate a specific course of action. Although spouses often do not experience this, there are choices open. In the above case, it was necessary to help the husband see that he could not eliminate his feelings of distrust through forceful efforts. One hope for him is that such feelings usually diminish as the partner exhibits trustworthy behaviors. Beyond the need to assist him in better tolerating the pain, the therapist must help him understand that he can best spend his efforts toward bettering the relationship, thus making it less likely that his wife will engage in the behaviors so painful to him. Although both tasks are hard and do not provide immediate relief, they constitute the best solution.

It is interesting to note that changing behaviors may decrease friction between a couple (which will have some benefits), but it will not necessarily change feelings. This does not negate the importance of working to change objectionable behaviors but points up its limitations in dealing with the hurt. In the above case, since the extramarital activity had ceased, we can infer that an early disturbance in basic trust predisposed this spouse to having continuous doubts and that problems in this area will have to be resolved before trust in the wife can be successfully established.

For the accused spouse, who feels trust can never be regained with the partner, there is frequently the temptation to say, "I might as well go ahead again; I'll never be trusted anyway." The point should be made that the choice and responsibility resides in the self, not in the distrusting partner. If the accused spouse wishes to increase trust, he or she should focus on what can be done in the present and over time and to explore how one can make the mate's feelings more positive.

In addition, individuals may need to learn a tolerance for less than absolute trust, since trust is often experienced in an all or none fashion. Perhaps the husband can never again achieve the degree of trust or confidence he once had in the wife, but this does not preclude bettering the relationship in the present and, indeed, achieving a satisfactory one.

Expectations from Marriage

In the course of working with spouses, the therapist often discerns implicit, or even explicit, expectations about what marriage should be like or what a "good husband" or "good wife" should or should not do. Along with our other values, mores, and morals, we have all formed culturally determined attitudes regarding our mate and the roles that spouses play in marriage. The unfortunate part of these expectations is that they often have a low probability of fulfillment. Whenever one becomes aware of these untenable beliefs in therapy, a constructive educational stance must be taken to show what is thought to be realistic.

One expectation is that things should stay the way they were in the early days of the marriage. Changes in the relationship cause strain, and spouses often struggle against accepting reality and its inevitable changes. This is illustrated in the following comments:

> [The wife has been talking about the changes in the way her husband talks with her and treats her now compared with when they were beginning their relationship.]

H: At that time, I came to see you or called you. I wasn't with you twenty-four hours a day.

W: That's what I'm saying. I liked the way it was—it was fine with me the way it was. I really liked it, and I thought that that was the way it was going to be, and O.K., well, now it's changed, and I have to readjust and understand how it is now.

T: What you're talking about is that during the courtship days the way of relating to each other was different than what happened when you were married, and part of that has to do with being together all the time.

W: Yes, and it changed then, and it's constantly changing and changing more often than I thought it would, and [my] not being prepared for it . . . not knowing what it is . . .

H: But now we are two people in the world, like I love you and want you to be my wife the rest of my years.

W: What it seems like you're saying to me is, "You're my wife. I love you, but we are two separate people. Let's keep it that way. Let's just have a small relationship with some depth, but not too much depth between us."

H: I love you, but I do not want to be with you twenty-four hours every day.

W: What time do you want to spend with me?

H: I love to spend a lot of time with you, but I don't want to have to say I have to be here with you these many hours.

It is obvious that much has happened to change this relationship, and the wife is struggling hard with her disillusionment. The therapist tells them that things are different now than they were in the past, and that it would be profitable for them to pursue a discussion of where things are now, what they want from each other, what they can and cannot accept, and what they are and are not willing to do. In other words, the therapist is suggesting a renegotiation and redefinition of the relationship.

> H: I just want you to love me and accept me for what I am . . . just take me for what I am, if you will accept me. You married me, I guess, because you loved me. I am still that same person. I have changed some. I have matured some, and my mind is in a different place now . . . and you know what I want out of life . . . I want you to help and not hinder me.

In these brief excerpts we can see that the therapist has just begun to guide them toward the mammoth task of working out the basics of a new relationship. Before this can be done, the spouses need to accept the reality of their disillusionment, mourn for and give up their loss, and move to a new willingness to find new solutions for a more gratifying marriage in the present.

A second expectation of marriage, related to the first, is the belief that one should be able to maintain, or at least recapture, the honeymoon. For example, approximately seven sessions into therapy, after some initial gains had been made, a wife commented on the improvement in her marriage but wondered if things would ever be like they were in the beginning; she referred to the "romantic glow" of their early marriage. The therapist replied, "No, things probably will never be like they were in your courtship days, but that is unrealistic to expect." The therapist went on to contrast the early years with the heavier responsibilities of the couple's life now with children and the accumulated tension between them as a couple. The freedom that each had, which enabled them to give to each other previously, is difficult to achieve now. Lest this have been discouraging, the therapist tried to replay for the wife some of the things she values now in her marriage, which were the product of long years of work together. The therapist also emphasized what the couple could hope to achieve through further therapeutic work. The focus was on realistic versus unrealistic hopes.

The perennial honeymoon does not exist. If most couples are honest, they will acknowledge this; occasionally, under special circumstances, some of the romance and glamour can be recaptured, but not every day. Some couples combat the routine, sometimes monotonous nature of everyday life by going off to a motel on occasion without the kids and responsibilities, to savor their love and the meaningfulness it holds for them. Couples can find other ways to regain some of that long lost ecstasy, such as the change of scenery and the break in routine offered by vacations or special outings.

Beyond the legitimacy of pleasurable moments, however, it is important to help spouses learn the value of day-to-day living. Although not exciting, loyalty, caring, and respect for both the spouse and the children are not to be undervalued. A task common to couple therapy and individual therapy is helping individuals give up their hope for reunion with an all-powerful, all-knowing, and all-giving parent who will forever love, protect, and administer solely to them.

Another unrealistic expectation that spouses often have is the belief that, "If you really love me, then you would intuitively know what I want, need, and expect, and will do all in your power to make sure that my needs are met." This expectation often arises out of the unconscious assumption that the mate is part of the self, and thus there is no need for verbal communication. The more this is so, the less effective a cognitive approach will be; other measures will be necessary. It is crucial to correct this expectation, since it often interferes with the therapist's efforts to help spouses state their needs, a primary task in couple treatment. Although one can agree that spontaneous recognition and anticipation of the needs is gratifying and that it would be preferable not to have to make a request for every desire, it is unrealistic to expect that one should never have to express one's needs or dissatisfactions. Our observation is that the ideal is far from what one should anticipate. In the first place, we are not dealing with just the wishes of one person but of two, who may have conflicting needs. Furthermore, failure to fulfill a desire may occur for many reasons, none of which necessarily convey the message, "I don't love you." One must help couples see that each spouse is trying to take care of the self as he or she functions in the various roles of parent, lover, and worker. It is no wonder that a spouse will not know the partner's every desire, or be able or willing to respond to it. In most marriages, a spouse will anticipate and fulfill the partner's desires without a reminder or request some of the time; at other times spouses will have to "take up the mantle" and "do battle" for their own satisfactions and needs.

Our advice to spouses is that if some important needs are not being met, it is each spouse's personal responsibility to bring them to the attention of the mate. To sit back in silence and wait, only to be disappointed, hurt, and disillusioned time and again, when one can make an active effort to achieve one's goal, is a grave mistake. When a spouse feels neglected sexually, for example, the therapist should encourage the spouse to initiate sex and to make known to the spouse how important this is. Of course, the spouse should check this out with the partner to see how it would be received. If it is well received, so much the better. If not, then it is incumbent on the spouse to negotiate with the partner to see what may be done for more receptivity.

Another common expectation is that spouses should be alike if marital harmony is to be achieved. When marriage goes sour, spouses often see their problems in terms of their differences: "Our problem is that we're just so different"; "He's affectionate and I'm more reserved"; or "She's more serious and I'm more carefree." One can take several different approaches when presented with the problem of differences, which is serious to spouses, since the opposite nature of their personal characteristics makes it seem inevitable that they cannot get along. The therapist can start by agreeing with them about their differences; in fact, one might go on to say that these very differences probably had something to do with their initial attraction to each other. Then one can encourage the couple to explore what it was that attracted them to each other. What usually emerges is that the very characteristics that are now viewed negatively were the same characteristics, or are at least related to the same characteristics, that were initially so captivating. For example, one spouse commented, "I think that the things you liked most when we met, you have really picked on and undermined my confidence in." These points are illustrated further in the following interchange, in which a couple were talking about their reasons for marrying:

W: I thought I was marrying someone who was really very stable—that I could count on like a rock.

H: Why did I get so much disapproval from you if I was what you wanted? I got the impression from you that I was unstable.

W: What I meant when I said stable was I could count on you. You weren't guilty of some of the things you're afraid I'll do in running off here and there.

H: Well, that's very strange, because I've got the feeling all through the years that you haven't liked the way I've been stable . . . that you found all that too compulsive and too inhibiting, and that you wanted me to be more carefree . . . but you married me for the things I thought you didn't like!

In exploring this, the wife clarified what seemed confusing to her husband. Indeed, she was attracted to him because of his stability and dependability, and she still valued these. However, some of the offshoots of these traits, which tended to make their style of living conservative, were irksome to her. It is important for the husband to be able to make this distinction, lest he feel that he is being completely rejected. This method allows spouses to explore specific behaviors that would be more mutually gratifying.

From this point, one can go in two different directions. One is to view the negatively viewed behavior in terms of the whole personality, which was originally viewed positively. As seen above, what is perceived positively, strength and reliability, may be allied with rigidity and compulsiveness, which are seen as objectionable. However, one can point out that if the spouse had chosen a mate who was more impulsive and changeable, this person might not have been as reliable. In other words, one tries to help the spouse see the personality from a larger perspective and accept the inevitability of some behaviors occurring together, all of which will not be equally valued. To get some things of value, we may have to give up other things; we cannot have our wish for the ideal person.

A second direction is to state that it is not the fact that a couple are different that is "the problem"; in fact, differences in spouses are the rule. Our cultural conditioning has shaped many differences between the sexes, many of which are highly recurrent. Men and women learn different roles and different ways to deal with stress. It is often important to point out the importance of our cultural-familial upbringing:

W: I don't cry that much, but I do cry when it gets to the point that the situation gets where I can't handle it. I don't know how to handle it, and I'm distressed—it's an outlet.

T: You don't have to apologize for your crying. You have a right to cry if you feel like it.

W: [To husband] You remember that!

T: [To husband] Just like you have a right to rage; women cry more than men, and men curse and rage more, so she has a right to cry and you have a right to beat on the walls and curse. You've learned a different reaction, and part of it is because you're different sexes.

The ways in which couples are usually alike is with regard to such characteristics as education, intelligence, and socioeconomic level. Our contention is that it is not personality differences that are the problem; they would exist no matter what mate one might pick. What a person chooses to do about the differences is what counts. (As George Bach has said, "It's not conflict, but conflict management.") We have come back to the core of therapy—how to help people learn ways of resolving differences without hating each other.

Another misconception by couples, which they espouse behaviorally if not verbally, is the feeling that they should spend all of their free time together. One should try to work toward underlining the separateness of the couple, and the rights of each to use free time for projects or for involvements which may not include or even be valued by the mate. Each spouse has not only a right but also a responsibility to the self to set aside some time for self-interests. Feeling compelled to always do things together can only lead to resentment and anger. To minimize guilt, the therapist can stress each individual's rights and needs, giving this equal weight to each spouse's respecting the rights and needs of the fellow spouse; the therapist should also work toward both spouses being able to accept some degree of separateness as both desirable and healthy. In the process, the therapist can substitute the negative connotations ("He or she doesn't want to be with me") with positive ones; that spouses have differing needs, which, if respected, will lead to more satisfaction for both of them, and that for one not to always want to be with the other is not a bad but good thing, although it may present problems at times for the partner. Such behaviors do not necessarily indicate a lack of caring, which is the assumption often made.

This issue is illustrated in the following excerpt:

H: I want you to be your own person, and I don't want you to do anything or be anything because of me. I really worry about you some because I'm the way I am. You know I've got my things that I do. Well, a lot of things that I do don't include you.

W: That's good, you should be . . .

H: But I feel guilty, you see, because when I don't include you in things that I do and you don't do anything . . .

W: I do things.

H: Yeah, you sit at home all the time. I feel really bad about that.

T: [To wife] Do you work?

[The wife responds that she does work, but that during evenings, if her husband has to work overtime, she frequently goes over to someone's house. But sometimes she does not like to go out and prefers to stay home.]

H: I just don't want you sitting. I don't want to feel guilty when I do things without you, I guess. I don't want to have to feel guilty because I'm not doing something with you, and the way that I will not feel guilty is for you to be doing something without me. Sometimes when I'm off, I want to play golf or something, and I feel guilt when I

do it, because you're saying you don't care if I go, but
you do. You always say, "Why don't you stay home?"
I always know that you want me to stay there. I guess I
would not feel guilty if you were sitting home knitting
or something. If you would say, "I'm going to do so and
so or such and such," I guess I wouldn't feel so guilty
about what I do. I do a lot with you. You know we do a lot
together, but we don't too, and I don't want to feel guilty
when I go do something without you. Because the only
way I don't feel guilty is for you to be doing something,
because . . . at the same time, I guess. Sometimes we
could be home together and you say, "Well, I'll see you.
I'm going somewhere." You never do that. Well, you
could say, "I've got to get over to do this," or "I want to
do this," and let me sit home, and I probably wouldn't feel
so guilty about what I do. When I feel guilty, that makes
me feel even worse about things.

[The wife comments that she does not have that many
things that she is interested in doing away from home.]

T: Let me interject something here. [To wife] Of course, it
would be convenient if you did have some of these going
interests that worked out just the way you wanted it; that
would be perfect. But I think if you [the husband] put
pressure on her to do things, that she can experience
this just as much as a burden as you experience that you
shouldn't go out and play golf. I think you sort of have to
wrestle with your feelings and make your decisions independent of what she chooses to do. In other words, you
do have the right to spend some time out doing something that makes sense to you, and I think you need to
make that decision and do it. You may have to struggle a
little with the feelings, but I think it's better to do it that
way and then let her make her decision independently
of how you choose to spend your time, if you're not
there . . . so that she doesn't feel the burden that she's
got to go out to relieve you of the guilt. You may have to
struggle with that yourself. You see, you can put an equal

pressure back on her. Each of you has the right to some time of your own to spend the way you wish.

[The husband says that one of the problems is that he does not have much free time left over from work. The therapist acknowledges the limits of time and goes on to emphasize the rights of each for some time to use as they decide, independent of what the other person feels or is doing. The therapist also tries to point out realistic limitations.]

T: [To wife] And then I think you will have to struggle with your feelings that you can't have all of him, and there's not too much left over when he gets through, and maybe it would be great if you could, but the reality is that he would come to resent it.

W: Sure he would, I would.

[The therapist goes on to encourage the wife to make her decision independent of her husband. If that includes sitting home twiddling her thumbs, this is her choice and should be in terms of her needs and not to alleviate his guilt.]

W: I guess I feel like when people get married they're supposed to spend all this time together and stuff. I guess that's the concept I had.

T: On the whole, I think people have a lot of misconceptions about what you both "should" do when you get married. Some of these notions you find out quickly in reality don't work. You know, like you should be together all the time . . . I don't know where we get all these "shoulds," you know, they're in the air. Everybody picks them up about what they're "supposed" to do, but I keep hearing you [to wife] use that word, and I wondered if you were aware of that, how much of this is in terms of what you should do, rather than what you want or what your husband wants, or what makes sense for the two of you, because that's where it is. What can you two live with comfortably so that you don't make each other feel guilty or burdened or where you're not close enough?

Perhaps the problem of time together is directly related to the misguided notion that one can get everything one needs from one's marital partner. A major therapeutic task is to get spouses to give up this unrealistic, infantile belief. As one spouse commented, "I just don't think I have to be able to talk with you about everything. One time I thought I did, primarily because I supposed you were the other person who . . . we had kind of made this little cohesive unit that I thought was going to suffice for the rest of the world, and I don't think that is realistic." Along with these comments, the spouse acknowledged some sadness at the loss, an appropriate feeling that usually accompanies acknowledging unrealistic notions, and recognized that she would have to reach out more to others.

There is no way that any one person can meet all the wishes of another. Desires and needs accompanied by the notion that one deserves to have what one wants must be acknowledged for what they are—archaic feelings and wishes from the past which impede realistic expectations in the present. Once spouses can accept this, one can stress the importance of diversifying ways in which each spouse gains satisfaction, lest they be overly dependent on each other and accrue resentments. This is not to say that they should not expect some of their desires to be met; expectations that some needs be satisfied are both legitimate and appropriate. The difficulty is when expectations exceed realistic possibilities (and this, of course, varies with spouses). The persistence of infantile fantasies presents major, and sometimes insurmountable, obstacles to achieving mutuality in the relationship.

We would be remiss if we did not mention a cluster of common problems associated with spouse roles. Expectations are often widely divergent between spouses on how each should fulfill the role of husband or wife. With the changing nature of the family and of spouses' roles, discontent with traditional, culturally determined roles has increased, especially with women, who are making bold efforts to forge new roles for themselves. This often creates havoc between spouses, especially if one maintains a more traditional role.

One of the difficult problems, often seen with younger couples, emerges when the wife does not work but resents and feels burdened by having total responsibility for the household. On the other hand, the husband, regardless of his attitude towards the wife's role, often feels that since he is engaged for many hours at work, his wife should be able to get the housework done. As one husband expressed it:

> H: Now you have forty hours a week keeping it [the house] up. I feel angry because I feel that, you know, you're not working, you're not doing anything except like buying groceries, cooking meals, and cleaning up, and yet for some reason that seems to be more than you can accomplish.

Although, on the surface, the husband presents a reasonable, logical point of view, from his wife's perspective the matter is quite different:

> W: I think that he feels like because I'm not working, I should do everything. In addition, I hate housework as bad as you do.

The wife then detailed how her husband is unaware of much of what she does and how many things she does just for him. One can see that the resolution of this division of labor dispute is not easy because of the lack of awareness as to kind and amount of time involved in activities and the comparisons as to their importance. What usually happens is that the couple begin to criticize each other for their failures to hold up to their past agreements, and working out new solutions becomes an uphill battle.

Another problem is that a spouse (often the husband), in his disgruntledness at his wife's perceived failure to keep the house up, is prone to do one of two things—both of which are bound to compound their problems. One is to criticize the spouse for the way a job is done; for example, one husband's complaint about his wife's housekeeping was that she was not organized. Complaints disguised as "how-to" suggestions can be equally irritating, since they carry the same message that the wife is not capable of doing the job without help. Spouses do not take kindly to such comments, and they frequently derail efforts to work out an agreement on the division of labor. Secondly, to add insult to injury is the husband who goes one step further to point out how much better he could do the job in less time. ("I have the feeling that if I were running the house, just me, if I wasn't working . . . I could accomplish a lot more in a day's time than you . . .")

One of the therapist's tasks is to help couples focus on working out the labor dispute and to point out that criticisms and comparisons will undermine the negotiating. Most spouses do not want suggestions, but active participation in sharing tasks.

> T: Why don't you talk to him now about what you think that you two could agree on that would be a fair split of the workload in the house? See if you two can reach some kind of agreement about what would be fair to both of you.

It is essential that the therapist help the couple check out with each other the acceptability of suggested proposals, lest one spouse agree and later resent it. This does not mean they have to like the work, but that they do not feel coerced.

> T: [To husband] What I hear your wife saying is that she feels like maybe she would be willing to do—[To wife] you correct me if I'm wrong—you might be willing to do more things if you thought he was holding up more his end of the job?
>
> W: I never thought of it as exactly like that, but sometimes when I try to do things and he complains, I would be more receptive to complaints and suggestions if I felt like he was.

In this case, the couple had spent some time dividing up household chores. Further complaints from this session illustrate other previous points:

> T: [To husband] You might be able to do it in less time, but that is irrelevant. You're very different people; you cannot expect your wife to do what you could do.

W: [To husband] Your standards are a lot different from mine about what you want done, so that's no good.

H: I guess it is unfair of me to say that I could do it in such and such a way.

T: Well, I don't know if it's "unfair," but you can be sure how your wife is going to hear it . . . she'll hear it as a criticism or put-down.

H: I think the hard thing is just saying I've got to accept that it's irrelevant whether I could accomplish more or different things, because I think that's something that I've very much been doing is saying that I could accomplish this much in a given period of time and that's the major complaint really. I'm saying you're not accomplishing what I would have accomplished, and I want you to do it the way I want it done.

T: She can't be you, there's no way.

Pressures by a spouse for the other to live up to a set of standards and expectations weighs heavily on someone who is already struggling with low feelings of self-worth. Here again, the therapist must work toward maximizing separateness and helping spouses to establish their own standards and to find ways to feel better about themselves:

T: Maybe you want some feeling that he's not always perfect or that he can transgress too, or whatever. But if you could feel better about yourself, you won't have to worry about whether he is perfect, imperfect, 100 percent, medium, or whatever he is; he is—that's him. But you're you, and you're a different person. You don't have to ultimately live up to *his* standards . . . but if you're going to be married, you do have to hear what is important to him, just as he has to hear what is important to you.

What may be an equally difficult problem is for spouses to let go of their criteria of how a job should be done, once the mate has agreed to take it over. At this point it is essentially the mate's responsibility to decide how it is to be done, even if it is not done to the other's satisfaction. If the work agreement is to function, each must be responsible for his or her own jobs without interference.

Sometimes it becomes apparent in therapy that the original rules and assumptions about role expectations that were worked out early in marriage are no longer working. People change, and what they expect from marriage is also likely to change, although they may continue to operate by their original rules. When discrepancies become apparent, it is useful to focus on this, so that renegotiation can occur:

T: Obviously, you had some, as you say, "inexplicitly," some expectations you both were not agreeing on. What I hear you saying is that, correct me if I'm wrong, you might like to renegotiate with just exactly what kind of, using your word, "responsibilities," what kind of commitments you're each willing to make and then perhaps working with it explicitly, so you both know where you stand. Do I hear you correctly as saying you are not sure you want to go by some of the old expectations?

W: I think that we haven't been, and I think this is probably . . .

T: Are you saying you don't want to?

W: I say, I know, yes, yes, I am saying I do not want to [go by old expectations].

T: O.K., say that quite clearly to your husband, so he knows where you stand. [To husband] In some way or another the rules that you are playing by, she wants to change. Am I correct now?

W: Yes.

T: O.K., it's going to be important to talk about what these are so you both know where you stand.

[The work proceeds to establish new rules.]

T: So what I hear you saying, correct me if I'm wrong, to your husband is you want a new rule now where there's kind of sharing the household and "It is as much his thing to do as mine."

W: Yes, and it's as much my responsibility as his.

In this case the wife was pushing for more equality in household responsibilities. Since the husband did not find this too distasteful and was willing to assume more responsibilities than he had previously, renegotiating was possible.

Another difficult problem for some couples is when the wife does not find home and family sufficiently satisfying. Although many wives work because the household needs the additional income, it is sometimes hard for husbands to accept their working for other reasons, especially for men who have grown up in families where the wife's sole function was to be a homemaker. They feel that it reflects their own shortcomings if marriage and family cannot suffice. As one husband commented, "I really don't feel she enjoys me and the kids 'cause that identifies her as a married woman, and she wants to be a career woman." It is interesting that an assumption of causality is made (a wife cannot enjoy a family if she wants a career). It does not, of course, follow that a need for a career precludes enjoying a family; both interests can be present and often are. The discontent that some married women feel who do not work and who feel their identity is only in terms of their husbands is expressed well by the woman quoted below.

T: What's left out for you. What's missing for you?

W: Any real sense of worth for me.

T: So what I hear you saying is *not* knocking your husband, which is the way I hear you [to husband] have been interpreting it, but saying, "I need to be 'put up' 'cause I'm not doing anything to advance me."

Another wife stated her discontent more sharply:

W: I've always wanted to do something more with my life than what I am doing now . . . something that was mine, that you [to husband] didn't have anything to do with, and I really get angry when I think about that—that I want something that is all mine . . . something that I can feel good about and know that you had absolutely nothing to do with.

It is important for the therapist to help the husband not hear the wife's desire as a disparagement of him but as expressing a lack of fulfillment that one should not necessarily expect to be found at home. It is equally important to help the wife feel the appropriateness of wanting and going after satisfactions that cannot be fulfilled by the family.

> T: I feel you have a need beyond monetary consideration, above and beyond being a wife, and that's the part that is probably hardest for you [the husband] to hear, because you would like for you and the children to be enough.
>
> [In further comments, it was clear that the wife's self-worth was tied up in functioning in roles beyond the wife and mother ones, with an additional need to feel less guilty for spending money without contributing to the family income.]

Another wife expressed her feelings quite graphically about fulfilling the husband's expectations of her family role, which she had incorporated to an extent into her attitudes of how wives "should be." "I feel really trapped and hemmed in. I feel when he and I are together, especially in public, I have no opportunity to, or even right to, talk to people and make my own friends, [to husband] because I was always your shadow and right by your side . . . and I felt that you felt that that's where I should be, and sometimes I enjoyed it and sometimes I didn't."

The issue illustrated in the above example is the problem of how much time a wife has a right to, to do some things she enjoys without her husband or kids. This can be interpreted negatively by both husband and wife—as selfish by the wife, if her superego is harsh, or as insulting by the husband. Women lacking self-worth will especially feel the pressure to find means beyond the family to boost their feelings; they will find taking a "back seat," as they experience it, as deleterious to their well-being. Out of this context spring numerous competitive feelings as the wife fights to acquire more space that is hers alone. But this same spouse may struggle equally with guilt feelings that she will inevitably hurt her husband and children, even break up the family.

As couples struggle to align role expectations, they frequently attempt to elicit from the therapist a stand as to who is "right." The therapist must make it clear that values are relative and vary immensely among individuals, and what is important for the couple is their views and values, and how they can work out solutions to points of friction. It is not important whether the therapist thinks the husband should do yardwork and the wife the cooking. Their solution may be one totally unacceptable to the majority of society, but this is irrelevant; what is important is that they agree upon a solution that they can live with comfortably. This is a relativistic stance that we have found most conducive to individual growth and marital harmony.

Extramarital Affairs and Vendettas

Directly related to unrealistic expectations of marriage is the matter of extramarital affairs. This is an age of experimentation with relationships—which we are in favor of. However, we think that extramarital affairs are ultimately detrimental to marriage unless they are agreed upon, experienced, and agreed upon again. (Many spouses, in their intellectual liberalism, endorse "open marriage" prior to experiencing it, only to find out that the actual experience evokes feelings of jealousy, competitiveness, and anger.) These affairs can remove involvement and the motivation to negotiate, while stimulating unrealistic expectations. A major therapeutic task will be to alter these patterns of thinking. It's easy to recapture romance in a brief, stolen evening with wine by candlelight in front of the fire, where none of the pressing problems of everyday living intrude and where the couple can pour all of their energy solely into pleasing each other. Affairs are intensive—marriage extensive. Marriage, in terms of romantic charm, cannot compete with an affair. Thus, the person having the affair adds to marital discontent and drains off energy that could be directed toward improving the relationship. The predilection to turn to a lover for reassurance and nurturance at times of tension between spouses works against the spouse's focusing on the problems constructively, negotiating around them, and learning to deal with pain.

An equally important hazard to marriage posed by extramarital affairs is the dissolution of trust on which most relationships are based. Once an affair has occurred, spouses struggle over and over again with the issue, "How can I ever trust you again?" The injury to the spouse is one that does not heal rapidly, especially to an individual who is extremely vulnerable. The incredible faith and blind trust that a spouse can build up in a partner may be a counterphobic maneuver against the possibility that hurts may happen again. If this does occur, the blow can be devastating. As one spouse said, "It's a destruction of my expectations of what we had and a blow to my trust in you." Another stated, "It's grief, it's a loss, it makes me feel like I'm at his funeral, like he has left me, it's just as if he had."

We discourage extramarital affairs for couples who want to improve their relationship, not on a moralistic basis, but because it decreases the likelihood of resolving existing problems. We try to help spouses determine what the price of an extramarital relationship will be, without telling them what they should do with regard to continuing the affair.

In some cases, infidelity springs not from any individual pathology but from dissatisfactions originating in the marital relationship. In these cases, work toward communicating dissatisfactions and efforts at negotiating are in order. An important part of the work is to help the other partner communicate to the spouse what the impact of the infidelity is and how this deters, through discouragement and anger, making any changes that may be desired by the spouse having the affair. One hopes to help both spouses see more clearly how each is contributing to dissatisfactions, so that they will be more knowledgeable about what it will take to improve the marriage. Additionally, one hopes to encourage them to find an alternative to infidelity, if they care enough about the marriage and are willing to make the required efforts.

Occasionally, we have encountered a couple in which the spouse having an affair claims to not know which mate he or she prefers and wants to maintain the extramarital affair because of this indecision. In most of these cases, this is not an honest statement; the spouse does know—both are wanted; the problem is that the marriage partner protests so much that the spouse cannot maintain both wants peacefully and feels forced to choose. It is useful to redirect the spouse to consider how realistic his or her wants are and how well they can be met in the marriage. No matter how overdetermined the needs, at some point the spouse will have to face the impact of his or her behavior on the partner.

One of the most destructive behaviors that we have encountered is the spouse who continually confronts the mate with the advantages the extramarital partner has over the mate. Inevitably, this creates intense resentments and minimizes chances for the mate to be willing to work on the marriage relationship. The mate is less likely to try to understand why the partner feels the need for the extra relationship and to be less willing to explore together what can be done to minimize this need. The mate who feels unfavorably compared and blackmailed when the spouse says, "If you don't meet such and such standards, I will continue with the affair," will rarely be willing to change. Whether defensive or not, the anger and bitterness that result usually dominate all other feelings.

Equally counterproductive is the spouse who uses guilt-inducing techniques to stop the affair. Although such techniques may work, they often breed resentments, which, in turn, interfere with mending the marriage. Where possible, it is the therapist's task to help spouses understand how to communicate their feelings and dissatisfactions in a way most likely to effect the cessation of the affair.

Prior to the interchange below, the wife had been barraging the husband with guilt-inducing comments. She had questioned how her husband could behave as he did when she was such a wonderful wife to him; she stressed his trying to hurt her (her reading of malevolent intentions was strong) and that he was "shitty" to do such a thing.

> T: Let me try to make a point that might be of some use to you. When I listen to you talk and hear you talking about what he has done to you, I think it would be much easier for him to hear if he didn't hear it in terms of what he is *trying* to do . . . anything that implies he is doing something bad, wrong, or whatever—stay away from evaluating him and talk about the effect on you.
>
> [The therapist goes on to say that the wife may "hook" her husband's guilt by statements about what he should not do, but that this will also produce resentments.]
>
> T: He is going to have to make his decision on other bases than guilt—otherwise, it is not going to go.

W: Yeah, that's what I hear him saying he cannot do at this point, is get away from the guilt, because it has been put on him.

H: [To wife] You know, I may be hearing you all wrong, but I think you want me to feel guilty, because that gets you partly what you want.

Note that the husband has probably read his wife's use of guilt-inducing techniques correctly. What she is not considering and what will be a responsibility of the therapist to help her see is that these efforts will not improve the marriage, even though her husband may give up extramarital relationships. His anger and resentment will affect many areas of their lives. Further comments by the therapist illustrated to the wife how she might respond differently to her husband to maximize her influence and minimize her controlling, guilt-inducing techniques.

T: Now, I don't know whether in your mind you are saying, "I'm going to make him feel guilty," but I do know that the way you talk about it, inevitably it's going to hook his guilt. And I know that you have some power to change that.

W: Just say I'm hurting and I'm crying inside.

T: Yeah, I think you need to communicate your pain—that it really makes it dreadfully miserable and unhappy. Now some guilt is going to get going over here [to husband] anyway because of him. You won't, you can't do everything to alleviate it . . . but you can help on this one issue by the kind of things you say to him, which means leaving out the "shoulds" a good deal. You could help him in another way by saying to him, "I understand that you are trying to find some way to get some things for yourself. I am hurting, but I do understand that. It's not just because you're some horrible man who wants to make me suffer."

Obviously, this is not all the wife needs to communicate—the limits of her tolerance and her decision about how she will choose to live will have to be explored by her and eventually shared with her husband, depending on his decision. It will be important for her to decide carefully if she is willing to live under the existing circumstances and then to make this clear—not on the basis of right or wrong, but on the basis of how she wishes to live. The issue really has little to do with right or wrong in any rule-oriented, moralistic sense; basically, it is what each can and is willing to live with—and the therapist can help them determine this.

The points above are made to stress the importance of eliminating guilt-inducing maneuvers as a means to control extramarital relationships. It is often necessary (and this sometimes can be worked on more readily in individual sessions) to assist the spouse having the affair to understand more clearly the nature of his or her own dissatisfactions. In many cases, although there are reasons for being dissatisfied with the partner, the extramarital affair is an effort to meet deficiencies in areas outside marriage. The greater the extent of unmet needs and lack of satisfaction in nonmarital life, the heavier the burden upon the marriage; and it becomes more likely that the partner will be held responsible for this. The erroneous conclusion often reached is that an affair with another person will alleviate the dissatisfactions; although an extramarital relationship may meet some of the spouse's unmet needs, it usually will not resolve all of the original problems. Particularly because the extramarital affair often places such a heavy burden upon the marriage and usually is not a tenable solution for resolving unmet needs, one must help the individual explore the self from a broader perspective, and if necessary, encourage individual therapy.

Unconscious determinants may stymie efforts to deal with extramarital philandering on any realistic, logical basis. For example, failure with a major developmental task occurring early in life may be responsible for this. In the ordinary course of events, the infant eventually realizes that both good and bad things are experienced with the same person (the mother who gives nurture is the same person who allows the infant to experience distress before tending it). Whenever the distress is overwhelming and the good is less dominant, fusing the attribution of good and bad experiences into one person does not occur. Individuals with this developmental defect are inevitably disappointed with whatever partner they choose and continuously search for the good mother. This kind of problem, although not hopeless, presents major obstacles to couple therapy, since no amount of external change by the marital partner will alter what is an internal problem. Because good and bad are maintained as separate qualities, they cannot be perceived in the same person for long. It is crucial to recognize the underlying dynamics in this kind of problem to determine the possibility for success of the ways one chooses to work. In this case, individual therapy would be warranted.

Because infidelity occurs for so many reasons, the therapeutic approach may well have to consider the many behavioral determinants and vary the therapeutic techniques accordingly.

Although not the only factor, extramarital relationships are a major source of spouses maintaining anger and being unwilling to forget the past. This may occur in couples even after a partner ceases such relationships. This is a difficult problem to tackle. Often it has its roots in disappointments and anger from earlier developmental stages which must be worked through before the present situation can be improved.

One approach is to help a spouse understand more fully the need to hold on to anger. If the spouse can be encouraged to encounter anger experientally and to explore its varying determinants then some progress can be achieved. Sometimes to forgive and forget is experienced as condoning the feared behavior, which is the last thing the spouse wishes to do. Continued anger can also serve as a constant reminder to the spouse not to go astray; if one lets up, then the event may recur. Related but different is the conviction that feelings of anger and efforts at control serve as a protection—to let go would be to expose one's self to further transgressions and to be vulnerable again. Thus one tries to stave off further hurts by various angry behaviors. A spouse may also hold on to resentment to make the partner "pay"—to have the partner suffer as the spouse has suffered. In order to center on this, we have at times asked how much longer the spouse is going to punish the other. If the answer is honest, both partners at least know what they are confronting and can hopefully deal with it.

Because of the complexity of the feelings, vendettas are not readily altered. Often the spouse who had the affair becomes so angry when there is no alteration in the mate's behavior that discouragement follows and he or she becomes less willing to work on the reality aspects of current transactions, which is necessary to minimize the problem.

Threats, Control, and Tolerance Limits

One of the problems the therapist encounters when attempts are made to help a spouse learn to state his or her needs and feelings, the importance of these, and how the frustration is contributing to difficulties in the marriage, is that the partner hears these statements as demands and efforts at control; this is especially true of individuals coming into marriages with a weak gender identity or a frail sense of autonomy. For some individuals, behind the fear of control may be the more pervasive fear of losing identity through merging or fusion. For these persons, the therapist will need to assess the underlying fears for appropriate interventions so that negotiating does not get fixated on the issue of control.

Efforts at interpersonal control are ubiquitous and often pose problems to the marriage. When this occurs, issues of control cannot be dealt with abstractly; they must be rechanneled into pragmatic issues, where problems of control can be worked out as a by-product. One of the things the therapist can do for the spouses is to separate the issues of limits and control. The therapist can support each spouse's right to have individual wants and tolerance limits, independently of whether these are experienced by the partner as efforts at manipulation and control. Separating these issues is crucial because spouses frequently experience their partner's statement about tolerance limits as an effort to control their behavior. Although the therapist may not be able to eliminate this problem, he or she can work toward minimizing it.

A way to work on the problem of a partner feeling manipulated is by helping spouses learn how to state their limits. If the spouse can express limits in an acceptable way, they may be more readily received. For example, if the spouse says, "If you don't do such and such, then I'm not going to have sex anymore," you can be sure that this will be heard not only as a demand, but also as a threat. The statement usurps the spouse's rights to choose and attempts to coerce the partner into a given behavior by promising disastrous consequences if the partner does not comply.

Although difficult, especially when the partner is already extremely afraid of being controlled, efforts to help the spouse come across in the most acceptable way are essential. Assume, for example, that a spouse is trying to get more expressions of love from a partner who leaves nightly to pursue nonmarital activities. The spouse should not say, "*If* you do such and such, then I'll do such and such," but rather, "*When* you leave me so frequently, I feel very lonely, unloved, and as if you don't enjoy being with me. This really bothers me to a point that I get so mad I just want to strike back. But that's not what I really want, I want to feel you care more about me. So what is happening is getting in the way of our relationship." Note that the therapist should encourage the spouse to express feelings, not consequences. "I feel so depressed most of the time that I feel like giving up. My work is not up to snuff, and I don't feel like doing anything for you anymore." The spouse leaves out any orders or commands and focuses on feelings and the ultimate cost of the behavior to the relationship. In this case, the spouse tries to help the partner to see how the frustrating behavior is feeding into other behaviors that will cause grief to the partner. How much of this takes place, the way it does, and what feelings are aroused in the spouse are crucial information for the partner. Then it is up to the partner to make a decision about the importance of doing what he or she wants versus what the spouse wants. The spouse does exert pressure and attempts to influence the spouse, but this is not the same as control or coercion.

If the partner's desire to avoid the spouse by being away from home all the time or having an affair is deeply rooted in unconscious factors, the anxiety of altering the behavior may be too great. In that case, therapeutic work may best proceed individually. On the other hand, if the anxiety generated is not intolerable, it may open up this problem area for the partner in the couple session and allow for some fuller awareness of what the behavior means. This, in turn, may help both spouses, since the offended mate also gains a fuller understanding of the partner's behavior. If the partner's anxiety is too great to alter the behavior, the spouses can still focus on the effects of this behavior on their relationship. As previously discussed, no matter how fixed the behavior of the partner, the spouse will need to decide his or her own limits of tolerance and communicate this—not as a threat, but as a statement of fact.

As already mentioned, one of the situations in which the problem of control emerges most strikingly is an extramarital relationship. Because of the hurts and anger, the offended spouse wants to dictate what can and cannot be done rather than what can or cannot be tolerated. These orders will be difficult to hear for the partner who does not want the extramarital activity to cease; any statement that comes across as a command can only be heard as an effort to control illegitimately. The more that this feeds into an existing sensitivity to feeling controlled, the greater the damage. In contrast, by using statements of limits and tolerance, the spouse can avoid issuing ultimatums. The responsibility for behavior remains with the appropriate spouse, the one who after hearing the mate's distress must decide a course of action.

The following examples will illustrate therapeutic interventions in dealing with problems of control. In the first case, the wife frequently objected to her husband being away so much in the evenings as well as his choice of friends; the husband experienced his wife as trying to control his behavior. It was important to deal with the wife's objections as two separate issues. With regard to the problem of the husband's frequent absences from home, it was suggested to the wife that the husband might hear her better if she told him of her need for him (rather than what he had no right to do), and that they might negotiate on the issue of time for himself and a time commitment to the family. Because of the strength of her feelings on this issue, she was encouraged to take a stand on this.

The issue of friends presented a more difficult problem. Any efforts to define friend choice would no doubt be viewed as control and as an infringement of personal rights. The therapist communicated the right of each person to choose personal friends (separateness) but also the equal right of a spouse to voice objections and feelings if the mate's friends were imposed upon the spouse. It was up to the husband to accede to his wife's wishes, to compromise, or to maintain his present position. Note that the therapeutic interventions are consonant with what is assumed to be an incompletely resolved conflict for the husband—failure with separation and autonomy, a conflict he is making efforts to resolve in the marital context. (An unusually strong need to be with male friends may also reflect homosexual needs.)

In another example, because the husband experienced the wife as "trying to control him," the therapist intervened to reframe the problem more constructively. Rather than the husband's viewpoint of the wife having a malevolent intention toward him, the behavior was presented in terms of her needs. What was experienced as a need to control was primarily an expression of her own overdependent needs and consequent clinging to her husband. It was a psychological deficit on her part that motivated the behavior, which was experienced as controlling. This is not to say that understanding the behavior will necessarily make it more palatable, but at least it deemphasizes the negative motivation attributed to the wife. If it can be seen as the expression of a need and a problem of the spouse, it may soften the aversive meaning. If this can be accomplished, then one can advance to a new front—helping the wife with her problems. If the behavior is not pathologically entrenched, the wife may be able, with support, to loosen her grip; perhaps the spouses can find other, more acceptable ways to gratify her.

Often what happens when one feels controlled is that the person begins to interpret many behaviors as controlling that may not be. It is useful to help the couple sort appropriate behaviors from controlling ones. This plus the diminution of anger that may follow when the spouse has a different perspective on the behavior can improve relations, even if the partner's behavior remains fairly fixed.

Limits of Power in Marriage

One experience that spouses must confront and have great difficulty accepting is not being able to control the external world. Much energy and time are devoted toward trying, often desperately, to alter externals (which most often includes the spouse) to make life more tolerable. A major therapeutic task is to help individuals learn and accept the limits of their power—the degree to which they are realistically impotent to effect change, and to be able to live with and accept this—a task not very easily accomplished.

Some things they may be able to influence, others not; some efforts are appropriate and have the potential for constructive influence, others can only frustrate further.

Sometimes dealing with this issue touches on some over determined aspects of behavior where impotence in the past was associated with overwhelming anxiety. These individuals will fight hard and refuse to accept the fact that they cannot change their spouse by efforts of sheer will. To accept this may mean putting them in touch with archaic feelings of catastrophe and overwhelming anxieties that must be defended against at all costs. For these people, prolonged individual work may be necessary to work on this unresolved, early developmental conflict. They will need help to understand these feelings and to gradually learn to tolerate them. In individual therapy, the therapist can offer greater support for this highly sensitive task than in couple treatment. For less pathological individuals, the problem is less pronounced. To accept impotence implies to accept helplessness, with its accompanying frustration, anger, and protest. One may even need to mourn for the lost power before moving toward a more accepting position.

Helping spouses deal with their personal limits of power fosters a more realistic conception of possibilities for change in difficult marital situations. One needs to help each spouse explore all appropriate means to influence behaviors, accept the limits, and recognize that sometimes even one's best efforts may not bring the returns one wants. The greater the pathology of the partner, the less influence the spouse will have on his or her behavior. For example, the spouse who seeks to gratify the symbiotic needs of the mate will find that it is impossible to gratify them all, no matter what the extent of the efforts.

For another example, the spouse whose partner consistently interprets all of the spouse's behavior, no matter how benign, as deliberately aimed at hurting the partner, will be dealing with insurmountable odds without some individual treatment for the partner. This partner exhibits narcissism and fixation at an early developmental level, where the infant experiences himself as the center of the world. A healthy spouse may be able to adapt to the individual, but the strain may well be great. The spouse will need to know the limits of his or her ability to influence the spouse and, if at all possible, to minimize the problems that arise. Beyond that, the spouse will have to assess the gains and losses of the marriage and decide whether to continue the relationship.

Reframing into a Positive Context

To conclude this chapter, we will discuss a major therapeutic tactic for altering ways of thinking—to rephrase or to change the context of (reframe) a point of view that is quite negative. In other words, the therapist offers a different way of looking at the negatively perceived behavior.[1] The examples below will explain this technique.

One wife complained of the husband's "manipulation" of her. One way to reinterpret this more positively is to point out the fact that all individuals make efforts to influence others to meet their needs. Therefore, within a marriage, it seems legitimate to expect that the spouse will do this with the partner. This in itself is not a problem; the problem arises when an individual expects all of his or her needs to be met all of the time by the mate, while not acknowledging the other's needs. In this instance, one might try to help both spouses sort out essential from unessential desires and continue toward negotiating. In doing so, the therapist must recognize the importance of both spouses' needs and the balance of the give-and-take, so that the wife does not feel that she is not being gratified or, as she experienced it, being manipulated.

Put in these terms, what originally begins as a complaint of the spouse's manipulation can be understood in terms of the legitimacy of spouses' efforts to get satisfactions from each other, as long as there is no major violation of individual rights. This point also illustrates a more general point previously made: When one labels one's partner with negative, derogatory terms (as "manipulative", "selfish", or as "having emotional problems"), these labels will be heard as criticisms and will not usually lead to any efforts toward change. If the therapist can reframe these terms more positively, meaningful work can proceed. Labels can be redefined in

---

[1]P. Watslawick, J. Weakland, and R. Fisch, *Change: Principles of Problem Formation and Problem Resolution*. New York: Norton, 1974.

terms of behaviors which get in the way of gratification, and spouses can learn to talk in these terms without use of such labels.

Another example of an effort to help a wife reframe the husband's behavior occurred as a result of a dispute over the wife's working. The wife interpreted the husband's objection to this as his need "to have control" over her. The therapist presented it differently:

T: I think he feels greater security when you're home, like he can really count on you, you're there for the kids.

[The wife strongly disagreed with this view and insisted on her husband's need to control her.]

T: As soon as you put it in those words, it's going to be something, of course, that you'd have to fight against, because it sounds like a very bad thing . . . but I don't think that's where your husband is at. What he wants is some assurance in terms of his emotional needs—that he won't lose you—that you'll always be there for him and the kids—and in that sense, you could call it control, but it's not to squash you, limit you, to hurt you.

W: It feels that way.

T: I know it feels that way, but that's not the intent. The intent is so he feels more secure, knowing that you're there.

W: [To husband] Is that true?

H: I think so.

T: I think if you could substitute the word "dependency" for "control," you would see a clearer picture of where your husband is.

W: You mean he needs me to be dependent upon him?

T: No, he's very dependent upon you. That's what appears to be control is all about [sic].

H: I can tell you why . . . for the first time in my life, my relationship with you has been one where I've got some emotional input into it . . . where I never had before in

my life—the first time I have felt the emotion love, need,
the desire to be with someone, and I never had it before, and golly, I'd fight like hell to keep from losing it.

Although helping a spouse see the need behind the partner's negatively viewed behavior may be useful, it is by no means a simple
solution to such complex problems as the above. Despite the wife's
understanding, she still experienced the husband's behavior as
"choking" her—as if his needs for her were insatiable and that
some of her very being was being sacrificed.

The therapist will also have to learn how to talk about troublesome aspects of a spouse's behavior without sounding critical
or blaming. Pointing up positive aspects of an irritating behavior
is useful. The following example is an effort, although not too successful, to talk to the husband about his authoritarian, hypercritical
style, which has proved so devastating for the wife. The therapist
first encouraged the husband to listen to the tape, hoping he would
become more aware of his harshness without having to be confronted with it. Then the therapist tried to comment on the husband's style by reframing the therapeutic comments—again not
altogether satisfactorily. The husband had been talking of problems
he and the wife have related and became critical of her in the
process.

T: And hear yourself in a more objective way, and I think
      you could become aware of some of the ways you come
      across . . . you have a very definitive style. I mean there's
      no question about what you feel or think, and that has
      great advantages to it, but when you are homing in on
      things she experiences as critical, then it adds extra
      weight.

Although the therapist hoped to sound impartial in the phrasing
of her comment, we infer that the husband thought he was being
accused, since he then comments that the wife's immaturity forces
him into a parent role.

T: That's probably true.

The therapist is not agreeing with his statement so much as trying to acknowledge that there is some truth in what he says with regard to the interactional aspects of the problem.

> T: I'm not trying to come in from the viewpoint of what causes what or who's to blame. I'm trying to come in where I think there's a possibility for some changes. You see, I feel like you're pretty much master of yourself, and you're not controlled by emotions as readily. And if you set yourself a course, I have a feeling that you could do it. [To wife] I just think you're more emotionally prone, and it's going to be harder for you to control some of the outbursts; this is not to say that therefore what you do is worse than this—I'm not trying to make any kind of comparison. I'm trying to move in where I think the most effort can be made quickly, maybe to help soften things a little.
>
> [The wife gives examples of things her husband asked of her that she could not do and described her feeling of desperation, as it she were going to "get it."]
>
> T: [To husband] She probably felt like you were her father, [to wife] like he was going to come in and scream and yell or like the heavens are going to fall out on her head or whatever. I think that you were pretty accurate about that parent thing, because I think that's what going on. You pull the child from her and she pulls the parent from you, instead of the two adults relating; and it's not saying who's to blame; it's just that this is what gets set up sometimes, and it doesn't make for the best of adult relationships.

Since cause and effect and a blaming orientation are often entrenched in the frame of reference of some spouses, the task of reframing may be insufficient to eliminate defensiveness. Sometimes, it may be preferable to help the spouse to observe and appraise his or her own behavior more accurately, for example, by listening to a taped session. This fosters self-reliance, minimizes the threat of criticism, and promotes better monitoring capacities in therapy and in life.

7

Continuing Therapy
and Termination

At this point we would
like to discuss what some authors call the middle stage of therapy.
In our view, a middle stage exists only in terms of the time sequence
rather than in terms of important characteristics that differentiate
the period from the initial and terminating sessions. Our position is
that therapy is a progression, in which the use of the tasks is varied
according to the couple's problems and capacity to use help. Many
of the tasks that are crucial to attend to early, such as altering a blaming orientation and eliminating an argumentative style, are difficult; they are never totally mastered and then replaced by new
tasks. Rather, these tasks, along with others, will need to be continuously focused on with the hope of eventual proficiency in as
many tasks as possible. The therapeutic process consists of continual
working and reworking with varying degrees of success; the therapist must be ever ready to reinforce forward progress but also
ready to soften the discouragement of temporary failure. One

hopes through this continuous process to develop a momentum that will eventually be strong enough for the couple to carry on without the help of the therapist. Expressed another way, this is to say that the couple will feel sufficiently confident with some of their increased awareness and newly learned skills to tackle their problems alone as they arise.

For couples with sufficient investment, therapeutic help, and adaptability, this kind of momentum will occur. The therapist will become aware of increased learning by changes in therapy as well as those reported at home, for example, the greater assumption of personal responsibility for problem-solving or the giving up of the expectation that the therapist can offer definitive solutions. One good indication is if the couple, when beginning a session, assume responsibility by either posing a problem for themselves or for the therapist to work on. Other evidence is a couple's willingness to begin using their new skills and awareness at home and to discuss their success or lack thereof.

As the therapist becomes aware of behavior that signals progress, he or she will also notice what therapeutic tasks must still be accomplished, that is, those more difficult for the couple to achieve; the therapist will then need to focus on these. In any event, the therapist is still well advised to use what emerges spontaneously in the session to promote whatever learning is necessary to change behaviors hampering the relationship.

Thus, each couple have their own particular patterning of problems and proceed in their own way. For some spouses, the development of trust and relinquishing belief in the therapist's total power occur early, and learning to negotiate and other tasks can proceed. For others, a workable therapeutic alliance with mutually acceptable goals and procedures for accomplishing these never develops sufficiently. Lack of trust, clinging to an infantile dependent position, or a refusal to assume any personal responsibility for change may prevail, so that therapeutic progress is meager at best. Wherever the spouses are hampered must remain the focal point until progress is achieved.

The delineation of stages also does not fit our conception of therapy because of our method of focusing and shaping our work to whatever material spontaneously emerges. The couple's own predilection, investment, and focus are good guides to where their attention is, and being attuned to this seems most expedient to effect better marital relations. In other words, one does not have a preset agenda through which the therapy will systematically proceed to a specific end point.

To illustrate the interim process of therapy as a segment of a continuous process rather than a stage in itself, two sessions will be presented of a couple who worked in therapy over a two-year period. One will notice that personal responsibility is good and the therapeutic alliance well cemented, but the overall problem of blame still remains. This couple had reported improvement in their overall relating at times, but they continued therapy because problems remained. The two sessions, recorded in the second year of therapy, are not dramatic in their content or outcome. They represent the typical, ongoing process of treatment for a couple who have sustained therapy over a fairly long period, and highlight the continuous work by the therapist to structure, direct, and focus, so that the couple can better understand each other and thereby learn how to negotiate more successfully.

It is acknowledged that even in these sessions, presented in their entirety, much will be left out. Voice inflections and speech patterns cannot be detected from the printed word. It is hoped that enough remains to make the principles described in the text more graphic.

> W: I came irritated this morning because we had a hard time getting here on time. I know we're not terribly late this morning, but we're later than I wanted us to be. We had a few words about that on the way over. It bothers me that when we have a commitment to go somewhere, to be somewhere at a certain time, there is always something that happens, and this morning it happened to be something regarding work. And I'm sure the reason is legitimate, but with a whole week to plan, it seems that we could get here on time.

The couple is familiar with the therapist's way of working, and the wife begins the session spontaneously without any direction from the therapist, indicating what is bothering her at the moment.

H:　Yeah, we could get here on time.

W:　What I mean is that *you* could get here on time.

H:　Yes, I think I could. [Pause] I could leave the office half an hour earlier or I could not even go down at all in the morning, but I only get four hours leave time for every two weeks. If I take four hours leave time once a week, then that should tell you what kind of vacation we might have.

W:　Jerry [the husband], you told me at Christmas time that you had like nineteen or twenty hours that you had to take.

H:　Nineteen or twenty hours that I *lost*, because I didn't take them last year.

W:　Well, you've always had an abundance of leave time, I don't think that is going to cause us any difficulty.

H:　Well, I have explained to you how the thing works, sitting right here, and this is the way it works. I've got nothing to do with it. That's the way it works, and if I take the leave time, then I don't have it left.

W:　Well, is this any different way of handling the leave time from the way it has been handled before?

H:　No.

W:　Well, you always have, every time, ever since you've been with this job, except maybe the first couple of years, you've always lost a lot of leave time or had to take some or you would lose it. Now, I can't see how that applies.

H:　Well, I haven't in years past, I haven't used four hours every week, where I was only getting four hours every two weeks.

W:　Well, there has to be some way we can get here on time. Can you make any suggestions?

At this point, the wife shifts toward the more constructive stance of asking the husband for suggestions.

H:　Yeah, I think if I had the gas put in the car yesterday or last night, and I think by getting to the house by nine o'clock and the kids being right ready when I got there, we could have been here on time. As it is, we were five to eight minutes late; I did have to get gas after I picked you up. By the time I drove into the yard and by the time I drove out of the yard, seven to eight minutes had passed. So we're seven to eight minutes late waiting on you. It's that seven or eight minutes late including getting gas.

W: Well, I don't know whose seven or eight minutes late it is, whether it's the getting gas or for waiting for me.

H: Well, either one of them would have made us late, but what I'm saying is that I'm not the only one who should of let some slack time in the schedule. [His voice rises.]

T: Rather than trying to . . . you know, the way you are going now seems to be a matter of who's to blame, which won't be helpful; maybe you could just concentrate and talk primarily on what each of you is willing to do to make things go better in the future. [To husband] I heard you offer one suggestion that maybe you could do.

The husband's previous comment and his rising tone of voice suggest that he is feeling blamed. The therapist intervenes to redirect the interchange, which shows signs of going astray from any constructive problem-solving.

H: Well, it would suit me much better if we could have meetings so that I could use an hour of leave coming over here and an hour for the discussion. And then at five o'clock my work time stops, so that I don't have to take any more time, so that would be two hours each week rather than four hours each week, so I don't lose any; I don't get in the hole.

T: O.K., would an end of the day appointment help?

H: That would help tremendously.

T: Would a four o'clock help?

H: Yes.

T: We can do that.

H: That would help quite a bit. That way I would have the whole day rather than just a half-hour to get things done for that day in the office.

T: O.K., let me look specifically. Does the day matter to you?

H: No.

T: One day is as good as the next?

H: Yes.

W: Well, no, the day doesn't matter, it's just the time. I would rather it be when the children are in school, because then I feel very responsible for them being out of school.

T: Oh, I see, then you have another problem?

W: I mean, they can stay by themselves. I would worry about them, however, but I guess they would be all right.

T: How long does it take you all to get back home from here?

W: It takes about an hour.

T: So that means if you left here at five, you would get home at six, and the children would have been home since three?

W: Two thirty, somewhere along in there.

T: [To wife] Are you willing to go that way in order to spare the leave time?

The therapist checks out the tentative solution with the wife; it is important that it be satisfactory to both spouses.

W: Well, I suppose I can make some arrangements. It makes it more difficult for me, but I guess I can do it.

T: Would this help you? Would you feel better about it?

W: It wouldn't help me, no. It would give me more problems, but I could work it out.

T: Well, maybe you want to talk together about which presents the most problems, because it doesn't matter to

me. I mean, you should work it out so that both of you
feel the most comfortable with the decision you come
out with. Maybe you should just talk about that.

Since the wife is hesitant, the therapist redirects the conversation to
focus on the couple's coping with the problem.

W: The reason it presents me with more problems is that I
have to find a ride home for the children in the afternoon; I have to find something to do for John; Mark and
Amy go swimming at four. [John, Mark, and Amy are
the couple's children.] I have to find them a ride to go
swimming at four and a ride home at six, and I can do
that, but it does give me . . . present difficulties.

T: Would a midday lunch hour help any?

The therapist offers another solution, since the problem concerns
all three present. The therapist would be less likely to offer possible solutions in ordinary circumstances.

H: I could make it then better than I could split up an afternoon or split up a morning.

T: Like if you left at eleven, had a twelve o'clock, and then
you'd be back at two, you would only miss two hours of
work, if you get an hour off for lunch.

H: I do.

T: O.K.

W: That's fine with me.

T: That wouldn't disrupt your afternoon schedule?

W: That would be better.

H: That sounds better than any of them.

T: O.K., now we have to find a time that'll work.

W: [To therapist] That will suit you now. [Laughs.]

T: I don't have any [noon times] without changing something, but I can work to change something. I have some

things . . . I don't think people will continue. Probably it would be between Tuesday and Wednesday. It could be on Monday; that would be O.K., because I don't have a one o'clock.

H: It could be on a Monday or Friday; that would be best. Some weeks I have to be gone.

T: O.K., Monday at twelve?

[More talk firming up the schedule follows.]

W: That's fine. I think I have really been difficult this week and last week. I've had terrific problems with depression that I haven't quite known how to handle, and I'm sure I haven't made life very easy for the people around me.

The wife shifts the focus to her own problems.

T: [To husband] Were you aware that she was depressed?

Although the symptom described is an individual one, the therapist chooses to focus on its implications for the marital relationship.

H: Yes, I was aware of it and tried to make things easier for her. In some cases I feel I succeeded in doing it, and other cases probably did not.

T: Were you aware that he was trying to make it easier for you?

The therapist hopes to have the wife acknowledge her husband's efforts to help her and thus reinforce his efforts.

W: Yes, I was.

T: Do you want to comment to him on that?

[The wife's comment is so brief that the therapist encourages fuller expression.]

W: I wasn't very receptive to most of the things. I found fault with a lot of the things that were attempted to be done. I have been very edgy, very short-tempered, and don't

know anything more to say; that's what I've done. I don't
know what's been wrong. I really don't. It's been difficult
to put my finger on it all.

T: You weren't aware that it was anything specific in what
      Jerry did. You felt it had something to do with you, and
      not because he was doing things that displeased you
      or . . . ?

The therapist tries to identify the extent to which the wife's problem is not experienced as caused by the husband.

W: Oh, I think a lot of it has to do with me. I do tend to be
      very short of patience with, you know, feel like . . . I'm
      not sure what causes it, whether I'm depressed because
      I'm irritated with things that you [to husband] do; or
      because I'm depressed, anything you do irritates me.

H: I think that's it, because other times I can be doing the
      same things and it seems like it's not making any effect
      on you at all. At least it doesn't cause any reaction. I think
      that your depression comes first and then your irritation
      with the things that I'm doing.

T: I think it's important for us to look at the things and how
      they affect you, but I think Jerry's right about that. Once
      you're depressed, then you're so easily irritable—it's
      really the way depression is—then it's very hard for any-
      thing to sit right.

Although the husband may not be completely correct, the therapist
is trying to highlight a point about depression that is independent
of the husband.

W: I've really tried to get myself out of it, but I haven't been
      able to do it. I haven't wanted to talk to anybody on the
      telephone, or go anywhere, or do anything. I've just
      mostly wanted to sleep and eat, read a book, and watch
      television.

T: Did this seem to start very recently?

W: Yes, it has begun here in the last three weeks or so. It has really been bad.

T: Since Christmas? Did you notice it around the time of Christmas?

W: Yes, around Christmas time. I guess I really noticed it, felt I was not aware of anything happening to me till right at Christmas Day, and Mark brought it to my attention. He said, "Didn't you get everything you wanted for Christmas?" I said, "Well, why?" And he said, "Well, you don't look like you're very happy," and I then began to think about it, and I began to realize that I had been exceptionally quiet and in some ways very depressed, with stress. Some of it is, I'm sure, in proportion, because I always associate at least the few days following Christmas with the death of my father, who died about four years ago, and he was extremely important to me; and then I have my very favorite aunt, last week—the week after Christmas—had a stroke and has been very ill, and I have been concerned about her, but I don't usually sit and mull over things like that, you know. They don't usually prey on me for weeks on end. I've tried to analyze why I would feel this way, and I think part of it may be that, but I don't think that's all of it. I think more than anything, after my job ended at the store, which you know, I wasn't that crazy about the job, but it did give me some regular schedule to be on, I just feel like I need to be doing something, to be going somewhere, to have some direction, and I don't at this point. It's not that I want to work full time—I've talked to you about this, But I do think that I need to be doing something—just fixing three meals a day, cleaning up, and doing all the laundry is not enough.

H: I realize that and I've realized that for three or four years. The only complaints that I have about your working anytime, anywhere, is that if your work lasts through to five, then it has an effect in one way or another, causing me to have to tend to the children in the afternoon when they

get home from school, and at the same time I'm supposed to be doing my work, and I've explained this to
you, too. On special occasions or if some kind of emergency comes up, I don't mind doing it at all, but I hate
for it to be an everyday thing. I can't tend to my job and
have to run back and forth to the house, too.

T: [To husband] Do you work beyond five o'clock?

H: No.

W: I can't remember a time when you've come home at five
o'clock or five or ten after. It's more like six o'clock.

H: Well, my work hours end at five, and occasionally I stay
a few minutes after five, but occasionally I'm home
shortly after five. The way things go around the office,
usually by the end of the day people will have run into a
couple of problems that you need to discuss with your
fellow workers. The work I do is involved in sales, and we
have some very good people, and some interested and
interesting people that are involved in the various phases
of sales, and a very informal discussion involving one or
two people at the end of the day, and I find those discussions interesting and in that somebody's coming up
with a solution that doesn't appear to be right and I throw
in my two bits, and usually those discussions end in fifteen or twenty minutes. Then I come on home, but occasionally I have some work that I'm supposed to turn
out and I stay after five. But what I'm speaking of, in
terms of having conflicts between taking care of the children and my work, is not in how long I stay at the office,
but occasionally it's necessary for me to leave the office
before five to take care of a spat between them or something like that, and then go back to the office. The ten or
fifteen minutes that I take doing that, by the time I get
back into what I'm supposed to be doing, is worth thirty
minutes. It's not just the fifteen minutes; it takes thirty
to get back to where I was before.

T: You think they can't stay home unsupervised?

H: Most of the days they do and they get along fine, but
occasionally, I mean it's not an everyday thing, but the

thing I guess I really want to say here is that I don't mind doing that kind of thing in an emergency. I don't mind it at all, [to wife] and I've explained this to you, too, that I think that if you could find a job there in Winchester that would allow you to work from maybe morning till two o'clock or from eight until twelve. That kind of thing would be fine. I would be willing to make any kind of adjustments that would need to be made, just as I've done before, of course, fixing breakfast in the morning so that you could get yourself ready. I didn't mind that schedule at all. You know I don't mind getting up a little bit earlier in the morning, but I don't like to get up early in the morning and everyone else lies around in bed, and I'm still late in getting to work.

W: You're losing me, I don't know . . .

H: Well, this is the way it's been when I would have to take the children to school in the mornings. I get ready to go. I have been ready to go by about seven thirty and the children aren't ready, and when I had to wait on the Brown children, they seldom get there before five till eight, and then I have to go take the children and then go to work and get to work by ten minutes after eight, and there's no way to avoid it. I don't mind taking the children to school in the mornings. I don't mind getting up early and I don't mind fixing the breakfast, [pause] but since you haven't had to drive to Winchester, I feel like my extra efforts in the morning have been taken advantage of.

W: What do you mean?

H: I mean that regardless of . . . now, I haven't fixed breakfast since you haven't been working.

W: You don't come downstairs to eat breakfast until twenty of eight every single morning, and the children are already eating before you ever come downstairs, I mean, which is fine, if that's what you want to do.

H: You are wrong. I do that occasionally. It's not every single morning, but I have found that when I get there earlier, that doesn't speed them up. I still don't get out of the

house. I'm out of the house before they are every morning. Regardless of what time I come down for breakfast,
they're always later.

T: I hear you are voicing some complaints about the way
      things are. Maybe it would be helpful if you could put
      that to Pam [the wife] in terms of some proposal of how
      you would like things to work out, that you could look at
      together.

The therapist tries to redirect toward negotiating rather than focusing too long on the negative. At this point, the issue of the wife's
depression has been shelved temporarily. The wife has been seen
individually in therapy and has that opportunity to work more on
her depression.

H: I would like to be able to get away from the house be-
      fore twenty minutes till eight in the mornings, but I don't
      think that has anything to do with your depressions or
      what's causing them or what can be done to get you out
      of your depressions.

T: No, but just for the moment I heard you throw in this
      comment about you feel like you've been taken advan-
      tage of, and I'm sure that would be something that would
      upset Pam. I thought maybe it would be better to put it in
      a form of, there's something you would like to have
      changed in the morning [that] you would like to work on
      with her to find a solution, where you wouldn't feel put
      upon and where there is some solution that she could
      accept, granted that isn't going to solve the issue of her
      depression.

H: Well, I would like to be able to leave the house by twenty
      minutes till eight—have the children ready to go, in the
      car, by twenty minutes till eight. Because if I leave much
      later than that, it takes me, because of the traffic, it takes
      me even longer [to] take the children down to the school
      and get back to my work; it takes me . . . if I leave after

twenty minutes till eight, it takes me almost half an hour to make that trip. But if I leave at twenty minutes till eight, it will only take me ten or twenty minutes, and that puts me to work on time. And it's aggravating to get to work every day late.

T: [To wife] Is there some way you could work it to get him out of there by twenty minutes till eight?

W: Well, I can get the children ready, but I can't get you [to husband] ready.

H: I know you can't get me ready.

W: I can have breakfast fixed, as I do every morning; it's fixed by seven thirty.

H: Pam, that's going a long way by saying it's fixed every morning by seven thirty.

W: Well, you wouldn't know; you're not down there. And you have been running later and later yourself. And this is the first time that I've had any inkling that it's bothered you. You've been running later, and all of a sudden it decided to bother you or all of a sudden you decided to talk about it, I don't know. But you've been running later and later every single morning, and it hasn't seemed to disturb you, so it hadn't occurred to me that it was an irritation to you.

H: I haven't seen the need to get downstairs and finish eating before the children are ready, because I have to wait for them anyway.

W: Now, I know that because I'm there and I don't have a job to go to, that you assume that the children are a hundred percent my responsibility, but I do think that you could talk to them and tell them that they are going to have to be ready, and press on them a little bit more. I'll do it, I'll do my part and I'll help and I'll try, but I don't think it's the fact that you need to come to me and tell me to adjust the children for you. I mean, you can talk to them, too; they're also yours.

H: I know they are.

T: Are you willing, also, that maybe both of you could take a stand with the kids that they are to be ready by twenty of eight . . . have eaten and be ready to go?

The therapist tries to promote their cooperation in dealing with the kids.

H: Yes, I would be more than happy to do that.

W: One thing is that you have been waking them up later than you had before, I mean, when I was working or even when I was working at the store, and you were getting them up at seven, and now sometimes it's not till seven-thirty, so I think it's unreasonable to expect them to be ready in ten minutes.

T: O.K., so why don't you decide on some time that you think would be a sufficient time to allow them to get dressed and have breakfast so that they can make it by twenty of eight, and then you can set that as your time to wake them, whoever wakes them.

W: Well, I should think that they would be able to get ready in forty minutes. If you woke up at seven, they should be ready twenty minutes before eight.

H: O.K., I agree.

T: Maybe you can sit down and tell the kids that you're going to make every effort to wake them at seven, and they are to be dressed, have breakfast, and be in the car by twenty minutes to eight. That you, mother and father together, will be working to get this done because you [to husband] need more time to get to work. Does that sound like something that can be done?

W: Yes, I think that can be done, and I think you can also tell them if they are not ready by twenty minutes to eight, they can walk; they'll be late for school. They've done this on a couple of occasions when they haven't been ready, and it's hurried them up the next two or three days.

T: Are you willing to drive off and leave them if they're not in the car by twenty to eight after a reminder or two?

H: If it's a day that the weather is such that they can walk. I won't if it's raining or snowing.

W: I could take them then.

T: So you're willing to do that to impress upon them that they should be ready?

H: In fact, I think someday it would even make me feel a lot better to drive off and leave them. [Laughs.]

W: You've done it on occasions; it hasn't even bothered you at all.

    [Laughs.]

T: Well, it's not a bad solution. It kind of impresses upon them they have to respect other people's timetables too. Does that seem a satisfactory resolution for both of you?

Again, the therapist is trying to encourage a common cause that will make both more comfortable.

W: It seems all right.

H: It seems pretty fine.

T: I mean, that both of you would feel pretty comfortable about it—you're not going to have some resentment that you're getting the short end of the stick or being imposed upon?

The therapist checks out the solution to determine if it is really satisfactory to them both.

W: [To husband] The only thing that I want to say about it is that it is difficult for people around you to know that this is important to you if you keep it to yourself, if you don't say anything about it. I mean, you have fallen very easily, it appears to me, into . . . [Husband begins to interrupt.] Let me finish! You appear to have fallen very easily into, you know, sitting back on the bedside and reading a magazine, or getting back into bed for just a few minutes and not getting up and not getting started until seven fifteen or seven twenty, and you appear to have fallen into this very easily. I'm not criticizing you for that. The Lord knows I'm the world's worst when it comes to getting up, but no one had any way of knowing it was bothering you.

H: Well, it *was* bothering me, and I had expressed that annoyance to the children.

T: You know, this is kind of a side comment on that. It's hard enough for each person to get himself up, most of us. It's a struggle to get yourself up and each of us has a tendency to hang in bed a few minutes longer, so you can appreciate that. Even if Jerry has done these things, that's part of the struggle with yourself, but since it's hard enough for you just on your own terms, it complicates it more if other people hang out, too.

W: I said I understand the difficulties. I'm just saying I didn't have any idea that it was bothering him, and I . . .

T: Well, Jerry, maybe she's not hearing you when you voice your complaints, I don't know. Or maybe that's because you don't do them often enough, or you don't make it known how important it is to you, because she said that she really didn't appreciate this as annoying you as much as you say it had.

The therapist is trying to stress the importance of communicating a complaint clearly to the spouse rather than letting resentment pile up.

H: I probably haven't made my annoyance very clear, but I do know that it's difficult for you in the mornings to do anything . . . that I don't feel like possibly I could have done it some other time. In the evenings when I come home, I can discuss it with you, but in the mornings I don't feel like hurrying you. "Pam, come on now, it's time to get up." I do come up and bring you a cup of coffee, if not right at seven, sometime before seven.

W: I know, and I appreciate it. I'm just saying that in the morning if you scream and yell at me, I probably wouldn't hear you. I probably would be very angry until I got a chance to wake up good, but that's not the only opportunity for bringing this subject up.

H: I realize that. That's what I just said.

T: So maybe you both agree that [for] those kinds of things you have to find the appropriate time, which might be in the evenings or sometime other than when she's sacked in.

Whenever spouses express a point of agreement, it is worthwhile to underline it.

H: That's true.

T: [To wife] But I also, if I'm wrong on this correct me, but I hear you saying that it would be important for you to know where you [the husband] stand in relations like this. Rather than have them building up.

The therapist again emphasizes the importance of spouses letting each other know their feelings.

W: I really assumed by the way you were acting that you were very happy with the arrangement because you had not said anything, at least not to me, about "I'm concerned about getting to work on time," and I just assumed that you were going along with everybody else being slow, and that you decided that you could make it at that time, and there was no rush and no pressure. I absolutely was completely unaware that this was bothering you this time. I know it has bothered you at other times. In the last several months, you seemed to have fallen into it very gracefully. I honestly didn't have any idea that it was irritating you.

H: Well, it does irritate me!

T: I think it's good to say that. Because if she doesn't know, then obviously it's going to keep building up in you more resentments and they're going to come out some other way.

The therapist reinforces the direct communication of feelings.

H: Are you going to talk about it in the evening sometime after everybody's asleep? [Pause] I think we need a schedule. I think you need a schedule that pushes you to do things on time. And I know from past experience that *I* can't set you a schedule.

W: Well, I wouldn't want you to; I probably wouldn't go by it.

H: That's exactly what I mean. I could lay out a schedule for you, but you don't want me to and you wouldn't do it anyway.

W: I certainly wouldn't.

H: The only schedule you go by is one that some work situation sets up for you. When you don't have a work schedule, [to therapist] she gets depressed.

T: Are you trying to offer some suggestions on how she might help herself out?

H: Yeah, I think she should get another job, but . . .

T: You would like for her to get a job?

H: I would. [Sighs.] No! I wouldn't like for her to get a job. I would like for her to be satisfied being there at the house, but she's not and I know that, and I would like for her to get a job as the second best thing. So far as I'm concerned, one that happens to fit the situation is the only thing that fits the situation, but I don't want the job to be . . . to run past the time the children get home from school. As I've explained, that interferes with my work. It's not that I mind doing these things occasionally, but for it to be an everyday thing is extremely disruptive.

T: I would like to . . . just for a moment, maybe it would help both of you if you would just pursue for the moment why you really would rather Pam like it at home and prefer to stay there—what this would mean to you, if you could tell her that.

The therapist was aware that the husband had said many important things with much feeling in this last group of statements and that they seemed worth pursuing.

H: It would indicate to me that what was at home was important enough to be in first place.

W: Jerry, suppose that there was some way that you could not make a living and I had to go out and work eight hours a day. Do you think you would be satisfied to cook, clean, do laundry, and take care of the children, and let that be your only life?

H: Probably not.

W: Then why is it so hard for you to understand that it can't be my only life?

T: [To wife] I don't think it is hard for him to *understand*. What he's saying to you is why it is important to him, because the way I'm hearing what he is saying, it would make him feel first place. And see, I think the dilemma is—you want to start out on an avenue that I don't want you to go on now—the dilemma is that there should be some way maybe that the two of you can find together where you [to husband] can feel first place that doesn't require her to be at home. I hear you saying that's really the important thing.

The wife's previous comment could promote an argument. The therapist tries to undercut this by stressing the husband's need for more caring rather than his inability to see why housework is not enough for the wife.

H: Yeah, that is!

T: You want to feel that you are the most important, and you've got that tied in with her staying at home, but you see, given the kind of person she is and with her feelings, you wouldn't feel most important even if she did stay home; I mean, it wouldn't give you what you want.

H: That's true.

T: So really what you're struggling with is for some way you feel like that you matter more and that you come at the top of the list. That's really what the issue is. It's not that he doesn't understand that cooking and cleaning and mopping floors is not enough for you; he understands that.

W: I'm not sure, I mean, I can hear you say it and I can hear him say it, but . . .

T: He understands it, but it's just not what he wants, because he's still struggling to get something he's not getting from you, which is the way of feeling really important. If you could do that another way, whether you worked or not wouldn't be the issue.

Again, the therapist is trying to focus on the issue of the husband's need to feel more important to his wife, and to separate this from the work issue, which only confuses the problem.

W: Maybe that's why it's always been a problem every time I've worked, because there's always been a bone of contention between us.

H: That may very well be it. I've heard you say lots of times, and I don't know whether to say dozens or hundreds, but when we were first married, that you felt willing to put our relationship, our family, in first place. But when I had to go out of town, and work out of town, all that stopped, that you felt put down and that I didn't give our relationship that same high place.

W: That's exactly right.

H: And that since you felt like I wasn't giving our relationship that high place, that you were never going to be trapped in giving it that high place again, and . . .

T: It sounds like initially that both of you had the same wish and hope; the relationship would be the most important and the family would be most important. It was not just you [to husband] wanting that. Pam wanted it, too.

The therapist tries to point up the same needs in both.

H: Yeah, I think she wanted it; I do.

T: Well, maybe some things happened along the way,

maybe, that made her concerned that maybe you were not putting her, as *she* felt you should, in first place. And maybe that was defined by the fact that he'd left you, saddling you with all kinds of kids and responsibilities, and at that time you were defining first as not leaving you under any circumstances.

W: No, not under any circumstances. I thought that there could have been some kind of reasonable arrangement made that would have allowed him to have a job and still make us feel like—or me, I mean there was Mark and me mostly—make me feel like I was in first place. I did not feel that way. I don't know what caused it, but I think I had good reason for not feeling that way, but it was not conveyed to me until way, way late.

H: Do you mean that you were more important or most important?

W: I would have sworn and put money on it that the job was most important. That's the point that I got. I never did . . . I never did feel from the very beginning that your family, and that I, and that our relationship was as important as your job. You gave us what was left over, if there was anything left over. That's the impression I have today of what happened then. I can give you examples of reasons why I had this impression. But I didn't feel that we were in first place.

T: What about now? I mean, whatever's in the past is in the past, but what about what's going on now? Are you missing out on feeling that you are important?

Although this is cutting off the wife's expression of past resentments somewhat, this topic has come up before and much work has been done on it individually and as a couple. The therapist chooses to focus on the present.

W: For the most part, I feel that we are central in Jerry's interest. [To husband] Often I feel that you're not . . . and you know, this happens when little things happen that you tend to forget or you can't remember or things that

I feel like your mind is not really with us—you know the things that I am referring to—like you forget. I give you a message, and you forget where I am and all this kind of thing, and I feel like though we're important, that there are times that you could make more evidence of it. And let's put it this way, I feel right now that we are probably as important as we have ever been, more important now than we ever have been. It may not still be exactly what I'm looking for, but it certainly is an improvement on what it used to be.

T: What are you looking for?

W: I suppose I'm looking for things that would indicate to me that Jerry is an aware person of what's going on in my mind and attuned to the children and attuned to the things around him, rather than fifty to seventy-five per-cent of the time he's home, he's in a fog and he can sit like this and the children will call his name three or four times, and I will finally go over and punch him, and he will finally wake up, and he will say whatever it is they want him to do. I mean, maybe you can't do any more than that. But this would be what I want. I would want someone who could be responsive and who could be attuned to what's going on around him while you're at home. In other words, if you're at home, I would like all of you at home, not just your physical body. I don't want your mind to be somewhere else. And I know you've had that, and I guess that that's part of the reason for your preoccupation. It does tend to be an irritation to me. I sometimes think . . . I know that you're not stupid, I really know that, but I sometimes think that you don't think when people talk to you. I can sit down and tell you that Wednesday afternoon I have to go so and so, and I've explained to you where I'm going and why I'm going and when I'm going, and Wednesday morning I can say "Remember this afternoon I have to do so and so," and you can look at me as blank as anything and say, "No, I don't remember," and that irritates me. It makes me feel,

"Oh, what the hell!" I mean, why bother to sit down and talk to you. It may go in one ear and out the other. So what I'm saying is that I think we are important to you, probably more important than we have ever been before, but still I would like to have *all* of you when you're home.

T: Would you settle for maybe *more?*

The therapist humorously modifies the word "all," but also introduces reality limits to wants.

W: Yeah, that would be an improvement. [Laughs.]

T: There's no way you're ever going to get all of him.

W: You're right.

T: I mean, there are too many competing things, you know, whether it's work or what have you, there's just no way you're going to get all of him.

W: [To husband] I would even settle for you being more tuned to the children, and this is one complaint. This would be an improvement. Two out of three have said to me in the last week that they find you difficult to communicate with. Both of them have said, "Sometimes I sit and say, 'Daddy, Daddy, Daddy, Daddy,' and he doesn't hear me."

       [End of session.]

Although the wife's discussion of her depression died out as the therapeutic work continued, one can see many resentments, which she was eventually able to voice and which may well have played a part in her depression. In any event, the couple were both working on communicating dissatisfactions and opening up possibilities for alleviating some of the problems expressed.

The following session occurred several months later:

W: [To husband] Waiting for me?

       [The wife begins the session by asking her husband if she should talk first.]

H: Yeah, I'm waiting for you.

W: I was mildly irritated this morning when you didn't remember that we had made plans to have lunch. I thought it was a kind of special type thing because you had a holiday today, and we had talked about going to this place off of Tates Creek Road. You asked me before we were getting ready to go, "did you want to eat today"—were we going to go somewhere to eat today? And I said that you had forgotten that we had made the plans and that that insulted me, irritated me I guess is a better word for it.

H: I've already explained to you I think what was going on. What I was actually doing was telling you to hurry up, let's get on the road, because if we were going to eat I needed to get a check cashed somewhere, and well, it's not that I had forgotten that we had plans to go eat, or that it had been mentioned that we would eat, and even that the particular place had been mentioned in our previous conversation; it was simply a way of telling you to hurry.

W: Oh, I didn't get the message.

H: I understand that you didn't. Again, maybe I need to be more direct in the way that I approach you, if that's what happened—not being direct and saying, "Pam, let's hurry up, we're going to be late. We have to stop and cash a check, and we need to cash a check if we are going to eat."

W: Well, I read it completely differently. I read that you had not remembered, or you hadn't found it important enough, or going out to eat was not important to you, so you hadn't remembered we had made definite plans.

H: I understand this is the way you read it, but what I'm telling you is the way it was.

W: O.K.

H: And your reading of it, even though you probably had a reason for it at that time, was wrong. I mean, I had not forgotten that we had planned to go out. It was a simple way of, well, it was a roundabout way of telling you to hurry up.

W: A strange way.

H: O.K., I'm willing to admit it.

T: Let me just ask a question here. [To husband] Suppose you really had forgotten, you know, you really had forgotten that you were supposedly going to eat out, and therefore your comments were based on that. How would you feel in response or what would you say or what kind of position would that put you in if she starts off in the same way? How do you think you would handle it?

At this point, it seems fruitless to establish what did in fact happen. So the therapist chooses to focus on what is an apparent pattern of interaction between the couple, that is, the wife's proneness to be critical and the husband's necessity to defend himself. The aim is to use their interaction to bring this into focus.

H: It would probably make me feel defensive if I had actually forgotten it, and I would feel like it put me on the spot, more or less.

T: O.K. So that it would be difficult for you to admit, if you had made a mistake, that you had?

H: Well, I think in the situation where more is at stake, I probably would find it difficult to admit. I don't think I would in this particular case, 'cause this happens plenty of times.

T: I'm trying to get across a point, Pam, that I don't know if Jerry experiences it that way, you'll have to check me out, but I experience it . . . the way you come across to him is almost as if you're out to catch him, and I think it is hard for all of us to admit mistakes just "period." But when we are having to admit them in a context where we think someone is going to use them to hang us with, it really makes it more difficult.

The therapist is using her own experiencing of the wife's behavior to suggest an interpretation of what is going on and invites the husband to consider this interpretation.

W: I think this is the circumstance. I think you're right; I'm very anxious to play the game "Now I've got you, you son of a bitch."

T: And I think, Jerry, you must sense that.

H: I do.

T: I'm not trying to talk about this specific incident. I don't know what happened; it doesn't matter. [To husband] But I know you must sense that, and it puts you always on the defensive, because you're going to be caught, like that's the big issue now—"Is she going to catch me or isn't she? Am I going to be able to defend myself or, you know, am I going to get it?" And I see this in so much of your interchange.

H: Yes, that's very typical of the way things go. I feel like I'm being examined under a microscope, so to speak.

T: What do you make out of this? You're both granting that that's the pattern, O.K., that you get into. O.K., what do you make out of this?

The therapist asks the spouses to try to focus on and understand better this pattern of behavior that they both acknowledge.

H: Well, I see it as an effort to put me down, to in a sense make me grovel a little bit.

T: Well, why don't you talk to Pam about that and see if you two can really talk together about this, to see what this is really all about. Can you tell her your impressions and invite some comments from her?

H: [To wife] I *do* see your method of approaching the situation like we had this morning as a way of seeking apology, as a way of being superior.

T: Notice your chin, Pam, at the moment, where you are.

The therapist calls attention to a nonverbal communication; the wife's chin is thrust forward in a defiant way. The wife laughs.

H: I don't like it, I don't like it.

W: I know where it is, I know where it was, just the second before you mentioned it; you caught me [referring to her chin].

T: O.K. I'm not trying to catch you. I'm trying to help you be aware of how your messages are getting across.

Although the wife feels "caught," the therapist's intent was to alert her to the nonverbal message.

W: [To husband] Well, I just disagree with you, that's why. I mean, you don't understand where I am in this situation, either. The thing that happens frequently—and I sensed it happening this morning, and I'm not trying to say that this morning you didn't actually try to tell me what was happening—but many times when this type situation has been repeated, something which is important to me—it may vary in degrees of importance—and we will have talked about it and said it and then when the time comes, it's completely out of mind; you've completely forgotten it. Now, I interpret that as you didn't give a damn, and you don't care enough to remember something that was important to me. Now I guess I'm trying to screw you to the wall and say, "Uh huh, you really don't care!" And that's what I was doing this morning.

T: You think he doesn't care and you're going to prove it to him, is that what you're saying?

The therapist underlines the wife's hurt as one determinant behind her behavior.

W: Yes, because when you forget things like that, I think you don't remember them because you don't care. And when

I do approach you with this and say, "Why didn't you remember it?", there are very few times that you can say honestly, "Well, I just forgot," or "It didn't seem important enough for me to remember." And I can understand why you don't want to do that, because then I can say, "Ah!" But what happens is that you give me a dozen different reasons why it was very logical that you would not remember it.

T: What do you want from him, what do you want him to say to you?

The therapist interrupts what is becoming a critique of the husband in order to refocus on what the wife would like.

W: I want you to say—when you actually have forgotten—I want you to say to me, "I'm sorry, I didn't realize it was that important to you." I want you to realize how important things are to me instead of being so defensive. I mean, I have said to you—I guess I haven't said it in the way that conveys the message—but what I want to get across to you is that you have hurt my feelings because you have not remembered.

The wife does a good job of admitting the hurt feelings behind her anger.

T: Did you know she was hurt, that this hurts her in these circumstances? I think you see the anger, but do you see the hurt?

H: I understand that; I think the anger is generated from the hurt. I understand this, I do. I don't like to hurt you; I don't want to hurt you.

T: Pam, would you tell him what you really want from him?

The therapist begins a series of comments aimed at helping the wife to ask the husband to care about her; because she has difficulty with this, the therapist eventually suggests a sentence for her to say.

W: I just did [tell the husband what she wants]. I said when I get the point across to you, when . . .

T: I don't mean that, I mean what's back of that. What do you want from him? I want you to tell him that, not what he's to do or say; what do you really want from him?

W: I'm not sure exactly what you mean.

T: What do you want from him?

W: You mean in this particular situation?

T: Not in a given situation, but in all situations. You're making inferences about his feelings about you. You're angry, so what do you want? I want you to say it to him.

W: I want you to be sensitive to what's going on with me. I get many evidences that you aren't, and one of them is your absent-mindedness.

T: O.K., can you say, "I want you to care about me?"

[A long pause follows.]

W: I want you to care about me.

[The wife then adds other comments that deflect this statement.]

T: Period.

W: No, I can't say that.

T: Stop with that—say that.

W: [Nervously] That's your period, not mine.

T: I know, I just want you to stop with that. O.K., try it again.

W: I want you to care about me. [Her voice becomes much softer.]

H: [Feelingly] I do care about you.

W: I want you to show me more, and I'm not happy with the way you're showing it. You show me in the big matters, but in the little matters. . . .

The wife becomes able to ask for consideration and caring.

H: By not forgetting that we had planned to go out to eat, by not seeming to forget, is this one way?

W: I guess being sensitive to what's going on with me; I mean that's one thing.

H: Well, sometimes it's hard to tell what's going on with you, because you hide what's going on with you pretty well sometimes.

The husband now introduces a heretofore missing part of the picture, that the wife plays a part in the husband's not tuning into her by hiding her feelings.

W: I know it.

H: Sometimes I would say it is impossible to know what's going on with you, because you deliberately hide it, I think, and other times it's just a matter of an action and a course that you've drifted into because I act like I do.

W: It's very easy to hide things with you, because you are so unaware of things that go on.

H: O.K., all right. But without having a basis to start on, how in the Sam Hill am I to know which way to look for what's going on?

T: Pam, I think your hiding your feelings has to be separated from whatever Jerry does. That's something apparently you choose to do for your own reasons.

The therapist tries to separate the wife's hiding her feelings from what the husband does.

W: I have done a lot of it. [Her voice becomes soft again.]

T: I wish you would, just the two of you, talk together. Maybe, Pam, you could start it by talking to Jerry why it's hard for you to show your feelings.

The therapist hopes to improve both spouses' understanding of what this is all about.

[The wife pauses before beginning.]

W: It makes me uncomfortable. That's the first thing that comes to my mind.

T: [To husband] Do you understand what this discomfort is about?

H: I feel it sometimes myself. I feel uncomfortable some-times, which is one reason probably. I go back to the very beginning of the conversation . . . that's one reason . . . sometimes it's difficult to come out and make a plain statement if I *have* forgotten something, when indeed I have.

T: Now are you saying that you feel uncomfortable about her expressing her feelings or about you expressing your feelings?

H: [To wife] No, I'm trying to put myself in your shoes. I feel uncomfortable at that point and I can understand why, and I can understand the feeling of discomfort in coming out and saying that I did forget or in saying some-thing that you want that you feel I would disagree with. I understand how you can be uncomfortable coming out and telling the truth, because I am myself.

T: Do you think she is expecting something bad from you the way that you're expecting something bad from her?

H: Yes.

The husband has suggested that what he feels may be behind the wife's reluctance to acknowledge her feelings. It is important to have him check this out with her, so the therapist suggests that he do this. It turns out that she is struggling with a different problem.

T: O.K., can you check that out with her? See if that's so.

H: Is it because you think that I would put you down? Is it because you would think that I would disapprove?

W: No, it isn't that, because I would think that you would think more of the same. In other words, if I tell you today, right now, at twenty-five minutes after twelve that I care for you, then tomorrow at twelve o'clock you will expect that same thing. I mean, it's not that. It's just that, well, I might know right now how I feel, but tomorrow it might be more expedient for me to hate you, and I don't know whether that makes any sense to you or not; I mean, I am trying, trying to express it, but it's hard for me to lay myself open to it—any kind of a long-term commitment.

T: Could you just talk with him about that second part of that statement, to where it might be more expedient to hate him. Can you talk to Jerry about that?

It seems important that the wife elaborate on her need to hate. When she does, her fear of hurt emerges, and she now begins to detail her efforts to avoid pain.

W: Yeah, because when you do something that pisses me off, it's easier to hate you than it is to be hurt. It's so much easier for me to say, "I don't give a damn and I don't care," than it is to say, "I care and therefore I'm hurt."

T: Another way of saying that is it would be easier to focus on him than it would be to focus on you . . . what that means to you as a result of whatever has transpired between you. Is that so?

W: Yes, it's easier to say, "I hate you for what you've done," than, "You have hurt me."

T: Rather than you focusing on your feelings, he becomes the object of different feelings.

W: I haven't quite been able to . . . when there is a good feeling between us, I still have a difficult time handling your unpleasantness or your irritableness or a difference of opinion with you. When you and I are feeling good and our relationship is going well, I still am not able to handle these things—you know, your irritation at something that may be well warranted or your irritation at the children or whatever, you know, if you and I have a difference of opinion, it's difficult for me to handle this. Do you know what I'm saying?

H: Yeah, I think so.

W: I guess if we're feeling good towards each other, I want it to be all the way through. It's hard for me to let you

have your bad mood and still continue to feel good toward you. I take them as personal—you know that. So
it's easier, it's easier for me. I guess you can say it protects
me, but it's easier for me to go along with an uncom-
mitted type situation and not to let my guard down at
all, and then when something does irritate you, say "Oh,
what the hell," you know. It's less painful for me.

H: I can understand that if you don't ever get involved with
anybody that you can't hardly be hurt by them; I can
understand that. That's about the same situation, same
way I look at some of the secretaries at the office. If I
don't let what they do or what they don't do bother me,
then I don't get upset by their inconsistencies, by their
inefficiencies, by their not getting their job done. If I
go on day to day expecting them to not do what they're
supposed to do, then I'm not disappointed when, in fact,
they don't do what they're supposed to do. I can understand that, but I don't see any reason why I should . . . in
the business situation, I think that's a perfectly acceptable way of looking at something. In a business situation
and a work situation, you always have to keep in the back
of your mind some alternatives as a simple way of getting
the job done, but that's not the way I look at what we're
supposed to have. I'm not looking for an alternative; I
don't look for an alternative.

W: Now I'm telling you the way I feel.

H: O.K., but what I'm saying to you is, you're telling me this
is the way you feel and I'm having a hard time [pause]
figuring out why you find it applicable to our situation.
God knows it's easier.

W: Do you know me?

H: It's easier on anybody not to be committed.

T: Pam, why don't you just start with this sentence; just try
it on for size. Just say to Jerry as a start of some talking
with him that you don't want him to let you down ever
again.

The therapist brings the interchange back to the wife's hurt.

W: [Softly] I can say that very easily.

T: O.K.

W: [To husband] I don't want you to let me down ever again.

H: I don't like to let you down.

T: And add to that . . . "because . . ."

W: [Softly] Because it hurts me.

H: [Eyes tearing] I don't like to have you hurt.

T: Can you tell Pam what your tears are about?

H: I feel like you've been direct with me, I feel like . . . and it touches me.

W: [Softly] I have a hard time with tender feelings, too. I just can't express them as well as you can.

H: Sometimes when you don't express them, I think they're gone.

T: Are you feeling any tender feelings now, Pam?

W: I am, yes.

T: Could you express them to Jerry?

W: I'm feeling a response to your tears and you know that tears are not . . . [long sigh] my way of expressing my feelings often, but I know that you can't hide them, that they just come out and they do have an effect on me, at least they do right now. Did you bring a handkerchief? [Laughs.]

T: What was the last part?

W: I was wondering if he brought a handkerchief. That was what I was feeling.

T: You had to break it up, didn't you? [The therapist jokes about the wife trying to break up the tender moment.]

W: I'm sorry, I was trying, trying to say what exactly came to mind. I mean my tender feelings may have been more of a motherly type feeling, but that's really ex-actly what went through my mind. I really wasn't trying to be funny; I know that you think I was. [The wife and the therapist both laugh.] But I wasn't. I know I do that; you're very right about that. [Pause] I'm sorry, I really am. [Laughs again.] Sometimes I don't react to your tears like that; sometimes they irritate me, they embarrass me.

The wife has experienced her tender feelings fully, and this is hard for her. She shifts the focus away from herself to criticizing her husband.

H: They embarrass you because you feel like a man shouldn't do that?

T: Do you feel that way?

W: Well, I don't think you ought to as often as you do, I mean, maybe that serves your purpose, but I think it comes more often than the situation calls for.

T: How do you judge that, Pam?

W: I guess I consider it a sign of weakness.

T: How about a sign of feelings?

W: You mean tender feelings?

T: Whatever—that too.

W: Well, it usually happens when your, often when your tender feelings toward me or toward, I guess, toward other people are expressed; this is a manifestation of it. But I don't consider tender feelings weakness; at least, I don't think I do.

T: Sounds like . . .

W: I know it, I know it—I know what was going to be the logical outcome.

H: Well, I believe you do and I can't . . . I feel . . . don't try to hide my feelings or my reactions to them, but I find sometimes that I hide myself in your presence.

W: Well, it makes me uncomfortable; I mean there are times when you. . . .

H: Well, that's the reason.

W: You have tears and I can't see the reason for it; I can't.

H: Sometimes I look at the children and I see them growing up and making mistakes that all children are supposed to make.

W: But if I see you go weak and cry, then I think, "God damn, I've got to really be strong." I feel like I can't reciprocate with tender feelings to you because I guess there have been occasions when this has happened, and the more that something has bothered you, that's made you unhappy or something that we've talked about, and you have cried about it. And on several occasions, the more sympathy I've given you the more you've reacted in the same way, and the more tender feelings I've expressed, the worse you got.

The wife now shifts to another problem, related to her husband's expressing feelings. This allows her to avoid focusing on her own difficulty in expressing tender feelings.

T: So you think he's going to fall apart if you show your feelings?

W: Yes, sometimes I do have this feeling.

T: Did you know that? She thinks you're really going to just disintegrate, become a babbling idiot, can't function, or do anything.

H: [Seriously] No, I didn't know that.

W: Sometimes I don't have a lot of faith in your strength, and I do consider . . . I mean, there are times when tears are appropriate, I know that, but from my way of thinking of it they come much more frequently than they should; and I do consider it some sign of weakness, and I feel if I reciprocate and cry along with you or if I pat you on the back and say, "Oh, you poor little thing," that you are going to fall apart.

H: [Annoyed] I don't want any old "poor thing."

W: Well, I'm . . .

T: [To husband] Is that what you want?

H: No, I don't what that.

T: What do you want if you're crying?

H: It's according to what the situation is. I do want some understanding; I don't want the "Oh, poor thing" business.

T: O.K., you want some acceptance?

H: Yes, I want some acceptance. I want your feelings . . . some way of recognizing that my feelings are valid.

T: Are not bad. I bet Pam's saying to herself that they are bad because they carry a message to you [to wife] that means that he's weak and therefore you have to be strong. Why don't you tell Jerry why that's particularly bothersome to you; maybe he doesn't understand that.

Obviously the wife's interpretation of the husband's expressing feelings as meaning weakness and her need to be strong is rooted in strong past experiences, as will become apparent. The therapist encourages her to talk with the husband about this.

W: Well, the only things that I know to say is the fact that all my life—and I know that you're not responsible for me before I married you—but all of my life the people around me couldn't take it when anything happened to me. You know, if I was unhappy or I was hurt, I didn't dare approach them with it, because they fell apart more than I did. So I put on a very, very strong front, and I ended up comforting my mother and both of my sisters. In some degree I still do it, and I guess I've got it in my head that I've got to put across this strong front. And there are many times when I would like to lean on you, and I would like to be able to have you to be the strong one, and if I evidenced any tender feelings and you come out with tender feelings accompanied by the tears, then I do, I do fear that you will fall apart, and I won't have anybody to lean on. [Long pause and then softly] Do you know what I'm saying?

H: I can understand why you wouldn't want to depend on somebody who wouldn't be there, who wouldn't be able to hold up. I can understand that thoroughly.

W: Then can you understand why tears and crying comes on as a weakness to me?

H: Yes, I think I can.

T: Do you lean much on Jerry?

W: Probably more than he thinks or more than he knows.

T: But you mean he's not aware of it?

W: I don't think so.

T: When you're hurting and really feeling bad, can you go and tell Jerry about your hurts?

W: No.

The above is the beginning of a series of comments to enable the wife to explain the ways in which she can and cannot turn to the husband for help. The outcome is that the wife elucidates how she has to avoid details of problems she is facing because her husband, rather than sympathizing with her, feels compelled to problem-solve for her.

T: [To wife] You don't do this [tell the husband of hurts].

W: I can say something bothers me or I'm really feeling bad about some things, and sometimes I can talk about them and sometimes . . . most of the time I can't.

T: Can you go to him for comfort?

W: Uh huh.

T: Well, what happens if you go to him for comfort? What does he do?

W: He usually gives it to me. I mean, I can't go and say, "I have this problem," and enumerate it and tell exactly what has happened, but I can say that, "I have some things bothering me." I don't do it often, but I have done it, and I have felt good.

T: Does he fall apart when you tell him you're upset or something's bothering you?

W: He doesn't fall apart when I tell him that something's bothering me, but I can't tell him what it is or that I don't feel comfortable discussing it right now. But when I do . . . sometimes when I do tell you exactly what it is, then you begin to fall.

T: [To husband] Do you know what she's talking about now?

W: We discussed this the other night.

T: [To husband] How you fall apart or what you do that she perceives as falling apart?

H: [To therapist] Yes, I can see what she's talking about. [To wife] When you come up with a flat statement: "I'm feeling down and out" or "I'm . . ." or something like that or something's bothering you without knowing what it is that's bothering you, it's easy to hold you and pat you on the back and say, "Now, now, Pam, everything's going to be all right, and we won't let anything get the best of you," and that's easy. 'Cause I don't know what it is, because I'm not involved in whatever particular thing that's bothering you, and that's easy to do with showing very little emotion other than treating you like I would the children. But when I know exactly what it is that's bothering you, when I see the source of your problem, that's the only time I can really be having any other than a feeling of sympathy for you. I can't put myself in the problem and see how it would be affecting me without knowing what the problem is. When I am able, when you do tell me what the problem is and I do put myself into it, I become emotionally involved, yes I do. But I don't just quit; I don't quit trying to solve a problem. I don't quit fighting; I don't quit trying; I don't throw up my hands and say, "Oh, I'm beat," even though I do show tears.

W: Well, we talked about this the other night. I talked about the fact that sometimes when I didn't communicate with you what was going on with me, it was because you couldn't listen to me and listen to all of what I had to say without at the very onset taking a stand. And then from then on out, no matter what it was I said, you defended that stand. Like if something is going on in my mind about what I should do or shouldn't do and is concerning me and bothering me, or something that happened that's really bothering my mind, and I come to you and try to talk to you about it, I can't come and talk to you about it while I'm still on the fence, because you immediately take, you take one viewpoint and then you just argue that viewpoint from then on out. And I feel compelled, I guess, to take the opposite side, and this is one of the reasons I don't communicate. If I have something bothering me, I have to settle it in my own mind before I can talk to you about it.

T: I'm not quite clear what that has to do with him falling apart, although that seems like a valid point.

The therapist tries to separate the "falling apart" issue from the new complaint.

W: It degenerates into an argument. You know, if I come to him and say I'm hurt by so and so, unless I have my position set or unless I have my own self defended very well, it usually ends up into something where it becomes more of a problem for you [to husband] than it is for me. I don't know if I'm making myself clear or not.

T: Yeah, I think that's something worthy of further comments, but I just wanted to clarify now that that's not your instance of how you think he falls apart if you come to him and want comfort, is it? I don't see the falling apart—I see the other points you're making other than he gets emotional. I don't know. Is that your definition of falling apart?

W: No, not really.

T: Are these examples of how he would be falling apart?

W: [Long pause] I don't know. I just don't get the feeling of strength from you when I come to you to discuss a problem with you. I . . .

T: O.K., maybe that falling apart is kind of something out of your past and these other things are the real issues that you're concerned with. It's not so much that you think Jerry is going to fall apart, I mean, maybe like your mother and everybody else did. But there are some other things that you are not getting from him at those times. Now I hear that. One of the things I hear, Jerry, that might be helpful for you is to be able to hear a problem without giving a solution to it.

The therapist tries to help the wife discriminate the present from the past and thus clarify her objections.

H: To be able to listen to the problem, [should I] say "Pam, I understand that you have a problem?"

T: To listen and show that you care that she's troubled, that you're willing to listen while she talks about the pros and cons of whatever she wants to talk about, and that you can feel for her as she struggles with it without giving a solution.

H: O.K., I understand that procedure. I'm trying very much in the last several months with our son . . . he asks my opinion on something I give it to him. And sometimes I can't keep from giving my opinion to him, anyway, but I understand what the process is.

T: O.K. I think it's helpful because a lot of times we get so caught up in trying to give a solution that we get out of touch with where the person is. You don't really hear anymore. You get wrapped up in trying to debate or stress why you think they should do "A" instead of "B" or whatever . . . you can get so caught up in that, that you can lose the person.

W: This does happen, I start to say this thing has been going on, and I've been wondering how I feel about it. You know, like right at the onset you'll say, "Well, I think so and so," before I've ever told you that I'm on the fence and why I think this might be possible and that might be possible—I really don't know where I am, but because at the onset you take a stand over there on that side, I have *got* to take a stand over there; at least this happens. [Laughs.]

H: I understand you do do that; there's no question about it. [Laughs.]

W: You know, you're so strongly on one way, then maybe if I get down and say how do you feel about it or what is your solution, you can give me that. But I do think that this is one of the reasons the children also don't communicate with you—because you get up in arms so quickly, so soon without ever hearing them out.

T: And sometimes when people want to tell you about a problem, it isn't really to get a solution.

The therapist underlines the point.

H: I understand that.

T: And I think you kind of have to let that person decide if they want help. Maybe when they get through about ten minutes later you say what you would do. Fine. What you would do is always different than what they *should* do, and I think you have to give your solution back in terms of what you would do. That doesn't come across as a dictate as what they should do.

H: O.K.

T: There being a difference, you know. Sometimes they might want to know what you would do, but it still leaves them the freedom of what they will choose to do, which may not agree with your solution. But I think what you [to wife] were saying is not so much really that you think Jerry is going to fall apart, but that he gets so overly involved himself that when he gets so emotional, you've lost him for support, for comfort. 'Cause now he's struggling with his own feelings and maybe all his energy is going into driving some horses that he wants to ride. At that point you're [to husband] lost from her, not that you're falling apart. You're just so tied up yourself in some horse you want to ride—that that's all you can do for the moment—that you're not available. I think that's what you're saying.

W: Yes, you're exactly right.

T: I think that's different from falling apart. I don't see Jerry falling apart, and tears to me are not indications of weakness. I think they're indications of feelings, you know, like women. I think something would be more amiss if Jerry couldn't have some tears, [to husband] but I think you need to hear Pam on this point. She's saying she wants some comfort at times; she doesn't feel all the time strong, you know. She'd like to lean, but it's hard for her to lean when this kind of interchange follows. And this shuts her off from coming back the next time.

[End of session.]

Our points about regarding therapy as a progression and refinement process which proceeds at a pace defined by the couple can be further demonstrated by examining examples of termination. Couples terminating at different points in therapy accentuate the uniqueness of each case. Individuals terminate therapy for many reasons; spouses are no different. As referred to in the beginning of the book, individuals come to therapy from varying vantage points, and this greatly affects whether they continue treatment. Many couples terminate after one or two sessions. Among these are those who are not really interested in saving their marriages, those who have waited too long and lack the patience and energy necessary, those who are quickly disillusioned when the first session offers no magical solutions and who fail to get the therapist to side with their positions, those whose relations with other significant people in infancy and childhood were so bad that they expect only bad things from the therapist and so cannot participate in a therapeutic alliance, and those in which one spouse perceives the problem as the mate's and does not choose to return.

The couple described below are an example of this last category, which is frequently encountered. The couple came because of the husband's dissatisfaction with his wife's lack of interest in sex. The wife, although acknowledging this, did not see this as a major problem and felt satisfied with herself. She was concerned with her husband's discontent but felt that this was his problem. The wife appeared somewhat rigid and was most assuredly not interested in changing her behavior. The husband returned after the first session, stating his wife would not continue. He wanted to continue with couple treatment, but being prone to blame himself for problems, he did not press the issue with his wife. With the therapist's encouragement he sought individual help. Since the husband was an overly dependent individual with problems in asserting his autonomy, individual help was warranted. However, one would anticipate that if, through help, he had become more assertive sexually, the couple's already strained equilibrium would undoubtedly become more unbalanced.

Couple treatment poses significant stress, particularly for individuals with poor coping skills. The numerous confrontations, which expose perceived deficiencies, may inflict repeated emotional wounds that are difficult to withstand. Thus the therapeutic work, because of a spouse's developmental flaws, may prove more destructive than constructive for ego building; such cases should be terminated.

In the example below, couple treatment was short-lived because of the extreme pathology of one spouse. Indeed, it is an excellent example of a case in which couple therapy is inappropriate. This case began with individual sessions for the husband, who came only after a year's effort by his minister to encourage him to seek help. He broke numerous appointments before he finally came for the first session, and he came only sporadically after that. He was a very distressed man and spent all the first session complaining bitterly about his marriage. So much anger was directed at all the things that were bad in his marriage that he was asked if he might like to bring his wife so that, together with the therapist, they could take a better look at what was causing so much unhappiness.

In the second session both came, and the hour was chaotic. The husband became uncontrollably angry at his wife periodically and raged about her behavior. She was more controlled and tried to tell the therapist about the husband's "mental illness." Therapeutic interventions were totally unsuccessful in structuring the hour constructively, and the couple devastated each other with their remarks. The husband complained about the wife's neglect of him and her violent rages, and the wife accused him of being insanely jealous and interpreting her behavior erroneously.

At the end of the second session, the therapist was convinced that couple therapy was not the best approach. The husband had many deep-seated problems contributing to his distrustfulness, almost to the point of paranoid projections; he had minimal frustration tolerance, extreme difficulty in controlling anger (direct discharge was the rule with minimal neutralization through use of thought), and an immediate need-gratification fixation. The therapist felt that individual therapy was necessary before marital treatment could have any success. Unfortunately, the husband would not maintain individual therapy. Threats of divorce were exchanged, and the wife made a final exasperated threat that if her husband's behavior did not improve, she would put him away.

There was intermittent contact with this couple for a period of several months as they dealt with the vicissitudes of their relationship. The husband made a pseudo-suicide attempt and was hospitalized briefly. The therapist had several phone calls, a few sessions with each spouse individually, and a final one jointly. The wife saw her husband as sick and wanted no part of couple treatment. The husband was unable to sustain individual therapy, and both failed to continue after the suicide attempt. Divorce proceedings followed shortly.

Although it became apparent in the second session that marital therapy was not appropriate, some joint sessions were held in the hope of involving the husband sufficiently to encourage individual help. The therapeutic efforts were unsuccessful, and termination was prematurely brought about by the spouses. Nine months later the husband returned for individual help.

One must also note that terminations may also occur because of the inexperience of the therapist and his or her failure to establish sufficient rapport with the couple to begin therapeutic work. The following case illustrates a badly handled first interview by a therapist in training. The couple did not return.

The therapist had seen the wife for one interview before the couple came together. During this interview, the wife primarily focused on her marital problems, including her husband's drinking, his refusal to work, and his lying around the house all day. Reported below is the interchange from the session with the husband present, which covers approximately half of the interview. The session was observed through a one-way mirror and notes were taken; consequently, there is some condensation, but efforts were made to preserve verbatim material, leaving out only excess detail. The following is the opening comment of the session:

W: [To husband] I gave my side of the story; now it's your chance to give yours.

Notice immediately the wife's preconception of what is to happen, that is, each will give a version of the trouble to the therapist, with the implicit assumption that the therapist will then pass judgment. The therapist misses an opportunity here to correct this by saying something like the following to the husband: "Yes, I have talked with your wife, as you know, but for now I'd like for the two of you to begin talking together about what's not working in your relationship. This way we can begin to see better what this is, and often you'll be in a better position to know what needs to be done." Initially, it seems particularly important to offset the husband's probable feeling that he is in a disadvantaged position.

H: [To wife] You're the one who is having problems, not me. [To therapist] In all probability, it's her parents—that's the way it started.

[The husband goes on to talk about how his wife has "angry jags," that is, the more she is angry, the more she eats.]

It is obvious that the husband already feels blamed, so he counterattacks. Furthermore, he dredges up a reason for the problem—her parents.

    T: She has lots of angry feelings?

The therapist does not deal with the issue of blame, which has already been introduced, but attends to feelings instead.

    H: She had them before we were married.

The husband makes sure that he is not held responsible for the wife's angry feelings.

    T: [To husband] Tell me your feelings when she's angry; what do you do?

Since none of their grievances have been discussed, this question is out of place. More important now would be to have the couple talking about the things that are unsatisfactory for each.

    H: I ignore her; it makes it worse.

Notice the therapist is now into a one-to-one mode, therapist-to-wife and therapist-to-husband, and is not promoting communication between them.

    T: [To wife] What makes you mad?
        [The wife begins a long list of complaints about the husband.]
    T: What do you tell him?
    W: I just complain. I probably go about it the wrong way and nag.

The therapist could have helped the couple to begin talking together by inviting the husband to respond to the wife's comment. Instead, the therapist repeats to the husband several things that the wife is concerned about and wonders what the husband does. All of the interventions are either about what a spouse does or what a spouse feels.

> H: She's been like that ever since we were married.

The husband continues to blame the wife.

> T: How do you like it [the wife's getting angry]?

The husband denies that the wife's anger bothers him and says that she has always had this problem. The husband's denial is consistent with his disclaiming any responsibility for the problem. The therapist makes a comment to the husband about his difficulty in expressing feelings. Efforts to confront the husband with his denial are unlikely to prove useful; from what has transpired, it is obvious that the husband is extremely threatened and guarded, and will defend against acknowledging this. Nothing has been done to help the husband feel that the therapist is there to help both spouses if they want it. The husband talks of his wife's anger again, continuing to externalize the problem. The therapist asks the husband how he has handled this in the past. The therapist is back to his stereotyped questions.

> H: Once she ran out; I didn't care if she came back.
> T: You must have some feelings.
> H: I didn't feel anything; I was in Canada, I didn't care.

Perhaps sensing he is getting nowhere, the therapist changes the subject, commenting to both husband and wife that they do not seem to have any fun. The wife, however, continues with her concerns.

> W: Maybe I expect too much—I get the idea he doesn't
>   care—he has no goals.

The wife states an important feeling. The therapist could have responded to this comment by encouraging her to give specific examples.

> H: You were having the same problem back then.

The husband is still blaming and does not hear his wife.

> W: You're trying to blame it all on my past; that's not all there is to it.

The wife talks about getting discouraged about the future. She assists the therapist by suggesting a need to look beyond the past.

> T: It seems like you're not satisfied; there is no fun in your life.

The therapist, heedless of the intervening interchange, makes further remarks about the wife's feelings and repeats himself.

> W: I think it's a lack of common understanding—no communication.

The wife bravely tries to talk of what is wrong.

> H: I think there is too much communication.

Her husband undermines her efforts.

> T: How is that?

The therapist gets caught in their game by not structuring toward a more fruitful interchange.

> H: She's always talking.

The husband goes on complaining. The wife begins to talk of their not going out together and suggests that maybe the husband is embarrassed by her. The wife seems to be making the most effort to focus on what is going on between her and the husband. Again the therapist could have invited the husband to comment, thus promoting an interchange between the couple. Instead, the therapist pursues another line of thinking.

> T: [To wife] Several times you talk of your husband's feelings; maybe it's better if he expresses them himself. [To husband] What do you feel? Happy? Lucky?

The therapist uses a correct principle of having each spouse speak for oneself, but it predictably backfires. The therapist already has sufficient cues (to which he is not attending) that the husband feels on the spot and will not disclose his feelings.

> H: I just get used to it; I don't pay any attention.
>
> T: How does it look—what do you feel about the situation?

This is a vague, unproductive question.

> H: I feel when she goes back to her childhood, she gets some strange things there.
>
> T: What would you like changed?

The therapist introduces a new comment that might have been productive if sufficient groundwork had been laid and the couple had been negotiating rather than complaining.

> H: Her nagging, her eating, her overdoing it.
>
> T: How about her nagging?
>
> H: She nags when there is no reason for it; she blames for a lot of things.
>
> T: So you have a lot of feelings about this?

The therapist has exhausted his repertoire and now returns to one of his previous responses.

As stated, this couple failed to return; they did not even call to cancel their next appointment. It was obvious that the husband felt on the spot and that he never shifted from his blaming position. The therapist's ineptness no doubt contributed to this, but it is possible, given some of the known characteristics of the husband (his drinking and refusal to work), that even with more skilled guidance he would not have returned. Also, the fact that the wife had already seen the therapist individually probably increased the difficulty for the therapist. The session is presented, however, because it demonstrates a series of bad interventions by the therapist and clearly shows how unproductive they were.

The next excerpt from a terminal interview is presented as one in which therapy never really got started. The couple were seen for only a few sessions, during which time they were not living together. They had decided not to resume living together, and the wife wanted a divorce; the husband was ambivalent. The couple were bogged down in bickering and in making assumptions about the other's feelings; nothing constructive was happening. This last session had been previously agreed upon. The therapist tried unsuccessfully to help them use the hour for some useful clarifications.

> T: Is there anything you can do with this session today to help you make some . . .
>
> H: [Interrupting] Other than some technicalities . . .
>
> [The wife begins to complain about the husband, and he defends himself. There are several unclear comments about what their relationship is to be, and the wife makes allusions to future contact with the husband.]
>
> T: [To wife] Is there some way you can make some statements clear to him in terms of what you plan for the future that would help him understand what you want? [To husband] You know, whether or not you'd even want to go with her in that direction.

The therapist is trying to help the wife state what she would like but is also acknowledging that it was up to the husband whether to agree.

T: [To husband] I mean, have you thought about it yourself in terms of what *you* want to do?

[The wife intervenes with a vague reply and again the husband becomes defensive.]

T: I don't think that's an answer to my question.

W: Well, try me again.

T: Well, I was trying to see if you could state explicitly to John [the husband] what you hope the course of events will be after you leave this session, so he has some way of knowing what's going on in your mind and where you intend to go with your relationship. [To husband] You may not want to go her way.

[The wife demurred with a long-winded speech.]

T: [To husband] I want her to, you know, she says she's done a lot of thinking and I picked up on these remarks about wanting to continue the relationship. [To wife] I wondered if you could specify to him under what conditions and how, so at least he knows where you are?

W: I stand ready to continue on any basis 'cause I like John.

T: Now, that doesn't include living together, so that's not quite correct.

W: All right, right, right.

T: Any other basis than living together applies?

W: Yeah, yeah, yeah.

The wife gave a conflicting message to her husband which the therapist clarified; she did not want to live together but was ready for some kind of relationship. The husband took this negatively and more bickering occurs.

T: [To wife] What would you like from John? What would you like for him to do?

W: Whatever he thinks best, I guess, is what I want him to do.

Note the wife cannot focus specifically on what she would like, which would help clarify in what way their relationship might continue.

The husband and wife begin to get away from the issue and to argue again.

This brief excerpt is presented to illustrate the difficulty in helping this couple make some constructive use of the session. The therapist made several efforts to redirect them, but they were not ready to work, and little was accomplished. This couple were later divorced.

Most individuals in our experience who come back after the second or third session are likely to continue therapy sufficiently to achieve some degree of resolution and comfort so that they can then continue on their own. This may be a temporary alleviation of stress, some short-term goal they set and feel they have reached; or it may be a more prolonged involvement over many months and, in some cases, years. The point of stopping is somewhat arbitrary, since the process of human living with its problems goes on, and couples rarely achieve the level of mastery of the varying tasks that they would like. However, couples may express confidence in feeling better able now to deal with problems as they occur; or in some cases, after prolonged efforts, they may decide on divorce.

Often there does not seem to be a clear stopping point. One good gauge is the couple's willingness and enthusiasm for continuing. On the other hand, we have occasionally seen couples who seemed willing to come indefinitely. In cases where we feel we have reached a point of diminishing returns, we confront the couple with this, especially if it is noted that their working has slacked off. In several instances, we have suggested that we become more contractual or take a break for several months to see how they are able to go on working at home. If things continue well, so much the better. If stresses begin to accumulate, resumption of therapy might be advisable. Some of the couples have not returned after the break. One couple returned several years later to report that overall their relationship had continued to improve greatly. They wanted some help with a recent problem, and a very brief interlude of therapy followed.

If couples do not wish to terminate but seem to have slacked off in working, it is helpful to focus on what is going on that is interfering with termination; a reappraisal of motivation is warranted. One couple acknowledged that although things were much improved, they were hesitant to terminate for fear that stopping might jinx their success. Continuing was seen as an insurance, which they could not afford to have lapse.

If the couple is not working and things are not better, the focus should be on the paradox of their coming for help but their unwillingness to proceed in useful ways. A therapist needs to be willing to stay with couples through lean spells, provided it is thought that some efforts are being made within their limits. We occasionally remind people of the amount of time and money they have invested and wonder what is preventing them from protecting this investment. Occasionlly, we mutually agree that therapy does not seem to be helpful and discuss the possibility of other help— either individual or marital with another therapist.

We think the dropout rate for couples should be higher than in individual therapy, since the motivational states of two individuals are involved, and so often the enthusiasm for working on the marriage with outside help is highly unequal. Not uncommonly we have had couples terminate when one spouse very much preferred to continue but could not alter the partner's decision. Some individuals are not psychologically minded and do not want to explore and evaluate behavior, however stressful their marriages may be. Individuals are able to tolerate varying degrees of stress, and this plays into their willingness to continue. Threats of divorce often bring spouses in but rarely contribute to their working constructively.

In some cases, the therapist, recognizing the difficulties posed by individual as well as marital problems, may settle for quite limited goals, which in turn influence the time of termination—often after only a few months of therapy. The case below is an example. With this couple, marital therapy was slightly successful, with some minimal gains after several months. It was felt that, barring further individual treatment, little more could be accomplished and termination followed.

The couple came for help after the wife got tired of the husband's periodic depressions, disorganization, and veiled threats of divorce. She was an extremely capable and charming woman, who was quite successful in her social life, work, and personal endeavors. She was a well-organized, logical thinker, who approached the world in a systematic, rigid, problem-solving way. The husband felt overawed by her forcefulness, was continually irked by her criticism, since he could not live up to her expectations, and varied between tempestuous outbursts and feeling sorry for himself and depressed. The problem in therapy was that the wife staunchly defended against seeing any of her behavior as difficult to live with. She felt justified in her criticisms of the husband and identified their problems as totally his—he should learn to be more organized and more effective in problem-solving.

The therapist decided that the wife's rigidity did not allow for much change in the couple-treatment context. Efforts were aimed primarily at helping the husband learn how to stand up to his wife, to voice his legitimate complaints, and to receive credit where it was due. He was by no means ineffective; he just could not live up to his wife's expectations. Some effort was made to help the wife see that the more she criticized, the more depressed her husband got; thus, it became more difficult for him to mobilize himself as effectively as he could. Specific supportive efforts were made to help him maintain areas of his life, separate from the wife, from which he could expect to get gratification. He was successful in a number of other endeavors; it was hoped that if he could enjoy his own achievements more, it would relieve some of the frustrations resulting from the wife's failure to provide adequate support and approval.

The rigidity of the wife's behavior, her authoritarian stance, and her need to be right (her impeccable logic was likely a defense against anxiety) were seen as unamenable for couple therapy. Her behavior was entirely ego-syntonic, and she had no need for personal change. Furthermore, she had no symptoms which were distressing as did her husband, and her defensive position was a great asset in her work. Very limited goals were set for working with the couple, and the husband was encouraged to continue in individual therapy because of his recurring depressive feelings. Although couple therapy was brief (several months), both felt some alleviation in the tension between them. No major changes were achieved; the supportive work with the husband and the encouragement of his gaining satisfaction outside the marriage may have been the primary therapeutic benefits.

Most gratifying are the couples who, no matter how severe their difficulties, come with no serious doubts about maintaining the marriage but want to improve relations and are ready to work. Over a period of ten years, we have seen many who were able to use couple therapy successfully. We might add that beyond the willingness to continue therapy, the single most important factor for success (as in all therapies) appears to be the degree of maturity and coping skills of the individuals. When these are present in both spouses, changes may proceed fairly quickly. Such couples, often already appreciative of the importance of mutuality and give-and-take, are able to learn to identify behaviors that hamper their relating and practice other, more adaptive ways fairly readily. Their caring and respect for each other and minimal emphasis on externalizing blame allow for rapid focusing on problem-solving through negotiation. Reinterpretation of behaviors from a more positive context reinforces these assets and facilitates greater empathy and understanding of behaviors as well as working towards changes.

Below is a final session of a couple who felt that therapy had been beneficial, despite the fact that they had only worked for four sessions. Termination was required because they were moving out of state. This final session is not typical, because of the brevity of the therapy. The therapist was aware from the beginning of the limited time and focused on reinforcing all learning as much as possible, however tentative. At the end of the third session, the therapist requested that both spouses think carefully about the work they had done in therapy and write a list of whatever had been meaningful to them and what they felt had been and hopefully would continue to be useful for them.

H: I learned to express how I feel, rather than to express things in terms of a situation as to right and wrong. It is an important thing and one I, especially me, hadn't been doing was to express my feelings [sic]. I have become much more aware, and it has really helped me a lot to tell Arlene [the wife] how I feel about certain situations. And the second thing I have learned is to avoid as much as possible a rehash of the past . . . to try to get to the feeling about the thing rather than get into the specifics of what had happened and how she saw it, how she interpreted it, and how I interpreted it, but staying away from judging the event—just don't bring up the past.

T: Especially if you are trying to establish the validity of what happened.

[The husband's next comment briefly stated that he had learned to turn to the wife for help; he had not relied on her at all in the past, and she relied much on him. Now, when she can see his feelings and help him with his problems, it makes him feel very good.]

H: I think it encourages me to be more open if I feel I'm not going to be attacked or I'm not going to get anything [bad] but [rather] some help or relief from the situation. Another thing which I think is the hardest thing to remember, at least for me, anyway, is to watch and not use attacking terms.

[The couple talked at length about how they avoided an argument on the previous night by temporarily removing themselves from the situation; they both recognized they were in bad moods. The husband talked about his tendency toward arguing, and how therapy had helped him control this. Both felt that now they were able to let a point of difference go, whereas previously they felt it had to be argued to a conclusion. The husband also went on to say that he had learned to get out of his parental role with his wife and that he now attempts not to judge her or instruct her, even though she may want this. He wishes to protect her independence and ability to decide things for herself. Both husband and wife recognized that frequently she asks many questions that appear to be seeking information. A discussion ensued about the purpose of asking questions and the importance of the response being based on the reason the question was asked. Since this was a frequent problem, the therapist attempted to intervene, suggesting possible alternatives.]

T: Maybe she just wants a point of contact with you. Maybe this is what she does to get you to respond to her. Maybe you could ask her questions [to explore the meaning of her questions] rather than feeling compelled to have to give a definitive answer, which for you might be yes or no.

The problem was clear that for the husband not to give a definitive, logical answer made him feel uncomfortable, as if he were being an indecisive person who could not handle a situation.

> [The final point the husband made was that he had learned that it was important to establish priorities on how he felt about different things that his wife did and to communicate these to her. The wife then went over her list, which was similar to but a more condensed version of what her husband had said.]

W: Explain how you feel and what is important to you. Compromise with the above [list] working. Discuss our fights without using attack as a weapon; discuss a fight, you know, a good fight, a real fight without attacking or using attacks as a weapon. We've been using them [discussions] all week, too.

Both the husband and wife actively participated and worked in therapy; they were both highly motivated to strengthen their marriage. These factors no doubt played a significant role in their feeling that therapy, although very brief, was useful. A short letter from the wife several years later indicated that the couple were still together and had had their first child. The tenor of the letter suggested that the wife was pleased and that things were going well in the marriage: "All is quite happy—joyful here. David [the baby] makes it all even more so. He's a beautiful gift and makes me very happy that I, we, worked things out. . . . Thank you for your helping hand."

8

Specific Problems
in Therapy

Married versus Unmarried Couples

A legal marriage contract is not necessary to work with a couple toward bettering their relationship. We are willing to do therapy with any couple who live together and seek help. In fact, we are struck by the similarity of problems that occur when two individuals live together, married or not. That this is so should not really be surprising, because once the honeymoon is over, the situation that emerges is fairly similar for all couples. When the rose-colored glasses through which one has been looking at the partner have been removed, one begins to see behaviors that have been ignored or not noted previously. Reality intervenes, expectations increase, and willingness to meet expectations decreases. All this requires is the closeness of living together every day—not a marriage license.

Since the problems unmarried couples struggle with are essentialy the same as those of married couples, techniques and ways of working with them are also the same. (The main problem that is different, which occurs on occasion, is the issue of whether to marry.) The therapist can help them to explore their problems, to assess their importance, and also to see which ones they can change. In some ways, it is to the couple's advantage that the early courtship and honeymoon are over, because they are now better able to make a more intelligent and informed decision about continuing the relationship, with or without marriage.

Living Arrangements—Together or Separate?

Although we have no hard rules regarding a couple living together if they wish to work on their relationship, we know that *not* to do so removes much of the impetus to work toward change; it also takes away many opportunities for the couple to try out some of the things they learn in therapy. The therapist must judge its advisability on the basis of the circumstances of the couple's living apart. In some cases, it may be dictated by practical matters, such as job arrangements. However, if it appears to be a way of trying to "have your cake and eat it too," which is acceptable to only one of the spouses, one should help the couple make a commitment either for or against working on the marriage. This is a prerequisite for treatment.

In some cases, indecision about living together will be one of the major problems of one spouse. The undecided spouse must be helped to make a decision, so that the therapy can proceed. A focal question for the undecided spouse to wrestle with is, "What is it going to take for you to make up your mind?" Often the response concerns improvement of the problems that have led to the separation. The therapist must point out how new problems attendant on the separation add to the originally unresolved problems and make the therapeutic work even more difficult. Often one spouse feels abandoned (frequently the wife) and so shackled by the responsibilities of children and home that the desired frame of mind for working together is not present. Much time and effort must be spent on the anger, hurt, and resentment which compound whatever problems existed originally. In many cases, if the couple truly want to reconsider life together, we tell them that the chances for working together successfully will be enhanced if the couple resume living together. Thus, the couple and therapist can work with the problems that originally drove them apart as they reemerge, rather than dealing primarily with the new behaviors and feelings that have resulted from the couple's living apart, which usually only serve to obscure and exaggerate the original problems.

In one instance, we set an arbitrary deadline of six sessions for a husband to decide whether to return to the wife. After that point, therapy was contingent on a decision to live together. This implied no permanent commitment for living together—it was only a commitment while they worked on the marriage. At the end of this period, the husband declined and therapy was terminated. The couple were divorced shortly thereafter.

Children from Previous Marriages

With the present high divorce rate, marital problems commonly occur between spouses over children from a spouse's previous marriage. The partner may resent the time the spouse spends with his or her children, whereas the spouse may be hurt and resentful because the partner does not express similar feelings toward, and interest in, the children. It seems important to help each spouse accept certain reality factors that are not likely to change. The reality is that the partner will have to give up some individual time with the spouse because of the children; it is understandable that the spouse would want to be with his or her own children. If the partner can also enjoy some time with the children, then that time can be shared with the spouse. If not, the partner will have to deal with whatever competitive feelings are aroused and accept not being able to get all that is wanted.

On the other hand, it is also unrealistic for the spouse to expect the partner to love and care for the children in the same way the real parent does. This partner has not had the advantages of time and of seeing the children grow to develop a bond of closeness. Although this opportunity may now be opened up, if the partner feels pressured to have interest in the children, which is increased by resentment that the spouse spends too much time with the children, he or she will be unlikely to develop positive feelings. One may need to aid the parent spouse to appreciate the reality-based difference in the relationships and any unrealistic expectations as to how the partner should feel.

If the way in which unrealistic notions are translated behaviorally can be identified, attitude and feeling change may be on the way. For example, the partner may make pointed comments about the spouse seeing the children too much, which elicits guilty feelings from the parent spouse. On the other hand, the spouse may berate the partner for not being more enthusiastic when they are with the children. If one can help each spouse see how their respective behaviors compound the problem and can help them to modify these behaviors, their feelings of resentment will likely diminish, and the opportunity for developing positive feelings will be provided. In this case, the difference in their initial feelings toward the children is not the problem; rather, certain assumptions about what should be and efforts to bring the expectations about create the problem.

The Mate Who Refuses to Attend

Occasionally a spouse comes with individual concerns but in the process reveals grave marital problems, which seem to merit attention. The spouse is reluctant, however, to have the mate come in for fear that this will make things worse. The strategic problem posed for the therapist is whether to work toward marital therapy. The example below illustrates the problem that may occur.

The wife was seen initially as a walk-in patient with complaints of vomiting spells and blackouts. She indicated major stress in the marital relationship but was reluctant to have the therapist talk with the husband or to have the husband come in. The wife was afraid to bring up with the husband the possibility of his coming in, let alone to reveal to him her dissatisfaction in the marriage. She stated her plans to endure marriage another seven years until her youngest child was grown and then to get out of it.

Along with acknowledging the difficult and unhappy situation of the wife, the therapist would need to point out the difficulty of effecting any changes in the relationship without both spouses present. At the same time, one would need to respect the wife's fear and concern of making things worse by approaching her husband with her dissatisfaction in the marriage and asking him to come in for treatment. A wife often knows much better than the therapist what disaster might result from this, and her self-protective strategy may be appropriate.

In this case, although the therapist indicated options and choices for her, it seems likely that the therapist also conveyed the feeling that the wife should ask the husband to come in and work on their marital problems. In any event, the wife did not return. One might suspect that the therapist was not attuned to the wife's concerns and fears. Perhaps it would have been more helpful to focus on these feelings and explore with her the pros and cons of her approaching the husband. With support over a more extended period of time, she might have felt more willing to make the effort to do so.

This shows a common problem that arises when the therapist attempts to impose his or her own idealistic notions of what would help couples—intervening as if certain conditions exist, such as the willingness of both spouses to improve the marriage. For these situations, we respect the person's judgment, although we continue to explore options in individual therapy. The therapist would do well to be firmly centered in his or her own beliefs about what would be most useful, but not rigid or coercive in their application, especially not in the beginning.

Divorce as Blackmail

Frequently when a couple arrive, there is already talk of divorce. In some cases, one spouse has already consulted a lawyer. Often, this legal action is held as a threat to the partner that if he or she does not change, the divorce will be filed and carried through. We believe that this is a bad way to begin therapy and tell the couple so. We try to elicit from them a decision as to their investment in and willingness to work on the marriage. If they wish to work on the marriage, it is suggested that they agree to withhold any more legal action or talk of divorce. We do not feel that any changes that occur as a result of blackmail will help the marriage in the long run. Hidden resentments and anger will emerge in subtle or overt ways as revenge on the blackmailing spouse. We try to indicate this to the couple.

In one early session, a spouse mentioned having consulted with a lawyer and reported that things seemed to go better after that. As this was explored, what one might have expected had occurred—the partner had made extra efforts out of fear. We are convinced that these efforts and such improvement will inevitably vanish, which occurred in this case.

Advice about Divorce

We are continually amazed at the ease with which therapists decide whether a couple should divorce. We suspect such ready wisdom springs from their feelings of impotence in aiding the couple and the wrath that is often unleashed by the couple, even when the therapist has tried to direct and structure the therapy carefully. We do not have that kind of knowledge, nor would we want to assume the responsibility for such a decision. To give advice on this or any issue works against a major therapeutic goal, trying to promote autonomy through individuals making their own decisions. What we are willing to do is work with a couple toward seeing if they can improve their marriage or toward exploring divorce, if they wish. If our efforts fail, then perhaps one of the spouses may decide to divorce. This is their prerogative. Or they may decide that, as bad as things are, they will continue; this is also acceptable. Each man and woman must choose his or her own path. Since only rarely is the path smooth, which rocky path is preferred can only be decided by the person experientially involved.

We feel we can be specifically helpful in aiding the spouses to understand the needs that tie them together, that is, the functions each serves for the other. A good rule of thumb is that no matter how great the surface frustrations and dissatisfactions, some needs are met. This fact may be extremely important; without help, individuals may realize this after irreversible decisions have been made. Inadequate appreciation of the unconscious drives satisfied by the partner may lead the spouses to repeat the failure by selecting a new mate who will serve the same functions and thus contribute toward the repetition of the previous marital problems.

We do not feel that awareness alone is sufficient for making the most mature decision. But it can alert the individual to another part of the total picture that had not been previously focused on and open up for exploration ways in which some heretofore unrecognized needs may or may not be met with the present partner, and what problems may be posed as a result.

It is usually useful to discourage hasty, crisis-oriented decisions to divorce, since time is needed to accomplish the above tasks. Since many of the bonds that have held spouses together are unconscious ones, the task of helping spouses become aware of these may require much work. One might also mention parenthetically that although it might not be a task for couple therapy, divorce may require much help for the individual spouses to mourn their loss and to give up their emotional investment in the previous spouse. Clinging to rememberances of things that were good and maintaining desires and expectancies that can no longer be fulfilled tend to obscure the legitimate, constructive reasons for separating and produce an unrealistic, overidealized picture of the lost mate. In contrast, some individuals, to defend against the loss and hurt, maintain an active hatred and disgust for their divorced spouse. Helping spouses achieve a moderate position so that the children do not suffer is a valuable service that the therapist can offer.

An additional responsibility is to bring up consideration of the divorce's effect on the children. We readily admit that this is a value judgment that we are willing to act on, because we feel ethically bound to help the couple think about the consequences for their children. We believe this subject should be part of the information they use for any decision making.

A major change is happening with respect to divorces and child custody at the present time. Whereas previously the mother was awarded custody almost without question (unless some grave evidence could be produced that she was unfit), efforts are now made to determine custody on the basis of what is best for the child. The father is now likely to be considered more objectively, and he may be the better parent and provide better living conditions. We bring up this issue because it often becomes a major source of contention. It is not fruitful for the mother, thinking she has the upper hand in gaining custody, to blackmail the husband into making changes she desires without any responsibility for making changes herself that he may desire.

There are a number of points we try to make to a couple seriously considering divorce. The synopsis of the discussion below comes from a couple in which the wife had already seen a lawyer and was pressing for divorce. The issue of child custody was already heated. The points that the therapist thought were important for each to understand and think about were as follows:

• It was clear that each parent loved the children and neither wanted to give them up.

• It was felt that each parent had equal rights to the children; barring some extreme circumstance that might alter the situation, it was felt that the sex of the parent alone should not determine rights.

• To the question of which parent would be better for the children, the reply was that there was no simple answer (that was to offset judgments already made by the spouses). For the most judicious decision, thorough knowledge of the various family members and the relationships among them would be necessary, with important consideration given to the age, sex, and developmental level of each child.

• The parents were encouraged to think carefully about the effects of divorce on the children: their loss, their feeling of being disadvantaged with other kids, and their possible guilt in feeling responsible for the divorce (a common child reaction).

• In answer to the question of the harm done to kids by quarreling parents, it was stressed that quarreling in itself is unlikely to be as damaging as one would think. More important are the extent to which a parent seeks to ally the children with him or her against the spouse and the use of the children to confide in or complain about the spouse. These are the most burdensome aspects of marital discord for children. They can weather much discord and even continuous tension between parents without significant harm, if the parents fight fair and keep the fighting between themselves.

• It was suggested that efforts should be made toward resolving the issue of custody out of court, because a legal battle would likely produce the greatest stress. Consultation with a neutral third party, emphasizing what would be in the best interests of the children and determining this through objective study rather than impassioned parental judgments, would be the most desirable course.

• It was stressed that any tug-of-war not resolved through the divorce would be likely to continue after the divorce and be just as harmful, if not more so, to the children than continuation of the marriage, especially if the children were put in the position of choosing sides.

Obviously, in the process of discussing these points, the therapist's role and strategy have shifted from those usually employed in couple therapy. However, once a couple has reached this point, a discussion of these issues is appropriate and necessary. Hopefully, if the couple continue therapy and do proceed toward divorce, the therapist can then help them to negotiate such difficult issues as custody and financial arrangements.

Individual Therapy and Secrets

Some years back we felt that neither spouse should confide something in the absence of the spouse that he or she is unwilling to share with the mate. Generally this seems like a good idea, since one goal in therapy is to facilitate open and honest communication. We no longer feel this as necessary. Frequently, we see one or both of the spouses separately as well as jointly. They may share information not brought up in the triadic sessions. Our stance depends a great deal upon the circumstances. In some cases, we think it helpful for the spouse to talk with the partner about the issue and we encourage this. If the spouse feels unwilling, we might encourage the spouse to talk with the spouse about the difficulty in sharing one's thoughts and feelings completely, the dissatisfaction that results, and whether change is desired. In some cases, the fears and expectations the spouse may have about open communication are unrealistic, and this type of discussion may improve communication considerably.

However, we can think of several instances where we thought opening up with some information (for example, with regard to extramarital affairs) would have been detrimental to the relationship and destructive to the progress already made. This is not to say that we condone the behavior, but rather put emphasis on what the consequences might be. Ultimately, we hope to help a spouse having an affair to understand the motivation to tell or not to tell. The motivation may be to alleviate guilt, to punish the partner, or in the case of not telling, to spare the self the possibility of retaliation. In some cases, the information is used to encourage the partner to behave likewise, so that the spouse's own behavior is justified. On occasion, we have agreed that to tell would be harmful. We have had more than one spouse emphasize that they would rather have not found out. But we have also tried to help a spouse having an affair see what price might be paid if the behavior were discovered. We do not feel that trust is an issue to be taken lightly; many marriages have foundered when a spouse felt that he or she could no longer trust the mate.

In one instance, the husband freely related to the therapist in a separate session his many affairs and his intention to continue them. His dilemma was whether to tell the wife the details of his affairs, which she had suspected and was continually pressuring him to do. The therapist was convinced that he had no intention of altering his behavior and that there was no useful purpose to be served by telling his wife. Indeed, the therapist was fully convinced that it would only torture her more than her suspicions already had and would be even more destructive to the relationship.

Although in some cases finally finding out the truth may be relieving to a spouse, details about such relationships are almost never helpful. Rather, the spouse will mull over the details and may make painful comparisons. This may not be rational, but it is how many people react.

Let us add one further point. In the case above, although the therapist stated explicitly the conviction of the destructiveness of a confession by the husband, this did not imply collusion with the husband. The stand was neither condoning nor disapproving, but rather, "Since you choose to continue, it would be to your advantage to consider the consequences of such behavior." At the same time, one would be remiss if one did not discuss the consequences, which had already evoked the wife's suspicions. Since the husband had chosen to maintain the extramarital relationships, the brief separate sessions were used to focus on how he could help the wife feel more loved (since he stated that he did love her), and the part he could play to make things more satisfactory at home. The briefness of therapy (for practical reasons) and the husband's stance did not permit more extensive exploration of and work with some of the underlying problems contributing to his behavior.

We now think it is possible to know something shared by one spouse seen individually and not have it interfere with the marital work. In another case, while we continued with joint sessions, the focus with one spouse in individual sessions was to improve the spouse's understanding of the compulsive need for extramarital relationships and how this interfered, through guilt, with the on-going marriage. However, one would want to be sure that the confiding spouse was not trying to manipulate the therapist into an alliance.

By now it is obvious that we often see spouses both jointly and individually. We have not ordinarily found this to present any major problems. Where it seems to present most difficulty is when one has been seeing a spouse individually, and then it is mutually decided that three-way meetings would be fruitful. In this new situation, it is somewhat difficult to maintain neutrality and not be overly identified with the person originally seen. However, this is less likely to be true if one begins with the couple together and later begins single meetings. This type of beginning helps maintain the interactional, marital focus.

Even if one does not experience any of the above problems, when beginning first with individual therapy and then shifting to couple therapy, one often finds that the second spouse may feel that an alliance has already been formed and that the therapist will be trying to work more for the interests of the original spouse. Besides being aware of this and being neutral, one of the most helpful things that can be done is to bring these issues and feelings out in the open with the therapist stating his or her present position, intent, and purpose. Beyond this statement, the actual proof of a nonpartisan position can only be conveyed through subsequent behavior towards each spouse.

Frequently, it is helpful in the early joint sessions to discuss with the couple how they would feel if the therapist were to see one or both of the spouses separately. In many cases, strong encouragement is given by a spouse. In other cases, objections are voiced, and it has been more expedient to refer one of the spouses to another therapist. We have found, however, that there is much advantage in seeing the couple jointly and one or both of the spouses separately. The extra perspective aids the couple work, and no problems in revealing secrets have occurred.

Spouses Who Have Previously Been Patients

Many times couples come for help in which one spouse has been identified as a patient either in a previous hospitalization or through previous psychotherapy. This may or may not present problems. Therapeutic efforts and directions are essentially the same. The set of the couple, however, may be very different from the case when neither has previously been identified as a patient. A common problem, found more often in the beginning, is that the partner who has not been treated often wants to talk of the couple's problems in terms of the mate's pathology. Whenever possible, one should try to redirect the discussion to what is going on between the couple. One must indicate that one does not accept that one spouse is the cause of the problem, and therefore only this spouse needs to change behaviors.

The therapist does need to recognize that one spouse may be vastly different in terms of ego strength, coping skills, or the presence of symptoms, just as with any couple. If the focus seems to settle on helping the less healthy spouse improve, the couple format may not be the most appropriate. If this is the case, the therapist should suggest that that spouse be seen individually in therapy. However, if the couple professes a wish to work on their marital difficulties, notwithstanding individual problems of either spouse, and want to be seen together, then we will persist as much as possible with a marital focus. As with all couples, but especially in these cases, the therapist must make special efforts to assess each spouse and the extent to which they can use direction and interventions.

We have worked with couples in which one spouse was far more incapacitated than the other. In one case, the psychological balance of one spouse was precarious. Although defenses were generally functioning, this spouse dealt rather weakly with major impulse pressures and feelings, and the defensive behavior was unstable. The course of the marital therapy proved to be more destructive than helpful, even with the therapist's early recognition of the questionable advisability of proceeding in the couple format and stringent efforts to provide maximal support. After a very short trial period, it was agreed by all that individual therapy for this spouse should be resumed (the spouse had been in individual therapy before). In another case, one spouse would have customarily been designated as a borderline personality and had decompensated to the point of requiring hospitalization on several occasions. Nevertheless, the therapeutic work with this couple proceeded quite successfully. Previous individual therapy probably contributed heavily to this success.

It might be worthwhile to restate briefly our premise for couple therapy. We employ a format that focuses on the marital interaction, operating from the assumption that neither spouse is the patient and working toward a more symmetrical relationship with give-and-take. However, we recognize that some drastic shifts have to be made in these assumptions when a spouse's pathology is such that the methods and assumptions previously detailed are virtually impossible to utilize. Whether couple therapy can continue under these circumstances must be evaluated carefully.

In some cases, it has happened that the techniques usually employed in couple therapy (for example, focusing on the relationship and asking spouses to state their own needs and to voice grievances) have produced so much anxiety for a spouse that any kind of negotiating, however handled, was impossible. But in other cases, with careful pacing, one could minimize the anxiety aroused. By this is meant that, although the therapist recognizes that one spouse is ready to confront more openly and directly what goes on between the partner and the self, commenting on this would be highly threatening and likely to mobilize further defensiveness in the partner. At such times, one proceeds slowly, inviting the less able spouse to observe and critique interactions as opposed to being confronted by the therapist. Where this is possible, the therapist should utilize the spouse's opinions more than comments originating from the therapist or the mate. Encouraging the partner to reflect on the self is both supportive and ego building.

Other kinds of problems may present themselves. For example, if the couple's therapist is also the hospital doctor who must assume responsibility for deciding whether hospitalization is necessary, or who is trying to urge one spouse to use special medication, problems concerning alliances are inevitable. Talking over these problems with the healthier spouse, which is usually necessary, undermines the role of the nonpartisan therapist attempting to work toward symmetry. In these cases, it is better for one therapist to focus on the interactions and another therapist to deal with the reality problems that identify one spouse as a patient, with all the contingent problems this presents. This is not to say that couple therapy cannot be done. Should one not be able to obtain an additional therapist for such couples, one may continue by shifting goals and changing some of the usual assumptions of couple therapy. For example, rather than trying to establish full negotiation skills, one might use the session for the couple to discuss such formidable problems as the need for hospitalization or special medications and to clarify the purpose of these (particularly in the case of paranoid suspicions).

Another example of difficulties was presented by a couple with widely discrepant coping skills, in which the wife had suffered several severe but not incapacitating physical illnesses. Her belief was that she was a total physical wreck about to die. Efforts to focus on the relationship were almost totally defeated by her unwillingness to even be approached on any basis that involved give-and-take. Her stance toward any issue was, "Do not expect anything from me; I am physically unable to assume any responsibilities." Efforts by her husband for her to meet some of his needs were met with resentment, anger, and further entrenchment in her position of being totally incapacitated. In one of the few attempted joint sessions, the therapist was trying to help the wife understand the husband's sexual needs. Even when the husband stated his willingness to forgo his sexual fulfillment for "just a little affection," the wife adamantly refused to discuss the matter. It was felt in this case that the wife's psychological response to her previous illnesses interfered with her functioning so much that there was no way to focus on the marital problems until some help could be achieved for her individually.

Monologues

Occasionally a spouse will monopolize an hour by discussing issues primarily related to himself or herself. In one instance, for example, regardless of the focus of the interchange, the husband always brought the conversation back to, "It's all because of my feelings of inferiority." This maneuver is designed to expound on a self-acknowledged problem to the point of excluding any opportunity to focus on marital transactions or even the effect of the individual problem on the relationship. If it is thought that the spouse's pronouncement is valid and may well be one of the major deterrents to a better working marriage, one might acknowledge what this spouse is experiencing and encourage individual help. However, such self-accusations are sometimes defensive maneuvers to avoid focusing on the actual part the individual plays in the frictional interrelationship. In this case, although one can agree with the spouse that inferiority feelings may play into some of the problems, one can help both spouses understand how such feelings lead to behaviors which impair the relationship. If successful, the therapist can resume trying to help the couple focus on their transactions, because only by identifying and understanding these can change occur.

Sexual Problems

It is rare in our experience that a couple comes in primarily for sexual problems in an otherwise intact marriage. We assume there are such couples, who may be helped by educational techniques with minimal therapeutic emphasis. However, most of the couples we have seen fight in bed just as they do elsewhere, and we have come to view their sexual dysfunction in many ways as no different than their general interactional dysfunction. In some cases, sex causes the most distress. However, it is usually just one indication of the status of the rest of the marriage. Or as one husband said, "I see what's going on sexually as just symptomatic of other things."

Some spouses find it difficult to sort out the sexual problem from the rest of their problems, and confusion may be expressed as to whether the sexual problem is a symptom or a cause:

> H: Are we having the problem because we feel a certain way about each other or is it more isolated than that . . . if we could solve some of these problems in sex, would we feel better about each other? Which way do you go ahead?

> T: You can try to go ahead in both ways. I don't think either one is where you necessarily *have* to start. Obviously what's going on between you is just a mirror of the way you feel put down, criticized, and negatively valued in other ways. [The husband has previously discussed such feelings.] I hear you saying something very important to your wife. If some way sexually you could experience more value for yourself, then also you might feel different about it.

The therapist essentially is trying to communicate that the sexual problems are part of the spouse's general feelings about himself, and that work needs to be done on that area, whether the focus is sexual or not.

Often the sexual area will become the focus of therapy. However, unless the couple emphasizes this in the beginning, we do not see the need to do so; we expect in most cases that dissatisfactions in this area will eventually be expressed. We view sexual problems as a subsystem of the general patterns of how partners communicate. In this area, we particularly recognize the importance of the unconscious nature of multiple determinants of their feelings and attitudes. Generally, we look askance at the use of any simple mechanical instructions to resolve sexual problems. We are not, however, opposed to giving technical assistance when the couple need educational knowledge, and this specific assistance is imbedded in the general context of therapy.

We have seen couples improve their sensual satisfaction without focusing on their sexual problems. On the other hand, for some couples much of the focus is on their sexual problems, which have been used to help the spouses understand more about how they communicate to each other generally. This is most appropriate when the couples themselves wish to begin their focus here; hopefully, we will move toward a broader understanding of why their behaviors conflict in other spheres.

To illustrate the variation in working with couples, we will mention one couple where much of the friction was sexual. The husband was occasionally impotent, but more stressful to the wife were his frequent ejaculations a minute or so after intromission; his difficulties left her extremely unsatisfied and contributed to the problems of the relationship. It was thought that it might be useful for the husband to obtain help quickly for his sexual problem. He was referred to a therapist who saw him eight times, using a structured, cognitive-behavioral approach (rational behavior therapy). The emphasis was primarily on helping him to eliminate the anxiety that aroused thoughts of failure once sex was initiated and to substitute thoughts of sexually arousing stimuli. This brief, extra-couple intervention provided some temporary relief for him and some improvement in the couple's relationship. This allowed therapy to proceed to other issues that were more basic to the couples' friction. The husband's sexual problem could be seen as symptomatic of the overall dissatisfactions in the marriage, but it disrupted any progress. The wife tended to use sexuality as an external focal point, which obscured the necessity of working beyond this. With the sexual problem somewhat alleviated, we were able to move on to the wife's anger about past grievances, and this facilitated the wife's wish to work more in individual therapy.

The brief, sexually oriented therapy did not produce any permanent improvement in their relationship. In fact, the husband's sexual problems recurred from time to time when things were bad between the couple. However, at the time this therapy was initiated, it served several useful purposes: the husband's self-image was not further undermined; the emphasis on the sexual area as a source of the wife's dissatisfaction was decreased; and sex was no longer viewed as the sole cause of the problems. The reader may notice the conviction that there were many other problems to resolve before the couple were in a position to have good sexual harmony.

On occasion, an impasse is reached in therapy where one

spouse wishes to talk about sexual problems and the other refuses. This may be out of embarrassment, unwillingness to discuss such an intimate subject with another, or any number of other reasons. We usually try to encourage the spouse wishing to discuss the problem to stress the importance of having the partner do this also and the frustration resulting from not being able to work on it together. Sometimes we even suggest that the spouse ask the partner what could be done to make it easier to explore this area. We have usually found reluctance to result from feelings of inadequacy and the fear of blame. Whenever the therapist can discern the possibility of these attitudes being present, it is important to focus on them, perhaps by acknowledging that many of us grew up with beliefs and values that may have contributed to sexual problems and that this does not make us freaks—we are all products of our learning and experiences. Sometimes with support, understanding, and stringent efforts to avoid any denigration by the spouse, the hesitant partner may become more willing to discuss sexual problems. In other cases, both spouses may be reluctant to discuss sexual problems, although they indicate discontent. It is often an area of great sensitivity in which individuals feel especially exposed and vulnerable. The therapist will need a solid therapeutic alliance with most spouses before they will discuss this area freely.

Individuals who already suffer from feelings of low self-esteem and are sensitive to disapproval from their spouses are especially vulnerable. One husband expressed it well:

> H: I don't know what to say—just my same fears at not doing things right. I'm clumsy, inept. I haven't reached that level, like all the other areas I've talked about. I feel a great deal of disapproval—[with the wife] kind of waiting around for me to reach a certain level of performance, and I just feel extremely self-conscious and uncomfortable.

Spouses are also prone to see their marital partner's lack of satisfaction as a direct reflection on them, and they often use this to conclude that there must be something seriously wrong with them.

H: I see us as really being in a jam. I'm very aware of my wife
being uptight, and it seems like I feel very bumbling.
We've been married fifteen years and surely by this time
I could have been more helpful to her and obviously I'm
not—so that must mean I'm some kind of schmuck.

Because of the tendency for spouses to draw unnecessarily
bleak conclusions regarding themselves if their mates fail to achieve
satisfaction, therapeutic efforts will need to emphasize the separateness of spouses in the sexual interaction, that one is not necessarily
responsible for the other's distress. At such times, exploration of
attitudes and feelings often reveals ingrained factors producing
sexual difficulties independent of the individual spouse and the
spouse's interaction. This is not to minimize the importance of the
interactional aspects but rather to stress that helping spouses to
carefully sort out what is going on between them and how this might
have come to be are usually useful. Inevitably, both present and
past factors are involved.

To clarify some of the aspects mentioned above, the following
interchange is presented:

T: Maybe each of you could be of help to the other in the
sense of telling what does feel good and what doesn't
feel good—how you'd like certain things to be or not
to be.

W: Well, I'm probably a little sensitive about this anyway.
I know I've picked up a lot of attitudes from my parents;
it's hard for me to forget all these, to approach things
differently.

T: I'm sure that's probably true—that you will have certain
kinds of feelings and attitudes as a result of your upbring-
ings, but that doesn't rule out what each of you can do to
make things go better for the other, even if you have
some attitudes that make it more difficult.

For some couples, one of the most helpful things one can do
is to increase verbal communication in this area; spouses frequently
comment that this is the one area that they have never really talked

about. Often there are confusions about wants, assumptions about what is appropriate, and unstated feelings. Helping couples begin to talk together about such topics is at least a start, and for couples with less severe problems, this alone may be greatly facilitating.

The following will illustrate some of the above points. The wife had just related that she and the husband had never been able to communicate very well on a personal, intimate level.

T: [To wife] Why don't you ask him questions as to whatever confusions you might have on what he said to you—to help to clarify by asking him some questions about things you're not sure about.

W: Well, the two of us have never talked that much about it. But I think probably for most of our married life that I have initiated any sexual activity that we have engaged in, and [to husband] I have always wondered a little bit if that doesn't bother you.

       [The wife goes on to say that she does not know enough about men to know what women are supposed to do.]

T: What are you asking?

W: I expressed the question, I believe, [to husband] how do you feel about my initiating sexual activities?

H: That is . . . that does not bother me, but obviously you feel that you shouldn't have to initiate. I guess one of the biggest problems I've always had [is] a fear in all areas of being rejected, and I suppose that is a part of what I have, you know, underneath, you know. For a period of time, there were moments when I thought you weren't inter-ested in me initiating sexual activities.

W: Well, why did you let that stop you?

       [The therapist interrupts the question and attempts to have the wife make a statement of what she is trying to express. Since the wife's comments do not pinpoint this, the therapist adds another version.]

T: I thought I heard something else behind the question.

You can correct me if I'm wrong. It seemed to me what you were trying to indicate to your husband was that you wanted him to initiate sex.

W: Yes.

T: I don't mean exclusively, but you want him to.

W: Yes, I have always wanted that; I have asked you for that before.

T: Can you tell your husband why that is important to you?

W: Well, I think at least culturally I was led to believe that the man was supposed to initiate sexual activity, and as a result of your not [doing it], if I wanted sex, I had to initiate it.

It is clear that the wife has left off the meaning of how she felt when her husband does not initiate sex.

T: Which made you feel how about yourself?

W: A little pushy . . . it would make me feel more wanted, more desirable.

[The wife mentions that she has been attracted to other men because they went after her. More interchange follows.]

T: O.K., one of these changes I hear you requesting is that he chase you some?

W: Yes.

T: [To husband] If she wants to feel wanted, then sitting back waiting for her to initiate everything doesn't make her feel wanted, and the less she feels wanted . . .

[The wife, in a lengthy series of comments, tells her husband in essence that whenever he initiates something, even though she may not be interested at the moment, that he should try harder and that he should not assume that if she says no, that is the end of it. The husband expresses concern that he will not be able to tell when she really means no.]

T: Maybe you won't be able to recognize it, maybe you will just have to take a risk. Maybe fifty percent of the time when you go ahead it will turn out to be a real no, and the rest of the time you can talk her into something. But there is another point I am making. Noes are not necessarily dichotomous—it really means that or it really doesn't; half the time she may not know herself.

[The therapist then says that the response has a lot to do with the amount of stimulation and investment put in the seductive efforts, no matter what the mood.]

T: And whether the no changes into a yes has everything to do with the initiator.

[Several comments follow.]

T: She wants to be sought after, she wants to be coaxed, to be loved, seduced, or any way you want to put it. You should go after her with, like you really want it, like you would do if you were dating. But of course, that is one of the hard things you have to learn; [if] someone says no, you may get your feelings hurt and easily withdraw, but that's not necessarily what has to happen. If you come back once in a while loving and caring, it's hard to resist for anybody.

W: Well, loving and caring and just a little bit of self-assertion, too.

[The therapist encourages the husband to voice needs he may want to have fulfilled so that he can request these of the wife. This is to make for a greater willingness on his part to attempt to gratify the needs the wife has just expressed.]

T: What's it going to take on your wife's part to make you more in the mood to do these things? We have just been working on one side of it, but I suspect there's another part of it.

H: Well, I think maybe the fact that I've heard it expressed may help . . . with something that I don't know, I don't guess . . . I haven't thought about it in that sense. I think

> probably I took you for granted—I didn't know how . . .
> I didn't feel you needed much. Just recognizing that
> might help.

At this point the husband does not seem to wish to state any of his
unmet needs.

In many cases that we see, sexual interest in the partnership
has reached a low ebb, usually because the otherwise unsatisfactory
relation between the couple has affected the physical relationship,
and the partners have implicitly agreed to avoid sex. Their dissatisfaction with this solution, however, may remain marked and an
area of continuing resentment and anger.

The following is a condensed version of the therapist's efforts to help a husband get in touch with more of his feelings and
understand more about his backing off sexually. Both spouses had
acknowledged their dissatisfaction with practically no sex, and both
had expressed little interest.

T: [To husband] What would it take to get you interested?
     Maybe you can talk with your wife about that.

H: I don't know . . . I don't understand what's going on with
     myself. I feel a lot of anger.

     [After several more comments, the therapist focuses on
     helping the husband experience his anger.]

T: O.K., now let's start there, then. Are you willing to try
     some things? [The husband looks suspicious.] You want
     to know what they are first?

H: Yeah. [Laughs.]

T: What I want you to do is just start out and say to your wife,
     "I am angry with you because . . ." and look at your wife.

H: I don't know. I can't put my finger on it.

     [The therapist says the sentence again emphatically.]

T: Let what comes, come. Don't stew and think and get too
     rational.

H: I really can't—I don't know.

T: Look at her and say the words, even if you . . .

H: I'm angry at you because [pausing] you monopolize my
      life—you take my individuality from me. I think . . . oh,
      that's not right!

Notice that as the husband begins to voice his resentments, he immediately feels he should not and he censors himself.

T: Just keep going with that.

H: [Pausing, to wife] I guess I just think everything pretty
      much follows your way.

T: One of the things you seem to have difficulty with is
      really standing behind your feelings.

H: I can't identify them. I don't know what they are.

T: Well, just assume that they are real—you said, "I'm
      angry."

H: Yeah, I find myself feeling angry.

T: And I believe you—I think you're very angry.

H: And I don't understand it—I try to pin it down and I just
      can't pin it down.

T: Well, I think you should take your anger seriously. There
      is something very important going on there with you and
      really making for problems.

      [The husband now reveals that one reason he is afraid
      to pursue his feelings is that he fears, "it's all my prob-
      lem."]

T: You may have many reasons why you're angry. I'm not
      implying anything about blame. I'm just saying your
      anger is an important thing going on between you. I'm
      not trying to talk about whether it's justified or not. I
      assume you have good reasons for being angry.

      [The wife comments that she understands the husband's
      anger and believes her efforts are toward not changing
      anything but rather toward trying to get the husband not
      to be angry.]

T: To me the importance of getting in touch with what that's all about is it can help us focus on what needs to be altered in the relationship. We want to identify more what's going on between you that's playing a part in that, if any, and I assume that there is something. I don't know how much; there may be sources independent of the marriage—I don't know.

H: I guess my reaction . . . is I've really done a lot of thinking.

[The husband talks of the good qualities of the wife.]

H: So I can't figure out what in the world it is I feel angry about.

Note that the husband has already made some comments about feeling monopolized but with little or no accompanying feeling.

T: Well, let's go back to your statement—just say again, "I am angry at you because you monpolize me"—say that to your wife and look at her.

[The husband does so weakly.]

T: Say it again and feel it as much as you can.

H: But I don't know what that means, though.

T: That's one of the ways you can try to understand what it's all about is to take a look at it—just look at her straight and tell her that.

H: I don't know how.

T: Don't worry so much about how—just say it again with all the feeling you can experience—or if you want to say something different, that's O.K.

[The husband expresses discomfort, and the therapist acknowledges "putting him on the spot."]

H: I think it's a crock of shit what I just said. I really do.

[The husband is trying to undo the implication of his anger toward the wife.]

T: You may think that, but it may not be what you're feeling.

H: I don't know what to do.

T: Where are you now—what are you experiencing now?

H: Frustration—I don't even want to be here.

T: Can you just stay with that feeling for now?

H: I really think I made a mistake fifteen years ago.

This opens up a new area of the husband's feelings. The therapist helps him pursue these thoughts and feelings to recognize more fully his ambivalent feelings toward the wife. This leads to a feeling at the core of his anger, his fear that the wife will leave him despite his need of her.

[Further work intervenes; then the therapist feeds sentences to the husband.]

T: What I need is . . .

H: What I need is to feel sure of and not have all the frightening uncertainty.

T: What I'm afraid of is . . .

H: What I'm afraid of is [to wife] you're just going to get a whim and just destroy much of my world, without any thought.

T: And I need . . .

H: And I need you badly.

T: Say that with feeling.

H: I need you badly!

Although the focus started on the sexual disinterest of the partners, note how feelings behind this disinterest, once pursued, showed intensity and complexity—anger the husband has trouble experiencing, ambivalence, and intense fear. As the session continued, it became clearer why the husband was so angry at the wife. He referred to the many times she failed to hear his needs and was inconsiderate, despite his protests and his lingering fear of further hurts. It becomes apparent as one works in this fashion why focusing on sexual techniques alone might miss out on the prevailing feeling from which the sexual dysfunction emanates. In this case, the therapist utilized some gestalt techniques for helping the husband get in touch with and be able to communicate his feelings.

9

Therapy with
a Divorced Couple

The therapeutic approach described can also be used successfully with divorced individuals whose fighting continues, usually with the children as the battleground. In many ways, it is easier to help these couples, since they are no longer as dependent on each other for gratifications. The issues are more specific and usually center around the children, visitation arrangements, or finances. We have not worked with a divorced couple concerning faulty child support or alimony and would assume this is primarily a legal matter.

The couple to be described in this chapter were seen jointly to work out problems primarily concerning their three children, ages 10, 8, and 4; they were referred by a lawyer for divorce counseling. At the time they came for help, the couple were divorced and had been separated for two years. The ex-husband was remarried and had children by the present marriage. The ex-wife had not remarried and was in school, working toward a degree in education.

Their problems centered primarily around how to work out arrangements with regard to the children. Their divorce granted the ex-husband unlimited visitation rights with the ex-wife having custody. There had been much fighting over the arrangement of visits. In addition, the ex-husband violently objected to the fact that the ex-wife had planned to move to Georgia (her state of origin) with the children when school was out for the summer. She stated this was necessary for financial reasons; teacher's jobs were hard to get since there was a large supply of teachers from the training program at the local university. The ex-husband insisted there was no reason why she could not find a job in the vicinity. He felt that his rights as a parent would be violated if she moved to Georiga, hundreds of miles away.

The couple began therapy with a stalemate: her refusal to reconsider moving to Georgia, and his strong opposition to the move. He pointed out that in their divorce agreement, it was legally stated that she could not take the kids out of the state unless it was for religious, health, or economic reasons, and he did not feel that she could prove that it would be necessary for economic reasons. Thus, the battle was initially waged around legal issues with an implied threat from the ex-husband that if necessary, he would resort to legal proceedings to win his case.

The couple were seen jointly for three sessions, and the ex-wife was seen individually for two. The latter was suggested by the therapist, because the ex-wife appeared to have many lingering, bitter feelings that were interfering with her helping the children and herself; she willingly agreed. Therapy with this couple was brief, yet the outcome was quite positive. The relationship between the two had been altered from a tug-of-war to an agreeable relationship, in which their interchanges could center on working out arrangements without argument.

Below we shall detail some of the therapeutic interventions and goals. Notes were taken on each session immediately afterward to preserve the accuracy of the material as much as possible. From these, the points below have been distilled.

The therapist acknowledged the ex-husband's understandable need to have the children remain living in the town where he resided, but attempted to separate the issue of his genuine concern for the children from the struggle with the ex-wife over control and who was to make decisions. The therapist also tried to help the ex-wife hear his caring, which had been hard for her to tune into. Out of her rejection and feelings of anger, her position had been, "You didn't want us, so now we don't want you." In separate sessions with her, the therapist focused on the positive aspects of the children having their father in town and what they would miss if they moved away. Here, efforts were made to separate the children's needs from the ex-wife's needs; it was stressed that the ex-husband did not reject the children—only the ex-wife. This required efforts to alter her conception that when the ex-husband divorced her, he divorced the children, also. These seem to be issues many ex-spouses confuse; they consider themselves and the children as one entity, treated as such by the ex-spouse. This interferes with their hearing the ex-spouse's caring and concern for the children.

The therapist worked to help the ex-husband see that if he had a chance to influence the ex-wife's decision regarding leaving or staying, it would come through him helping her to be convinced that living nearby would not involve the current hassle. This meant being able to see the power plays that he was utilizing and giving them up. The ex-husband was a bright, articulate individual, who could outargue the ex-wife and, through his logical reasoning, prove his points and justify his positions. The ex-wife, also bright, felt unable to argue back successfully and was frequently frustrated in trying, but did not feel moved by his arguments to change her position. For the ex-husband, it was necessary that he realize that his argumentative style hurt his efforts to influence her. To accomplish this, it was necessary to encourage the ex-wife to feed back to him *what* he did that bothered her—that she felt overpowered by his heavy-handed ways and angry as a result, and that she felt she could never really be heard, particularly when she expressed her feelings. Hearing feelings was somewhat difficult for Paul, the ex-husband, and some work was necessary to help him appreciate her feelings rather than using her responses for further debate.

To illustrate these points, the therapist had them focus both on a successful negotiation and on an unsuccessful one during one joint session. The therapist then tried to aid them in exploring and learning substitute behaviors for their red flags, such as each stating personal feelings regarding needs to plan for the children as opposed to arguing over whose plan was the most logical. The therapist suggested that their final decision be made on the basis of strength of convictions and feelings rather than of logic; if both felt equally strong, they might have to use some arbitrary tie breaker.

The therapist challenged the ex-wife to think more in terms of the children's needs rather than being swayed by her anger at the ex-husband, where she would operate more from a position of wanting to retaliate toward him, hurting the children in the process. This is a tricky point. Many parents, very concerned about their children's best interests, are not able to see how they use the children in their continued war with their ex-spouses. With the ex-wife, one main point focused on was the dilemma children feel in being placed in the middle and pressured to choose sides. The therapist tried to explore with her ways, however subtle, that she might be contributing to this; it was obvious that she genuinely did not want to hurt her children.

The therapist aided the ex-wife to evaluate realistically the pros and cons of moving and staying. The issue was discussed of what marriage failure. Initially the ex-wife was quite vituperative in blaming the ex-husband for their marriage failure, and her continuing angry feelings interfered with her working out plans with him as well as their being a source of discomfort. After some time detailing ways in which the ex-husband was at fault, she began intermittently to wonder how she had failed, stating that she must have done some things wrong as well. The therapeutic work was aimed at derailing efforts to place guilt and, instead, trying to understand the marriage failure from another view—two individuals who, with time and change, failed to mesh sufficiently to satisfy each other. It was necessary to alleviate some of the anger (which was possible once blaming was not the focus) before the ex-wife could work more constructively and be able to understand the ex-husband's needs as well as maintain the importance of her own.

The therapist aided the ex-wife to evaluate the pros and cons of moving and staying realistically. The issue was discussed of what the children would miss with a father so far away and how much more they would gain if they lived in the same town, provided that their parents were not at war and they were not caught in the middle. On the other side was the ex-wife's need to get away from reminders of what had happened and the attraction of moving to where the family was present to support her emotionally. With continued venting of her feelings and a genuine concern to do what was best for the children, the ex-wife began to feel that she did not have to get away and could live in the same town as the ex-husband. The advantages for the children were very obvious to her, and she did not want to deprive them of their good relationship with their father. There was also the advantage of owning her own home.

The therapist helped the ex-husband to understand the children's questions about divorce and their feelings about it. During therapy, the ex-husband had expressed concern about the persistent questions the children had voiced. The therapist focused on the meanings of these and was able to illustrate via the questions the ex-husband's general problem with understanding others, which was to use logic without feelings. His son had repeatedly asked him why they had gotten a divorce. The ex-husband had spent considerable time giving a logical and what he thought to be a satisfactory answer. He was thus puzzled why it did not seem to satisfy his son, who repeated the question.

The therapist helped him hear the question not as a request for information but as a complaint or protest with much feeling behind it. Translated it meant, "Why did you have to do it—I wish you hadn't—I don't like it." Hearing feelings rather than just content was new for the ex-husband and improved his communication with the children as well as the ex-wife.

Due to technical difficulties, only the last half of the third and last couple session was taped. By this time, the therapeutic work was primarily accomplished. The exchange from this tape is presented to give a clearer conception of the couple and to illustrate the successful way they were able to communicate by this time. Rather than showing therapeutic techniques, it illustrates a couple who are terminating therapy with a relationship markedly different from when they arrived, and in this sense it indicates the success of the therapy, brief as it was.

H: I've made commitments to try to help, and this is one way of my saying to you that I am concerned about what happens to you all. I'm concerned about what happens to you. I think this experience is the greatest thing that could have happened as far as each of us individually is concerned, as well as the children.

W: You mean . . .

H: The fact that we're able to get into a counseling situation where each of us can find some guidance and help, not only as we relate to the children, but as we relate to ourselves and to each other. I mean, it's worth every penny that it cost. This is saying that, you know, I'm concerned about you. On exceptions that we're not together, I'm much more hopeful that you're dealing with things that are making you comfortable, not just dealing with things related to the way the five of us [including the children] interrelate, because I care what happens. I know that, or I think that what you're seeing is that my behavior two years ago or subsequent before that negates the fact that I care what happens to you. It doesn't—not as far as I'm concerned—and so, you know, when you get sick it concerns me. It concerns me not only because the kids have a hard time but because you're sick and I want to help, not only because of the children, but in ways that I can help you. I want to do that because I do care what happens to you.

W: I hear what you're saying and I appreciate what you're saying, but by the same token I find that there are, other than the fact, the very specifics of the children needing certain things, like for example, if I'm sick in bed and can't do, or you know, if they need care, so calling you would take care of them, things like that. But as far as calling on you for my own—something that's just something I need, I just can't do that. I find that impossible. Maybe it's because I depended on you so much when we were married. I don't know why, or maybe it's just the phases I'm going through. Maybe I will find this easier to do in a very short time from now, but I have this feeling of . . . not that I can't depend on you, but that I must not depend on you, but of course that just concerns me, but that I must find other more appropriate

ways of handling that. Now if it is obvious that it's something that I need to do for the children, then I find it no
difficulty at all to call on you, but if it's just something
for me, if I've just had it or, you know, something like
that, then I find it very difficult to—I realize that I have
a very double standard here, because with things with
my school, which is very much me, I don't mind calling
on you for that. But if it's just a matter of whether I can
cope or not, I just can't do that.

T: You know, I think it would be helpful for Paul [the ex-
husband] if he knew more what that was about.

W: What do you mean?

T: Why it's difficult to ask him for help just for you, if you
could talk with him just about that.

W: Well, it's a very personal thing, and it goes back, of course,
to the fact that, well, I don't want to do this. [Laughs.]
Well, it does relate to the circumstances of the divorce.
You didn't want me, you left me. Fine, O.K., I'll take care
of it from here on out. I think that's what's in back of it,
but these are things I'm working through, so see, I
don't . . .

T: O.K., well, if you need him now, therefore what?

W: What do you mean?

T: Therefore what does that mean, if you could talk to him
about it?

W: Well, that I still have some dependency on him, or at
least the feelings are there that I do. You know, a short
time from now when we're further down the road, so to
speak, as far as my development and working through
these things are concerned, then I won't see it that way,
but that's the way I see it now, because I still have these
hang-ups.

T: Well, I don't know if they are hang-ups, [to ex-husband]
but what I hear her saying, which I think would be helpful for you to know, is that she doesn't want to need you,
because she feels like, in essence, she can't really have

you, and that continuing in that vein is uncomfortable for her now.

H: Well, I can understand that now.

T: It's like it raises hopes of something that can't be, and [to ex-wife] I'm going a little beyond what you said.

W: Yes, you are. [Laughs nervously.]

T: But I think that's in there.

W: Could be.

T: That's part of it; it can't really be, and it's sort of like her taking a little of it and that's hard for her now. See, I hear you saying that it would really make you feel good if Jana [the ex-wife] could turn to you for help. Am I misquoting you on that?

H: That's stating it in a little different way, but I guess that's really what I'm saying.

T: That's what I hear you saying, and it makes sense to me that you would say that, because I think there has to be some uneasiness about the divorce, about leaving a person, about giving up responsibilities, and I don't think you've given it up. The divorce doesn't mean that you've given it up. I think you feel some responsibility and some concern, and I think in some ways that would make you feel—I don't know if the choice of words is best—but maybe less guilty if you felt she could turn to you for help and you could give her some help. I think it would really make you feel better. [To wife] And I understand where you're coming from, because turning to him for help is too reminiscent of like being married again, and it's sort of like you feel like you've got to sever it; it's one way or the other, and . . .

W: There's appropriate ways. Like he said, I have asked him for extra money and that's always come through, and I have asked him to keep the kids when I take the field trips, and he's always done that. There are degrees of appropriateness or maybe that's the wrong word, maybe it's degrees of comfortableness.

T: I hear what you're saying, but I just wanted each of you to know where the other was on this, what each is struggling with, because they're different kinds of things. [To ex-husband] You're struggling with a different thing than she's struggling with, and I heard you say, "I hear what you're saying, you know, and I acknowledge that, but hear where I am." It's hard for her to take help from you, unless it's something for the kids.

H: I think I have a fairly clear understanding. I think I identified this a long time ago.

W: We even talked about this.

H: I think what I'm saying now is, "Look, if you can reach a point where you're comfortable with it, I can be comfortable with that and I'm willing to help any way I can— however you can feel comfortable.

T: And it may take some time, like you suggested.

W: Yes.

T: As things go on in the relationship, the relation between you continues positive in terms of working out arrangements, you know, it may be much easier to be friends— other than just making business arrangements.

[The ex-wife laughs. A long pause follows.]

W: [To ex-husband] There is something I would like to say. The sessions she [the therapist] and I have had alone have been very helpful, and I appreciate that, too. [He has paid for the sessions.]

H: Well, I'm pleased that you all have met. Some of the frustration I was feeling, as far as your decision making about going to Georgia, for example, I can identify for my own self, the fact that I really wasn't comfortable with the kinds of input that I saw going into the decision. Over the last two or three weeks, I've accepted the fact that I've become more comfortable with the fact that when you make your decision, that it will be made with the kinds of input that I'm comfortable with, I guess is really what it boils down to.

W: Maybe.

H: Well, I feel like that in talking with Dr. Tydings [the
     therapist] that you—I really don't have any idea what you
     are talking about or where it's going to lead to—but I feel
     like I'm more comfortable with your making the decision
     in this kind of context than just making it in the con-
     text of just input you might be getting from friends or
     family or just from yourself.

This comment could be inflammatory, because it implies criticism.
The therapist redirects the flow.

T: Well, let me put that another way. It may not be exactly
     what you were going to communicate, but I think the
     optimal thing for her is to make a decision not out of
     frustration and difficulties with you.

H: Yes.

W: Yes.

T: That's the thing, it doesn't matter what friends or any-
     body else says, but that it not be done because she just
     can't tolerate this. You know, that there's so much fric-
     tion between you and so much discomfort in negotiating
     with you that she just wants to get away from it. That was
     my goal, one to me that seems most helpful to both of
     you. Because once it's not embroiled in the context of
     anger and just wanting to sever completely, then she can
     make it on the basis of considering all the factors, the
     children, economic reasons, her comfort, availability of
     relatives, availability of you, put them all in there to-
     gether and try to make hopefully for her what would be
     the most livable decision, and hopefully it would be one
     you can accept.

H: I think what I'm saying is I think this kind of thing is
     happening, which makes me more comfortable. I still
     don't know what decision you will end up with. I've got
     a pretty good idea after the long talk.

T: Would you like to tell him where you were on that?

W: I haven't said anything to him about it, but I am looking

at jobs here, and it's an either-or. It's either here or in
Georgia, because if it's somewhere halfway in between,
then we've accomplished nothing. The children don't
have you, and I don't have any family, either, but I feel
like that if I could find a job here that would be economically the same as one in Georgia, that I can personally, can stay. Then, say, I don't feel like I need to run
away anymore, and also I've been talking with Dr. Tydings about specific things the children need right now,
and if I can find a position here, then they'll have you
and this is in terms of what I'm thinking. Dr. Voight
[someone in her field] was somewhat helpful—positive
that I could find something. He had something specifically in the back of his mind, but he did not tell me what
it was. Economically—at first I thought—well, my uncle
said that I could get a very good job in Georgia with the
schools, but we checked and the information is not all
that correct. But this is what I'm thinking, I'm checking
both places with a very open mind. Considering the eco-
nomics here and that we have a house and I know what
it's going to cost to get it, things like that. That does not
mean that we may not move. At least, I have been looking in both places very actively, but only in these two
places, not two hundred miles down the road.

H: I can understand that, and that makes sense to me. To
me the only advantage of living two hundred miles down
the road is to provide you with the kind of distance that
you were wanting to get, like the eighty-five miles to
Louisville provides a whole lot of distance, too.

W: This is another thing that Dr. Voight said, because he's
got a lot of contacts in Louisville and Cincinnati and that
still puts the children close to you, but it involves the
move and so forth, which takes the economic factor
there.

H: That of course pleases me very much; it surprises me,
but it does please me very much.

W: Well, I still want to go home, but I can wait a few years;
the children are so happy. They enjoy you and your

family, and I'm glad of that. I can give them a little bit more time and Peggy [a daughter] graduates from high school in thirteen years. I can go home in thirteen years. But it could be that nothing will open up. It could be that there would only be some consulting jobs, and I have to make that decision.

H: Well, I think what I was trying to say to you initially [was] if you decide to move to Georgia, I can be more comfortable with it now than four weeks ago. I still don't like it, you know, because it does present some real problems. I can understand that it would also present some problems for you to stay here with a lot of angry feelings.

W: If I work through those angry feelings and a job comes up . . .

T: And it would be very hard to move to a strange place, you know with no friends, no family, no husband, just you and the kids, 'cause you would have to start all over and that's hard.

W: Yes. That's why those things in Georgia, like the specific town where my aunt and uncle are, just seemed beautiful, because they have friends. That may not be very realistic, either.

T: I don't know, but I can sure understand that just having some relatives can make a lot of difference . . . and people you care about and people who care about you versus going to a totally strange place where you don't have friends, you have to start from scratch. That's really not very much fun for anybody under any circumstances— it's always unsettling.

W: So that's some of the things that I'm working on.

H: Well, that's good, I think. The way I feel in this decision . . . anything I can do to try to help it along. [Both laugh together.]

W: You'll go out and knock on doors and look for jobs [for me].

T: [To husband] Sure, that [a job here] would be great for you—it really would—there's no question of it. It will be a big loss for you and for them if the move comes to be, which is a possibility.

W: They're either on one side of the fence or the other. Mother's just devastated, but we will work it out.

T: Did she kind of think that you would move into the same town that she lives in?

W: No, but see, she's going to retire and she's gonna follow me.

T: Oh, I see.

W: When I talked to her on the phone, I shouldn't even have brought it up, but I thought I've got to let her know about moving and I threw it out, and you know, I could just hear doom and desperation and the negative, you know, "Well, I'll probably just stay here then," and that's the worst place in the world. She's in a little town about like that, and she's allergic to everything that grows and blooms around there. She should get back down to Georgia, where she can get some help from my grandmother.

T: When does she retire?

W: Two years from right now. But mother has a tendency to flip into the negative pretty easy, and I'll have to help her work through it. Of course, her thought . . . she says, "Whatever's best for the kids," but that's not what she really, really feels. She wants me, because I'm her only child. So she's thinking of me and I'm thinking of my kids and it's kind of a vicious cycle.

T: Well, it's quite understandable, because she lives in a different town and she's going to have a loss, too. A loss of all the things that make her feel important, her work and so forth, she's going to be needy. I can see she would want very much to have you there.

W: But when she does retire, this climate up here is bad for her because she has arthritis, but the summers are nice, a lot more pleasant than they are in Georgia, so she could split her time. I mean, there are a lot of things if you can get beyond the initial hurt and get up and do it. [A pause follows.]

T: Well, where do you folks want to go from here?

H: I personally feel comfortable with the way things are right now. I don't have a lot of things now that I feel like it's real important to talk about. I'm still open to being here if there are some things we need to talk about. I'm also open to kind of leave it where it is right now, and if problems start developing again, let's check back in on it again. I'm comfortable with this, but then I'm open to be here to talk any more about some things. [To ex-wife] You know, I may not recognize some problems that you're feeling, and I want to sit right down and talk about them.

W: I had certain goals, I think we had certain goals in doing this and I think they've been met, and one of them was that we find a level that we could communicate [on], and if we have to we'll just stick to that. Just that one level from here on, because it is a level that I think we can function at.

H: I'm not sure I'm hearing what you're saying.

W: Well, we have discovered some ways in which we can sit down and talk.

     [The last interchange of several minutes was not recorded because the tape ran out.]

Although the couple worked through their problems sufficiently to enable them to continue living in the same town, this did not come to be. A good job opportunity materialized for the ex-wife, and she and the children moved away. However, individual contact with each of the couple approximately a year after therapy indicated that their work in therapy had paid off. Although disappointed with the distance from the children, the ex-husband accepted this, viewing the decision to move as not dictated by anger but as best suited to the practical considerations. Both ex-spouses felt the child visitation arrangements were pleasant and that the tug-of-war had dissipated. She seemed pleased with her new job; he talked of the warm reunions with the children, which were frequent.

10

Couple Therapy:
A Summary

We are currently witnessing marked changes in the styles of living among individuals. New patterns of relationships have become prominent with open marriages and the more prevalent pattern of unmarried couples living together. The current rate of divorce has risen alarmingly. The traditional stable family has been questioned as an acceptable model for relationships that can function effectively and be maintained in our present society. Increased mobility of individuals, which makes it difficult for them to put down stable roots, and the shrinking of the extended family as a source of support have added to the pressure placed on marriages to provide the emotional security and support individuals seek.

Within this context of a changing society, the values and roles of which are no longer clearly defined, couples are experiencing increased strain. How well they withstand this stress depends in large part on their success in mastering previous developmental tasks. However, such success is always relative, and individuals are rarely free from problems. The close relationship of living together often rekindles previously unresolved conflicts, which now come more fully into focus in the transactions of the couple. In addition, specific crises or problems arise as couples progress through the normally varying "stages" of life, with their shifting requirements and stresses. Solutions to marital problems that were functional in the past may cease to be so, as interactional behaviors take on new meanings within the context of changing experiences, needs, expectations, and satisfactions. Societal, individual, and relationship problems often coalesce to produce stress with which couples cannot cope without help. Increasingly, such individuals are seeking to find ways to alleviate their distress. Professionals attempting to perform this function have found the more traditional, individually oriented methods limited and have pushed to explore more effective means. This book focuses on helping couples in distress resolve their difficulties.

In the previous chapters, a treatment approach has been advanced that describes problems posed for the therapist attempting to work with such couples and the principles and methods useful in dealing with them. An important basic assumption is that a couple's behavior can be understood both from an interactional and intrapsychic point of view. This assumption has important implications both in understanding what goes on between the couple and in guiding the therapist in his or her work.

From the interactional point of view, it is important to recognize that couples influence each other both in eliciting and in maintaining behaviors. An interlocking interaction often exists because it serves certain important functions, healthy or otherwise, for each individual, thus contributing to a stable equilibrium. The implication is that attention to, and understanding of, this "contractual" arrangement, which may not be in conscious awareness, aids the process of working toward the change necessary for improving the relationship. Helping spouses become aware of the functions served by their behaviors, as well as the spouses' cues that trigger and contribute to their reoccurrence, is part of the unraveling process necessary before change can occur.

Equally important is the assumption that behavior is not controlled solely by these interactions. Pressures from previously unresolved conflicts may contribute to, and shape behaviors independent of, the spouse's behavior. Current expectations in a relationship and present coping skills depend a great deal on previous experiences. In some cases, external changes on one spouse's part may effect little or no change in the mate. Armed with this understanding of dynamic and etiological factors, the therapist can better appreciate why the present behaviors are so rigid and, in turn, can understand both the advantages and limits of work on the interactional aspect of behavior. In addition, the therapist can help each spouse appreciate more fully the extent and limits of his or her impact on the mate. Greater appreciation of earlier determinants of present behaviors may also offer both spouses a perspective that minimizes guilt and blame.

Therapy proceeds both experientially and cognitively. The primary focus is on the interactions of the couple as each attempts to meet personal needs and as their need-satisfactions and expectations fail to mesh. The therapist addresses himself to the logical and reasonable aspect of each spouse, using interpretations, confrontation, suggestion, persuasion, explanation, or reasoning to promote awareness and understanding of individual and interactional behaviors, preliminary to the next step of spouses' making decisions as to whether they wish to initiate change. A change in understanding, however, does not guarantee a change in overt behaviors. The assumption is that behavior is not solely under the sway of the logical processes and thus not necessarily subject to change through rational means. Feelings often color thinking and the interpretation of behavior, as well as being powerful determinants of behavior. Mindful of these facts, the therapist recognizes the limits of the cognitive approach and works also to advance emotional awareness and understanding. In fact, overt behaviors represent an expression of myriad complex states involving feelings, satisfactions, attitudes, perceptions, and interpretations of the spouse and the spouse's behavior.

The therapist thus works in varying ways, concentrating at times on helping individuals change external behaviors and at other times focusing on attitudes and feelings. With some individuals, decrease in tension may result from alteration of irritating, external behaviors. With others, improvement in the relationship may result from change in the individual's perception, understanding of, and attitude toward the mate's behavior, without overt behavioral change. In other words, certain behaviors originally experienced as noxious may continue, but they may be experienced differently. The therapist makes decisions as to which changes have the best chance of being implemented, given the strengths and limitations of the couple, and sets goals accordingly. In some cases, helping individuals change external behaviors precedes the more difficult job of helping them become aware of, and attempt to better deal with, more pervasive, underlying conflicts. Certain external behaviors often have defensive functions, thereby obscuring a more basic problem, as in the case of the spouse who perceives her lack of sexual responsivity to her husband as a result of his sexual inadequacies in order to avoid looking at her own problems with being intimate.

In shaping interventions, the therapist needs to be aware of, and continually attuned to, the different attitudes, feelings, and ways of relating to the therapist that spouses present. These often reveal conceptions about how help is expected, as well as the couple's ability and willingness to work in the ways specified by the therapist. Thus the therapist is alerted to specific obstacles to establishing the therapeutic alliance. Some spouses are compliant, dependent, or helpless. Others may be ambivalent, defiant, suspicious, or resentful. Others maintain unrealistic expectations that the therapist will provide magical solutions with little required of them beyond a detailing of the problems experienced. For the last kind of individuals, it becomes especially important for the therapist to avoid assuming too much responsibility for problem solving or implying knowledge and powers beyond those possessed. For individuals who are excessively dependent and have difficulty in taking the initiative for the work and effort required in therapy, the therapist needs to be supportive and to offer specific help to change this style. These individuals must learn that therapy is not something done to them but rather a mutual assumption of responsibility to explore and work toward finding ways of enhancing individual satisfactions; it can work only if both partners are willingly involved. With some individuals, such willingness may need to be cultivated. This may take place only after the therapist helps the couple become more fully aware of the power they have to effect changes toward a more satisfactory relationship. Whatever the couple's orientation, the therapist needs to respect the problems and limitations set by existing attitudes and feelings and work toward changing them where necessary.

Such presenting attitudes and feelings often reflect specific developmental deficits, such as lack of basic trust or other rather fixed individual problems that have contributed greatly to interactional marital problems. Assessment, seen as a continuing and integral part of therapy, is particularly concerned with recognizing the kinds and severity of such deficits, since these are so crucial to selecting appropriate goals and therapeutic interventions. The more severe the deficits, the more difficult the work will be in a couple context where confrontation may be too anxiety-provoking to permit the couple to focus on their part in the interaction. In such cases, the therapist may need to modify the couple approach, supplement such work with individual sessions, or recommend individual therapy with another therapist.

In some cases, the therapist—recognizing the difficulty, time, and struggle involved for the couple to move toward greater growth —may choose more limited goals of working for minimal changes that provide some relief of tension. Specific limited goals, such as improving frustration tolerance and helping individuals learn better impulse delay, although difficult to achieve, may be set. When deficits are severe, the therapist needs to be aware of the limitations of a reality-oriented, problem-solving approach and the difficulty of working toward the goal of greater mutuality. Goals have to be modified in line with the spouses' present limitations, as well as their current capacity for change.

For all individuals therapy is, to some extent, stressful and arouses discomfort and anxiety, as spouses confront each other with their dissatisfactions and needs. In the face of such discomfort, it is to be expected that some spouses may be reluctant to bring conflicts into the open and may actively seek to avoid painful feelings. In addition, even with the therapist's stringent efforts to remain impartial, a given spouse may anticipate judgment by the therapist and thus be less than honest in revealing thoughts and feelings. Negative expectations rooted in earlier experiences make it particularly difficult to establish a therapeutic alliance. In any event, the therapist needs to proceed at a pace reasonably comfortable and at least tolerable to the spouses and needs to help promote a trusting climate. A reasonable balance of frustration and gratification should be maintained. The therapist may need to point out to the couple that some anxiety is inevitable if they are to achieve the improvement they seek. Although initially disquieting, bringing more veiled resentments and conflicts into the open may lead ultimately to a more vitalized and satisfactory relationship.

In furthering the therapeutic alliance, the therapist needs to convey respect for the spouses' feelings and an attitude that these are not seen as wrong, but as important phenomena that have a powerful influence on the individual's behavior and that cannot readily be willed away. The therapist needs to be especially alert to the potential problem of one spouse utilizing emerging knowledge of the partner's feelings and conflicts as ammunition to exonerate the self and support the contention that the partner is responsible for the marital problems. Work can proceed successfully on individual problems within the marital context only if both spouses are sufficiently dislodged from a blaming orientation to be able to be more sympathetic.

By personal conviction that therapeutic skills offer support and guidance, by careful attention to sparing spouses unnecessary feelings of being disadvantaged, and by the belief, where appropriate, in the ability of individuals to withstand stress and modify behavior, the therapist works to engender hope in the couple that they can alleviate their problems and that they are not helpless victims of unalterable circumstances. The therapist shares in the importance and seriousness of the feelings and the work, but, where possible, lends an occasional note of humor or lightness to make the work more palatable. The therapist recognizes with the couple the difficulty of modifying behavior and also recognizes that the successful completion of therapeutic goals often requires herculean efforts. Resistance to change is usually present despite a sincere wish to better the relationship. Therapy proceeds most efficiently if the therapist acknowledges this resistance but nevertheless feels confident that his or her repertoire of skills and knowledge of individual and interactional behavior and dynamics can be useful to the couple and can provide enough direction for facilitating therapy.

Within this context of support and guidance, the therapist works to mobilize in the couple responsibility for actively seeking to become aware of how they feel, think and behave in an effort to meet individual needs as well as the partner's needs, and of how these characteristic patterns of behavior lead to friction. The therapist works to promote curiosity and inquisitiveness to better understand feelings and behavior and to support the spouses toward altering the patterns of behavior which prove dysfunctional and which they wish to change. To fully appreciate typical patterns of behavior, a spouse needs feedback both from the therapist and the partner. As each spouse becomes more aware of such behaviors, he or she also begins to appreciate more fully the extent to which such problems are more individually determined, as well as how they interact to cause marital friction. This promotes the possibility of an individual's assuming responsibility for his or her own behavior, and ultimately of great appreciation for the limits of individual power in effecting overall change. It is often a difficult task to accept that one has limited power to change another, and it is also difficult to realistically appraise wherein one has the potential to influence, as opposed to changing, that person. Much of the difficulty in accomplishing this task resides in the discomfort of acknowledging and experiencing realistic helplessness, an experience of intrinsic vulnerability and impotence.

A crucial part of the therapeutic work is promoting the separateness of spouses within a context of an interpersonal union where mutuality and give-and-take are desirable. Although legally and psychologically entwined, each spouse must also maintain his or her autonomy if any successful relationship is to occur. The therapist works to help the couple define the boundaries of their marriage in a way that will be neither too constricting so as to inhibit individual choice and self-expression nor so loose as to permit freedoms that violate important individual needs. In the promotion of autonomy, the therapist helps spouses utilize aggression for the assertion of self-needs and self-interests, for communicating the relative importance of these, and for conveying frustrations and disappointments. Such communication is, hopefully, to help influence the partner toward change in better meeting the spouse's needs. The therapist supports the contention that efforts to influence do not necessarily represent attempts to control another but are legitimate and to be expected in all relationships. Such effort by a partner is often experienced as rejection of the total self. The therapist needs to help spouses view these from a different and more positive perspective. For example, a spouse can change certain behaviors and remain the same person; also, the wish for some changes by the partner does not imply rejection in an "all or none" sense. Specific help may also be needed to enable spouses to learn how to go about influencing their partners to change in ways least likely to be experienced as efforts at control. For example, threats (statements beginning "if you don't do such and such, then I'm . . .") most assuredly will be experienced as coercive. Spouses must learn how to state limits of tolerance for living with dissatisfactions and state preferences and choices in ways that are not threats. A distinction can be made between efforts to influence that are coercive as opposed to those that are not.

As the therapist works with the dissatisfactions of the couple at those points where individual needs clash, he or she works to sharpen differences, helping spouses become aware and accepting of them. A therapeutic task is to help spouses appreciate differences not only as inevitable but as "good"—and not as the primary source of problems. More accurately, what creates problems is how two partners view their differences and have come to deal with them. The therapist respects and encourages spouses' right to disagree, hoping to help them learn more effective ways of dealing with their differences.

A specific and important goal of therapy entails helping couples learn how to negotiate differences, that is, to reach some mutual decisions regarding how to deal with dissatisfactions and how to remedy differences in ways that respect both parties. But before they reach this point, most couples need to learn how to voice their dissatisfactions and state their desires in a constructive way. Many spouses typically view their difficulties from the point of view of "who's to blame?" Endemic to this view is a narrowness in focusing on a previous behavior of the spouse as the "cause" for the partner's behavior. Most spouses need specific help not only to become aware of the rigidity with which they cling to this blaming orientation but also to fully appreciate how this perspective obscures the inter-actional and intrapsychic meaning of many behaviors. In addition, it interferes with the ability of the partner either to understand the other's hurts and frustrated needs or to want to do anything about them. Most individuals, when blamed, become defensive and then counter-blame the partner. A major therapeutic task is learning how to state personal needs clearly rather than stating how bad the part-ner is for frustrating the individual. Once spouses can do this more successfully, they may then be able to move to the next stage of deciding the extent of their willingness to make efforts to satisfy the partner.

At this stage, the therapist may need to underline forcefully that greater receptivity and efforts of the partner will be encouraged by similar responsiveness. This style of accommodation and com-promise is not one, however, of weighing and measuring coldly to equalize effort but rather one that encourages individuals to make agreements or commitments, independent of what the spouse de-cides. Emphasis on each individual deciding how willing he or she is to change certain behaviors—willingness not contingent on prior changing by the partner—minimizes the frequent problem of "who goes first." At the same time, it promotes separateness and further recognition of the extent and limits of the individual's ability to influence the partner.

As the therapist works with the couple toward the goal of learn-ing to negotiate, the extent to which spouses can readily learn and utilize appropriate skills becomes apparent. Much of the therapeu-tic work is concerned with what interferes with a more tempered, problem-solving, negotiating approach. By the time spouses arrive for therapy, there is often much prevailing frustration, anger, and bitterness. Awareness and full expression of such feelings can help the partners appreciate the extent of frustrated needs and under-line the importance of attending to them. It is hoped that couples will learn in therapy to "express" feelings, with some measure of comfort and expectancy that they will be heard and respected. The therapist may need to help spouses identify the behaviors that dis-courage such positive expectations.

The advantage of ongoing communication of feelings to avoid emotional build-up and explosiveness also needs to be stressed. The therapist has the opportunity to help spouses not only to learn to become more comfortable in expressing feelings but also to learn how to channel their anger into more effective behavior or expression. Without direction, spouses often proceed with endless and pointless angry arguments and attacks that can only lead to further discouragement. The therapist must intervene to actively circumvent expression of such anger. Expression should be related to need-statements, need-dissatisfactions, frustrations, and the weight of the feelings that result. When anger persists and spouses cannot refrain from denigrating attacks, spouses have difficulty negotiating. The therapist needs to focus on the disruptive aspects of the anger and the problems it presents; explore with the spouse, if necessary, over-determined aspects of anger that may be confounding the marital problems; and, in some instances, meet with the spouse individually to work toward better management of anger so as to prevent the inevitable despair in the mate who is the butt of continuous attacks.

Ways that spouses typically communicate with each other often are intrinsic to their difficulty in negotiating. Not only do couples blame each other and call each other names, but often their communication of needs is expressed in such abstract terms that their partners cannot deal with them. Helping a spouse define needs in specific, behavioral terms is an assist to the partner. A further impediment to communication (and, in turn, negotiation) is a spouse's proneness to "read" or infer the intentions or feelings of the partner without checking their validity. The therapist should encourage partners to check out assumptions directly with each other. Feelings and nonverbal communication must not be overlooked. The therapist can pose as a model of effective communication by the clarity of his or her remarks and expectations and by being willing to listen and explore meanings with due respect for the feelings involved.

In all the therapeutic work, the therapist utilizes the here-and-now transactions as one of the most useful focal points. This implies deemphasizing the partners' rehashing of past events, often used to establish blame; instead, the spouses are directed to work on problems in the present. The therapist may need to encourage the spouses to talk directly to each other about how they currently feel and what they want, rather than talking *about* the partner to the therapist. Direct confrontation of one spouse to another greatly facilitates awareness of feelings and promotes a more fruitful interchange. Minimizing talk about the partner decreases experienced blame and resentment. Along with paying direct attention to more manifest behavior, the therapist should be cognizant of the feeling component to behavior, often less focal in an individual's awareness. Promoting greater awareness and expression of feelings is crucial to the work of learning to negotiate, because resistance to active reality problem-solving is often rooted in strong feeling states.

Further barriers to successful negotiation reside in patterns of thinking that will need to be altered. Most spouses have certain attitudes and beliefs about what marriage should be like and how partners should behave. Some of these ways of thinking are quite common in marriage, such as the belief and expectation of automatic need-gratification from the spouse rather than having to "work" for such gratification. It is assumed that if one spouse loves the other, then of course he or she will not only know the other's needs but meet them without delay. Many of these notions are often romantic, over-idealistic, and unrealistic, based on "shoulds" that are not functional to the relationship. Often such expectations, beliefs, or attitudes are not manifest but implicit in the usual patterns of relating. It is important for the therapist to help the couple become aware of the assumptions and implicit rules they hold regarding the roles each "should" play and how these "shoulds" are causing specific marital problems. Often such rules relate to who is in charge and who makes which decisions; problems of control, power, and competitiveness inevitably emerge as individuals struggle to protect individual rights. Together, the couple and therapist can examine what the assumptions and rules are; understand, where possible, their origins and functions; and, in addition, learn more about how they are translated behaviorally. A major part of the work may be toward furthering recognition of the myriad ways such rules are put into effect in everyday interactions. Knowledge of this hidden agenda of implicit rules allows spouses to question the utility of abiding by them when they are nonfunctional. When couples alter their implicit expectations, they may then choose to behave differently. Identification of the behaviors emanating from the rules allows them to know where change is needed; new behaviors can then be practiced and put in their place.

Bringing such thinking and attitudes into direct focus also offers the therapist an opportunity to guide the couple toward more realistic expectations and toward a better understanding of why some expectations are more likely to produce problems. The therapist lends his or her own conviction to statements about the feasibility of certain expectations being met in marriage and helps couples understand how certain behaviors significantly interfere with the rights, needs, and autonomy of each individual. In this context, the therapist may choose to use persuasive "logic" in the hopes of convincing a spouse that he or she cannot get needs met by present behaviors. The emphasis is not on giving advice in terms of how spouses "should" live and behave but rather in terms of how the spouse *is* living and behaving that is self-defeating. The decision to alter such behavior can only reside with the individual. It is hoped that with fuller knowledge of the dysfunctional aspects of behaviors, couples will have a greater impetus to change.

Because the therapist works from an implicit position of power, he or she must be careful not to use this position in a way detrimental to the couple. The keynote of therapy is to use this position of superior knowledge and greater objectivity to actively direct and structure therapy toward provoking and mobilizing the couple to change in ways that will meet the needs of each and minimize friction. This requires a nonjudgmental point of view that focuses on the dysfunctional aspects of behaviors rather than their "right" or "wrong" aspects. It does not mean that the therapist should always be completely neutral or that he or she must refrain from any statements that reveal personal biases and predilections. What it does mean is that the therapist acknowledges these as individual preferences rather than operating from an omniscient viewpoint that implies knowledge of what is best. To do this successfully, the therapist must be aware of personal attitudes, biases, values, role expectations, and ethical or moral convictions concerning marriage. Armed with this awareness, the therapist is less likely to fall into the trap of siding with one partner and pressing for specific changes consonant with personal beliefs. The ultimate tenet is to find what the couple can mutually agree on, and in this matter there is no right or wrong. A therapist needs to respect the rights of both individuals to decide and determine what goes on between them.

Although equal respect for the needs of both spouses is the rule, behaviorally the therapist may not at a given moment be able to demonstrate this. From time to time the therapist may take the vantage point of one spouse or the other, working to promote attunement of the partner to the spouse's needs. However, the overall shifting nature of such coalitions makes it clear that such siding is temporary and does not represent partiality in favor of one spouse.

One major, implicitly held belief of the proposed principles and methods of working with couples is that any successful relationship depends on a balance of both spouses' needs being met and that any system or relationship built on power will be dysfunctional. This point of view represents a judgment and conviction as to how interpersonal systems function best and with least friction. It holds to the tenet that each individual has a right to self-realization, to seek personal fulfillment through development and use of one's capabilities and talents, but also a responsibility to the spouse to respect his or her needs and to help the spouse likewise work toward such goals. This is not to say that marriages that depart from this point of view may not be functional and satisfactory to some individuals. However, such individuals are unlikely to come for help or, if so, it is assumed that the *status quo* has been disrupted and that the relationship is no longer satisfactory. It is on this basis that the therapist proceeds.

A final point concerns the qualities of the therapist. Of inestimable importance in facilitating the spouses' willingness to work is a commitment on the part of the therapist to continue with the couple through the lean and difficult times, when hope is dwindling and efforts most fledgling. The couple needs to draw strength from this commitment, through their experience of the willingness of another to share their pain and struggle and to lend to their mutual work all the power and skill available in order to find ways of altering dysfunctional molds and of helping them endure the inevitable pain before relief can be found and changes made. This covenant will be the foundation for the support and nourishment necessary for enduring the pain and anxiety aroused through attempting to alter behavior. It is this acknowledged bond of dependency and experience of trust that allows couples to muster the courage to proceed.

How therapy progresses depends ultimately on all three members of the therapeutic team—the two spouses and the therapist. With sufficient ego-strength to withstand the confrontations and inevitable discomfort of therapy, and with sufficient investment in the marriage, therapy can greatly assist a couple in improving their relationship. Equally important for therapy to flourish, the therapist must have achieved sufficient self-comfort and confidence in skills that can be translated behaviorally into helpful guidance. Successful therapy involves appreciating individual differences and the range of treatment problems posed, and it requires flexibility in employing different treatment strategies in response to these. When these conditions can be approximated, the principles and methods described in this book can be successfully employed for promoting growth for spouses and increasing relationship satisfactions. We believe that couple therapy is particularly advantageous because it provides a couple with the unique opportunity to become more observant of their dysfunctional interactional patterns of behavior than would be the case in individual therapy. Further, it provides an opportunity, as the couple's awareness and understanding develops, to modify crippling patterns of thinking and behavior. And, under the guiding hand of the therapist, it enables the couple to practice more adaptive behaviors.

Appendix

✳✳✳✳✳✳✳✳✳✳✳✳✳✳✳✳✳✳✳✳✳✳✳✳✳✳✳✳✳

Personal Data Form

This form has been found useful for understanding important developmental and relationship parameters of individuals entering couple therapy. It is administered either before or after the first session—whichever proves to be more practical. Both spouses fill it out separately but are not discouraged from discussing it with each other or with the therapist. However, it is not a primary focus of the treatment.

ANSWER BELOW TO THE EXTENT THAT YOU FEEL COM-
FORTABLE. YOUR ANSWERS WILL BE HELPFUL IN OUR
WORK TOGETHER.

NAME: _____ AGE: _____ SEX: _____

YEARS MARRIED: _____   PREVIOUS MARRIAGES: _____

NUMBER OF CHILDREN: _____

    AGES: MALES: _____

        FEMALES: _____

OCCUPATION: _____

EDUCATION: _____

RELIGION: _____

PARENTS:

    1. LIVING: MOTHER: __ FATHER: __

    2. OCCUPATION: MOTHER: __ FATHER: __

    3. YOUR AGE AT DEATH OF: MOTHER: __ FATHER: __

NUMBER OF BROTHERS AND SISTERS: _____

YOUR POSITION IN FAMILY (for example, oldest): _____

DESCRIBE BRIEFLY:

    1. YOUR MOTHER:

    2. YOUR FATHER:

    3. OTHER RELATIVES WHO WERE ESPECIALLY IMPOR-
       TANT TO YOU WHEN YOU WERE GROWING UP (for
       example, a grandparent):

WHAT IMPORTANT EXPECTATIONS ARE OR WERE HELD
FOR MEMBERS GROWING UP IN:

1. YOUR PRESENT FAMILY?

2. YOUR FAMILY OR ORIGIN?

CHOOSE THREE WORDS WHICH WOULD BEST DESCRIBE
EACH OF YOUR BROTHERS AND SISTERS:

CHOOSE THREE WORDS YOUR FAMILY USED OR MIGHT
HAVE USED TO DESCRIBE YOU WHEN YOU WERE GROW-
ING UP:

WHAT MEMBERS OF YOUR FAMILY "TEAMED" TOGETHER
OR SEEMED ESPECIALLY CLOSE IN:

1. YOUR FAMILY OF ORIGIN?

2. YOUR PRESENT FAMILY?

MOTHER'S FAVORITE:

1. FAMILY OF ORIGIN:

2. PRESENT FAMILY:

FATHER'S FAVORITE:

   1. FAMILY OF ORIGIN:

   2. PRESENT FAMILY:

SLEEPING ARRANGEMENTS:

   1. AT HOME PRESENTLY:

   2. IN YOUR HOME OF ORIGIN:

INDIVIDUALS LIVING:

   1. AT HOME PRESENTLY:

   2. IN YOUR HOME OF ORIGIN:

YOUR REACTION TO BEGINNING SCHOOL:

YOUR EXPERIENCE OF SCHOOL THEREAFTER:

YOUR EARLIEST SEXUAL EXPERIENCES:

YOUR EARLIEST MEMORIES:

MOST SIGNIFICANT PERSON IN YOUR LIFE PRIOR TO
MARRIAGE—DESCRIBE AND STATE WHY:

EARLY IMPORTANT INCIDENTS OR "TALES" THAT
STAND OUT IN YOUR MIND THAT YOUR PARENTS HAVE
RELATED TO YOU CONCERNING YOU OR YOUR FAMILY:

DESCRIBE HOW YOU SEE YOUR PARENTS AS GRANDPAR-
ENTS NOW COMPARED WITH HOW THEY WERE AS PAR-
ENTS TO YOU:

WHO TOOK PRIMARY CARE OF YOU AS AN INFANT?

DESCRIBE YOUR EARLY CARE, INCLUDING ANY PARTIC-
ULAR STRESS DURING YOUR INFANCY (for example, by
hospitalization of you or an individual who took care of you, losses
in the family, divorce, and so on):

PRESENT PROBLEM AREAS—DESCRIBE *HOW* INTERAC-
TIONS WITH OTHERS ARE STRESSFUL:

WORK:

SOCIAL:

CHILDREN:

SEXUAL:

OTHER:

MAJOR PRESENT STRESS:

GREATEST SOURCES OF GRATIFICATION:

Index

Abandonment, fear of, 24, 26, 124–125
Absence, of spouse from therapy, 302–303
Abstractions, avoidance of, 167–173
Accusation, assumed, 194–197
Adolescence, developmental tasks of, 23
Affection, expression of need for, 95–97, 118–121
Anger: constructive, 101; defenses against, 124–125; effective statements of, 153–155; encouraging expressions of, 130–131; and extramarital affairs, 230–231; rechanneling of, 105–109; right to, 83–84; and tug-of-war, 100–112
Annoyances: building up of, 100–101, 156–160, 256–258; hierarchies of, 155–156
Anxiety, 20–21; of being consumed, 27; as diagnostic tool, 30–31; of therapy, 60–66, 311–312
Approval, need for, 105–109. *See also* Positive reinforcement; Praise
Argumentative style, 73
Arguments: about expectations, 87–88; about work, 218–225
Assault, vs. confrontation, 91, 104–109
Assessment, 163—32, 37
Assumptions: of blame, 95, 99–100, 197–199; about spouse's feelings, 175–178
Attitudes: changes in, 341–343; and identity, 36; parental, 238–239; regarding treatment, 35–36; unconscious, 14, 349–350
Attracting characteristics, 2–5
Autistic stage, 21
Autonomy, 12; establishment of, as developmental task, 20, 23, 24; fostering of, 25, 87–89; and self-image, 26; as therapeutic goal, 32, 345–346
Avoidance mechanisms, 11

BACH, G., 8n, 118, 153, 156, 214
Behavior: alterability of, 66–67; 341–342; effects of changes in, 15; and feelings, 125, 204–208; identifying of, 175; maladaptive, 28–29; vs. personality, 115

Beliefs, unconscious, 14
BERGIN, A. E., 7n
BERGMAN, A., 20n
BERNE, E., 58
Blame: and anxiety displacement, 30; assumed, 95, 99–100, 197–199; and disguised anger, 173–174; role of, 90–100
Blaming stance, 13; as assessment tool, 18; need to control, 58–59; therapeutic interventions for, 46–47
BLANCK, G., 8n, 20n
BLANCK, R., 8n, 20n
Borderline personalities, 25, 29, 311–313
BOUVET, M., 27n

Career, woman's desire for, 223–225, 237–239, 259–260
Change: anxiety of, 60–62, 114–117; educating for, 66–67, 79–81; realistic expectations for, 234; in separate directions, 6–7; value of, for self-enhancement, 112
Children: custody of, 305–307; effect of divorce on, 305; and husband's symbiotic needs, 25, 200–204; as pawns after divorce, 325–338; from previous marriage, 301–302; shared responsibility for, 252–255
Choice, perceived lack of, 78–81
Clinging behavior, 25–26
Coercion, 231–234
Cognitive approach, 8–9, 12–13
Communication, 5–6; acknowledging of, 139; of content and feeling, 136–137, 347–348; direct, 167–173, flow of, 39–41, 48–54, 57–59; improvement of, 13; models of, 138, 178–179
Comparisons, and complaints, 121
Complaints: in comparison context, 121; statements of, 92
Compromise, and deadlock, 122–124
Concluding remarks, 59–63
Conflict, management of, 214
Conforming behavior, and deference to therapist, 49–50
Confrontations: and anxiety, 30–31; 180; vs. assault, 91; timing of, 70

Consequences, expression of. *See* Threats

Control: fear of, 231–234, 237–239; problems of, 57–59, 236–239

"Cooling off" period, 101–104

Couple therapy: approach to, 7–15, 340–341; beginning sessions, 17, 37–57, 59–66, 286–290; control issues in, 57–59, 236–239; drop-out rate in, 294; focus of, 12–15, 41–43, 67–71, 179–189, 192–204, 247–252; goals of, 34, 190–192, 210–211, 343; limits of, 24, 25, 29; and nonattendance of spouse, 302–303; pace of, 138; process of, 240–242, 341–343; sample sessions, 242–263, 263–283; slacking off of, 293–294; structuring of, 37–57; success factors in, 296; termination of, 65–66, 283–286, 291–298. *See also* Individual therapy; Therapeutic alliance; Therapeutic interventions; Therapist

"Courtroom" game, 58–59

Criticism: fear of, 140–141; and self-image, 134–135; statement of, 92, 178; and statements of need, 149–150

Cultural conditioning, and role, 208, 214

Deadlocks, 111–114, 327–328

Decision making, autonomy in, 87–89

Defenses, 20–21; as diagnostic tools, 29–30; functional limits of, 117; mobilization of, 30–31; of unwilling participant, 34–35

Denial mechanisms, 11

Dependency needs, 4–5, 234

Developmental failure: and extramarital relations, 229–230; and paranoid tendencies, 235–236

Developmental stages: interference with, 18; marriage and, 19–29; uncompleted, 3, 12, 339–340, 343

Diagnosis, conventional, 16–18; using defenses and anxiety for, 29–30; and responses to first session, 37. *See also* Assessment

Displacement, and anxiety, 30

Dissatisfactions, statements of, 92–94, 156–160. *See also* Criticism

Distance, need for, 26–27

Divorce: advice about, 304–307; children and, 305–307; emotions surrounding, 305; therapy after, 325–338; threats of, 294–295, 303–304

Dyadic relationships, and development, 20–24, 35

Early trauma, 18

Eclecticism, 7–8

Ego, 8, 12; and change, 114–117. *See also* Self-

Empathic listening, 144–146. *See also* Listening

ERIKSON, E. H., 19*n*

Evaluation, 16. *See also* Assessment

Expectations: agreements about, 87–88; facilitating statements of, 44–46, 146–152; of marriage, 4–7, 208–225; of self, 80. *See also* Attitudes

Extramarital relations, 206–208, 225–231, 233, 307–309

Face saving: facilitation of, 69–71; seeking therapy for, 34

Fantasy: in childhood, 14; in early marital stages, 2

Feelings: and behaviors, 204–208; control of and spontaneity, 151–152, 154–155; expression of, 41, 152–155, 270–281, 347–348; priority of, as issues, 155–156; recognition of, 58; respect for, 66–67; working with, 122–124

FIERMAN, L., 75*n*

FISCH, R., 236*n*

Fixation, 20–21, 26, 28–29

Free time, 214–218

Freedom, comparative of spouses, 117

FRIEDMAN, P. M., 8*n*

Friends, choice of, 233–234

GARFIELD, S. L., 7*n*

Generalizations, as red flags, 175

Gestalt psychotherapy, 8

Giving and taking, 26–27

GORDON, T., 92*n*

Gratification: counterproductive, 14; delay of, encouraged, 29; effective requests for, 147; exaggerated need for, 95–97; patterns of as assessment tools, 18. *See also* Symbiotic stage

GREENWALD, H., 79n

Grievances. *See* Annoyances

Growth: marriage and, 19–20; risk of divergent, 6–7; as therapeutic aim, 12–13. *See also* Developmental tasks; Personality development

Guilt: and blaming orientation, 90–91; of children for divorce, 306; manipulation of, 227–229

Gunnysacking. *See* Annoyances

GURMAN, A. S., 7n

Heavyweight, vs. lightweight, 118–121

Here-and-now emphasis, 11, 179–189, 192, 348–349

Homosexual needs, 24, 234

Honeymoon stage, 2–3, 210–211

Hooks, 148–149

Hopelessness, countering feelings of, 77–79, 83–85

Housework: division of, 218–225; and sex role, 122

Hurt: desire to, 110; helping clients recognize, 58

"I" messages, 92

Ideals, imposed, 117

Identification, opportunities for, in marriage, 20

Identified patient, 310–313. *See also* Individual problems; Individual therapy

Identity: and adolescent development 23; fear of loss of, 231–234

Illness, as a crutch, 312–313

Improvement: initial, 114; reinforcement of, 160–166

"In love" stage of marriage, 2. *See also* Honeymoon stage

Inadequacy, feelings of, 143–144, 313

Independence: and early development, 24; need for, 4–5

Individual problems, 42–43, 284–286, 310–313; clarifying, 94–97; convergence of, 10–11; and focus of therapy, 192–204, 247–252; and limits of power, 234–236. *See also* Individual therapy

Individual therapy: and anxiety of change, 116; drawbacks of, 62; necessity for, 29; and secrets, 307–310;

Individual therapy (continued)
for sexual problems, 315. *See also* Couple therapy

Individuality: consolidation of, 23–24, 346. *See also* Autonomy

Inferiority, feelings of, 313. *See also* Inadequacy

Intentions: reading of, 175–178; separation of from outcomes, 204–208

Interchange, 52. *See also* Communication

Interpersonal relationships, establishment of, as developmental task, 20, 23. *See also* Dyadic relationships

Intimidation, 118–121

Issues: identification of, 41–43; misconception of, 190–192; separation of, 121

JACKSON, D. D., 8n, 73n

KAISER, H., 75

KLEIN, G. S, 19n

KNISKERN, D. P., 7n

Labeling, 174–175, 177–178

Labor, division of, 218–225. *See also* Career; Housework

LAZARUS, A., 8n

LEDERER, W. J., 8n, 73n

Lightweight, vs. heavyweight, 118–121

Listening: effective, 138–139, 144–146, 181–186; and problems of overidentification, 83–85

Living arrangements, 300–301

MAGGARD, E., 189n

MAHLER, M. S., 20n

Manipulation. *See* Control

Marital problems, 17; and developmental deficits, 20–32

Marital treatment. *See* Couple therapy

Marriage: as developmental phase, 19–20, 32; early phases of, 32, 208–211; expectations of, 4–7, 208–225; limits of power in, 234–236; nature of, 1–7; role structure in, 25; stresses on, 339–340

Mate choice, 2–5, 25

Men, symbiotic wishes of, in marriage, 25

Message interpretation, 137–138

Mind reading, 97–98, 175–178

Misconceptions: of issues, 190–192; con-

cerning therapist, 36, 41, 48, 58–59
Modeling of communication, 138, 178–179
Monologues, 313
Mother figure, 18, 224
Mother-infant dyad, 21–22
Motivation, 33–34
Mutuality, 13; development of, 23; in therapy, 32, 67

Name calling, 174–175
Narcissism, 21, 235
Needs: anticipation and gratification of, 211–212; balancing of, 351–352; differing, 13–14; in early marital stages, 2–4; facilitating expression of, 53, 76–77; stating of, effectively, 146–152, 211–212; uncritical expression of, 115; unrecognized, 8–9, 304–305
Negotiation: and anger, 100–112; for assumption of responsibility, 75–90; blaming as obstacle to, 90–100; for change, 114–117, 346–347; of child custody, 325–338; through deadlocks, 112–114; of divorce issues, 305–307; failure of, 121–125; sample session of, 125–135; and separation of issues, 121; style of 13, 32; with unequal partners, 118–121
Neurosis, 11. See also Individual problems
Nonverbal communication, 128, 179, 267
Note taking, 74–75

Object constancy, 21, 22–23, 32. See also Separation-individuation stage
Object relationships, 20
One-to-one focus, 137
"Open marriage," 225
Opening comments, 37–39, 43–44, 54–56
Optimal distance, 27
Outcomes, vs. intentions, 204–208
Overdependency, 234. See also Dependency
Overidentification, with spouse, 25, 83–85, 141–146

Paranoid position: and blaming, 94–97; developmental basis of, 235–236. See also Individual problems
Paraphrasing, 137–138, 178–179, 236–239
Parental attitude, 150–151
Parental role, 238–239
Parents, psychological separation from, 20, 211
Passive-receptive fixation, 27
Pathology, of couple, 10–11. See also Individual problems
Perceptual apparatus, 23
Personal data form, 18, appendix
Personality: vs. behavior, 115; conflicts of, 91–94, 212–213; development of, 20–27
Physical illness, as a crutch, 312–313
PINE, F., 20n
POLSTER, E., 8n
POLSTER, M., 8n
Positive reinforcement, of changed behaviors, 113, 160–166. See also Praise
Power, limits of, 234–236
Praise: need for, 24, 105–109; spouse's responsibility to, 89; therapist's responsibility to, 69–71, 113, 160–166
Primary narcissism, 21
Problem-solution approach, 181–186, 281–283. See also Solution-response turn-off
Problem solving: approach to, 11; and fears of therapy, 64–65; as goal of communication, 40; sample sessions in, 242–263, 263–283
Projection, 28–29, 30. See also Blaming stance
Psychoanalytic developmental psychology, 19. See also Developmental stages
Psychological health, 9
Psychotic persons, 16. See also Individual problems
Questions, phrasing of, 39, 55, 173–174
Quid pro quo, 73. See also Negotiation
Reassurance, need for, 24. See also Praise

Record keeping, 74–75
Red flags, 174–175
Reeducation, 14, 190–239
Reframing, 236–239. *See also* Paraphrasing
Regression, 20–21; and stress, 27–28
"Rehashing," 179–180, 348
Rephrasing, 236–239. *See also* Paraphrasing
Resentments. *See* Annoyances
Responsibility: acceptance of, for improvement, 71, 345; for anger, 154–155; assumption of, 41, 75–90, 129–130, 133, 141–146; after divorce, 332; of therapist, 345
Revenge, 175–178, 230–231, 303–304; fears of, 120–121
Risk taking, change and, 110, 112
Roles: expectations of, in marriage, 208–225; parental, 238–239; sexual, 122; of women, 24, 218–225
Rules, internalization of, 23

Sample sessions, 125–135, 242–263, 263–283
SATIR, V., 8n
Secrets, of one spouse, 307–310
Self-: accusations, 313; assertion, 118–121; awareness, 12, 21–22; denial and early development, 24; determination, 81–82; enhancement and change, 112; esteem, 316–317; expectations, 80; image, 134–135; worth, 224–225. *See also* Ego
Separateness. *See* Autonomy
Separation: desirability of, during therapy, 300–301; anxiety of, 24–25
Separation-individuation phase, 22–23; deficits at, 124–125; and marital problems, 24; resolution of, 32
Sex roles, 122
Sexual problems: and assessment phase, 18; refusal to discuss, 316; and self-esteem, 313–317; verbal communication about, 317–324
Sexual relations: anxiety of, 27; withholding of, as punishment, 205–206
Sexual relationship, establishing of, as developmental task, 20

SHEEHY, G., 9n, 19n
Sibling rivalry, 117
Solution-response turn-off, 141–146, 181–186. *See also* Problem-solution turn-off
Solutions, therapist's facilitation of, 86–89. See also Negotiation; Problem solving
Spontaneity, limits, of, 151–152
Stages of life, 9–10, 20–29
Stalemate, 111–114, 327–328
Standards: imposed, 117; internalization of, 23
Stress, and regression, 27–29
Strokes, 160–166. *See also* Praise
Style, allowance for differences in, 91–94. *See also* Personality
Superego development, 23
Superior attitude, 151
Symbiotic stage, 21–22; fixation at, 26; resolution of, 32
Symbiotic wishes: and closeness in marriage, 27; of men in marriage, 25

Taped sessions, 75
Telephone calls, initiating therapy, 36–37
Temporary crises, 9–10
Therapeutic alliance: and communication flow, 48–54; formation of, 32, 37, 39, 57, 351–352; and individual focus, 192–193; secrets and, 307–310; strengthening of, 66–69
Therapeutic interventions: ability to hear, 28–29; with blaming behavior, 46–47; shaping of, 342; unsuccessful, 48–54, 286–290
"Therapeutic processing," 137–138
Therapist: anger directed at, 109; expectations of, 36, 41, 48, 58–59; as facilitator of problem solving, 86–89; as medical advisor, 312; as model of communication, 138, 178–179; perceived alliances of, 36–37, 67–69; responsibilities of, 75–76, 342, 350–351; supportive role of, 48, 69–71, 113, 160–166, 343–345. *See also* Couple therapy; Therapeutic alliance

Therapy. *See* Couple therapy; Individual problems
Threats, 231–234; of divorce, 303–304
Tolerance, limits of, 232–233
Tone of voice, 150–151. *See also* Nonverbal communication
Transactional levels, 122–124
Triadic relationship. *See* Therapeutic alliance
Trust: development of, 22, 32; and extramarital relations, 206–208, 225–226
Tug-of-war, 100–112; with children, 328

Unconscious determinants, 8–9; and extramarital relations, 229–230; of mate choice, 2–4; of unsuccessful marriage, 304–305

Unmarried couples, 299–300

Vantage points, of spouses, 33–36
Vengeance, 175–178, 230–231, 303–304. *See also* Revenge
Vulnerability, of unwilling participant, 34

WATSLAWICK, P., 236*n*
WEAKLAND, J., 236*n*
"Why" orientation, 192
"Why" questions, 173–174
Women: career choices for, 237–239, 259–260; roles of, 25, 218–225. *See also* Mother-infant dyad
Written commitments, 74–75
WYDEN, P., 8*n*, 118*n*, 153*n*, 156*n*

"You" messages, 92